Together and Apart in Brzezany

TOGETHER

and

APART

in

BRZEZANY

Poles, Jews, and Ukrainians, 1919–1945

Shimon Redlich

INDIANA
University Press

Bloomington & Indianapolis

This book is a publication of

Indiana University Press
601 North Morton Street
Bloomington, IN 47404-3797 USA

http://iupress.indiana.edu

Telephone orders   800-842-6796
Fax orders   812-855-7931
Orders by e-mail   IUPORDER@INDIANA.EDU

The paper used in this publication meets the minimum requirements of American National Standard for Information Sciences—Permanence of Paper for Printed Library Materials, ANSI Z39.48-1984.

Manufactured in the United States of America

Library of Congress Cataloging-in-Publication Data

Redlich, Shimon.
Together and apart in Brzezany : Poles, Jews, and Ukrainians, 1919–1945 / Shimon Redlich.
p. cm.
Includes bibliographical references and index.
ISBN 0-253-34074-8 (cloth : alk. paper)
1. Berezhany (Ukraine)—Ethnic relations. 2. Berezhany (Ukraine)—History—20th century. 3. Redlich, Shimon.
I. Title: Poles, Jews, and Ukrainians, 1919–1945. II. Title.
DK508.95.B48 R43 2002
305.8'009477'9—DC21
2001004948

1   2   3   4   5   07   06   05   04   03   02

In memory of
Tanka Kontsevych
and
Karol Codogni

CONTENTS

PREFACE AND ACKNOWLEDGMENTS

The writing of this book was not so much a matter of choice as of necessity. For some time I have contemplated writing about my childhood in Brzezany, a town in eastern Galicia. For those whose childhood ended abruptly and prematurely, clinging to the life before disaster struck is much like holding fast to an anchor of a drowning boat. I was a happy, secure, and loved child of 6 when the Germans occupied Brzezany. And it was to those few normal prewar years that I gradually and consciously started returning for solace and hope. I have been drawn to relive my early past.

The actual writing of my story faced insurmountable difficulties, not least of which is inherent in my craft. As a historian, I am well aware that relying solely on memory to record the past has many pitfalls. Moreover, my authentic childhood memories were rather scattered and scant. There was another reason for my reluctance. Did my own personal ordeal merit telling? Hindered by these obstacles, I searched for a way to fulfill my need to write. I soon realized that my childhood, or what I remembered of it, was the place, the sites, the landscapes, and, most of all, the people with whom I shared a life before the war. Indeed, it was through researching and writing about my hometown that I began to recover the childhood I longed to remember and the war experience that for many years I tried to repress.

In trying to persevere after a trauma, we often bury the deserving memories along with the tormenting ones. Some of the worthiest people in my life, those who saved it, were for many years casualties of my attempt to forget the past and build a new life. It was nearly half a century before I could express my gratitude to Karol Codogni, a Pole whose family provided us with food when we were hiding in the ruined Brzezany ghetto, and to Tanka Kontsevych, a Ukrainian woman who gave us shelter in her house in the nearby village of Raj.

Returning to the sites and people of my early life was delayed by more than the Iron Curtain. While the collapse of communism facilitated the journey, the psychological wall that many of the survivors have erected to separate them from their traumatic past also had to be vanquished before the return. Contemplating going back to Brzezany was not like traveling to London or New York. It uncovered memories of painful losses as well as recollections of exceptional human kindness.

Brzezany was for centuries home to Poles, Jews, and Ukrainians. The war and the Holocaust dismembered this multi-ethnic town, and what is left of it remains only in the historical record and in the memories of its former inhabitants. My attempt in this book is to reconstruct Brzezany of my childhood, its complexity and richness. Using written sources as well as interviews, I have tried to reassemble the Polish-Jewish-Ukrainian triangle as carefully and even-handedly as possible, allowing the different voices to be heard.

Those Brzezanyites with whom I met and spoke shared with me their memories of the relatively peaceful prewar years as well as those of the tragic events that came with the war. Despite the indifference, greed, hatred, and murder that my own people have experienced, I felt a certain sense of compassion for the difficult and tragic history of the Poles and the Ukrainians. This compassion can, apparently, be felt among some of those who were bound together by something that no longer exists. Half a century after we parted under the worst and most tragic circumstances, I attempted to recover the life that existed before darkness set in. It was also my obligation to tell how prewar multi-ethnic Brzezany came to an end.

* * *

The researching and writing of this book was possible only with the help and goodwill many people extended to me. My primary thanks and appreciation goes to those Brzezanyites—Jews, Poles, and Ukrainians—who have agreed to uncover their lives and memories. Without their generosity of heart, this book could not have been written.

I discussed the idea of writing about my hometown with Aharon Appelfeld, Yuval Lurie, Jerzy Tomaszewski, and Theo Richmond. I would like to thank them for their interest in my project. My colleague Gulie Ne'eman Arad read the manuscript in its various versions and provided me with valuable suggestions and much encouragement. Rachel Patron and Jolanta Brach-Czaina read the first version and made very useful comments. Eva Hoffman was very kind to read part of the manuscript and to make some very thoughtful suggestions. Jan T. Gross's enthusiastic response as well as Antony Polonsky's detailed remarks convinced me that I was on the right track. I am also grateful to Saul Friedlaender, Ezra Mendelsohn, and Roman Szporluk for taking the time out to read the manuscript and provide me with valuable comments. I would also like to thank David S. Rosenstein for his editorial help. At Indiana University Press, I thank Janet Rabinowitch, assistant director and senior sponsoring editor, who accompanied this project with great interest and wisdom from its beginning.

I would like to extend a very special thanks to Pieter Louppen of Ben-Gurion University's Geography Department for doing such a great job with the maps and to Shlomo Arad (Goldberg) for his help with the illustrations.

Menachem Katz was kind enough to let me use the maps of Brzezany originally published in his edited *Brzezany Memorial Book* (1978). Thanks also to Verlag J. H. W. Dietz Nachfolger for their permission to reprint the map of eastern Galicia published in Thomas Sandkühler, *"Endloesung in Galizien"* (1996). Yossi Regev, Margo Schotz, and Udi Sheleg assisted me in overcoming the pitfalls of word processing.

In conducting the interviews, I was assisted by Waclaw Wierzbieniec from Poland (who also accompanied me during a visit to Brzezany); Yaroslav Hrytsak, Victor Susak, and Natalia Narolska from Ukraine; and Eynat Rubinstein and Tehila Sagi from Israel. I thank them all.

I would also like to thank Mordechai Altshuler, Dmytro Bartkiw, Ryszard Brzezinski, Aviva Cantor, Ariel Cohen, Shlomit Cohen, Ludwik Czaja, Vadim Dubson, Marek Glazer, John Paul Himka, Kaja Kazmierska, Bela Kirshner, Yehudit Kleiman, Christine Kulke, Bogdan Musial, Joanna Nalewajko, Irena Plastun, Dieter Pohl, Monika Polit, Efrat Redlich, Gabriele Rosenthal, Zbigniew Rusinski, Daniel Terner, Jennifer Turvey, Ayala Yeheskel, and Roman Zakharii. All of them assisted me in one way or another.

I would like to extend my appreciation to the staffs of the following institutions: Yad Vashem Library and Archives and the Central Zionist Archives in Jerusalem, the Central State Historical Archive in L'viv, the State Archive of Ternopil' Region in Ternopil', and the Zentralle Stelle der Landjustizverwaltungen zur Verfolgung nationalsozialistischer Verbrechen in Ludwigsburg.

My Brzezany project has been generously supported by the Israel Science Foundation; the Memorial Foundation for Jewish Culture, New York; and the Rabb Center for Holocaust Studies and the Solly Yellin Chair in Lithuanian and East European Jewry at Ben-Gurion University. I also appreciate the friendship and support of Fanya Gottesman-Heller. Nachum Finger, rector of Ben-Gurion University, and Jimmy Weinblat, dean of the Faculty of Humanities and Social Sciences, were supportive throughout the project.

As always, I owe a great debt to my family: my wife Judy and my daughters Shlomit and Efrat. They have accompanied me throughout this long journey with their love, understanding, and support.

And last, but first, to Karol Codogni and Tanka Kontsevych, without whom I would not have survived to tell the story. It is to them, for their humanness in the midst of barbarism, that this book is dedicated.

A NOTE ON TRANSLITERATION

Transliteration has been simplified for the convenience of the reader, although I have basically followed the Library of Congress system for Ukrainian and Russian and the *Encyclopedia Judaica* system for Hebrew and Yiddish. Polish diacritical marks have been omitted. Polish spelling is used for geographical locations in eastern Galicia.

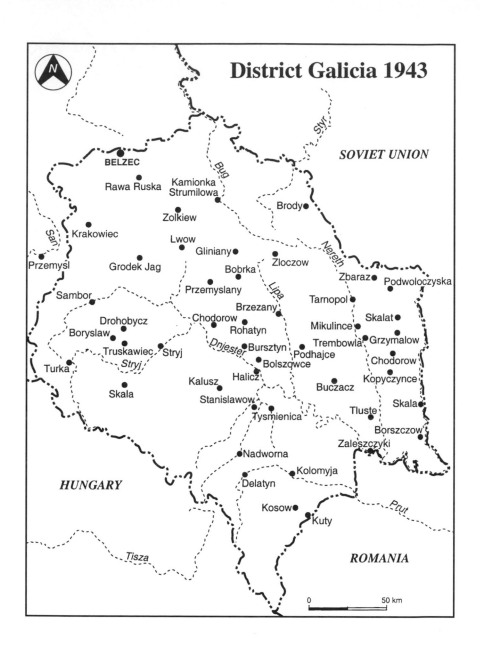

District Galicia 1943

SOVIET UNION

BELZEC

Rawa Ruska

Kamionka
Strumilowa

Brody

Zolkiew

Krakowiec

Lwow

Gliniany

San

Przemysl

Grodek Jag

Bobrka

Zloczow

Zbaraz

Podwoloczyska

Sambor

Przemyslany

Brzezany

Tarnopol

Skalat

Drohobycz

Chodorow

Mikulince

Grzymalow

Boryslaw

Rohatyn

Trembowla

Chodorow

Truskawiec

Stryj

Dnjester

Bursztyn

Podhajce

Turka

Stryj

Bolszowce

Kopyczynce

Halicz

Buczacz

Skala

Kalusz

Stanislawow

Tluste

Skala

Tysmienica

Borszczow

Zaleszczyki

HUNGARY

Nadworna

Kolomyja

Delatyn

Prut

Kosow

Kuty

Tisza

ROMANIA

Styr

Bug

Nereth

Lipa

0   50 km

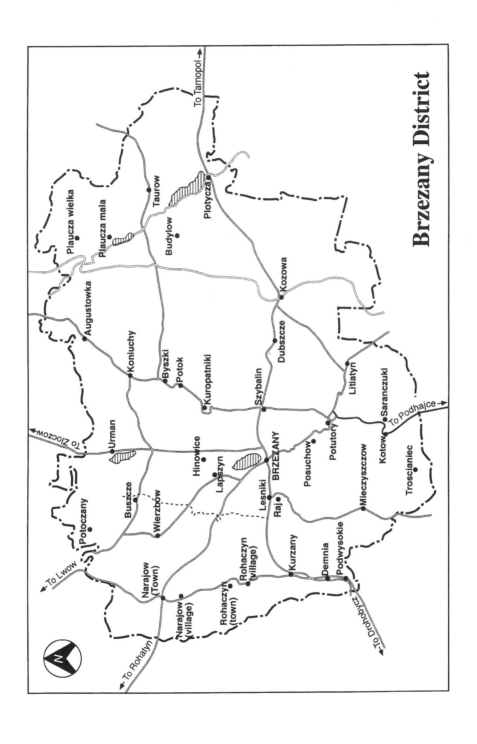

Brzezany District

To Tarnopol

To Zloczow

To Lwow

To Rohatyn

To Drohobycz

To Podhajce

Plaucza wielka
Plaucza mala
Taurow
Budylow
Plotycza
Kozowa
Augustowka
Koniuchy
Byszki
Potok
Kuropatniki
Szybalin
Dubszcze
Litiatyn
Saranczuki
Kotow
Urman
Hinowice
Lapszyn
Lesniki
BRZEZANY
Posuchow
Potutory
Mieczyszczow
Troscianiec
Buszcze
Wierzbow
Potoczany
Raj
Kurzany
Demnia
Podwysokie
Narajow (Town)
Rohaczyn (village)
Narajow (village)
Rohaczyn (town)

N

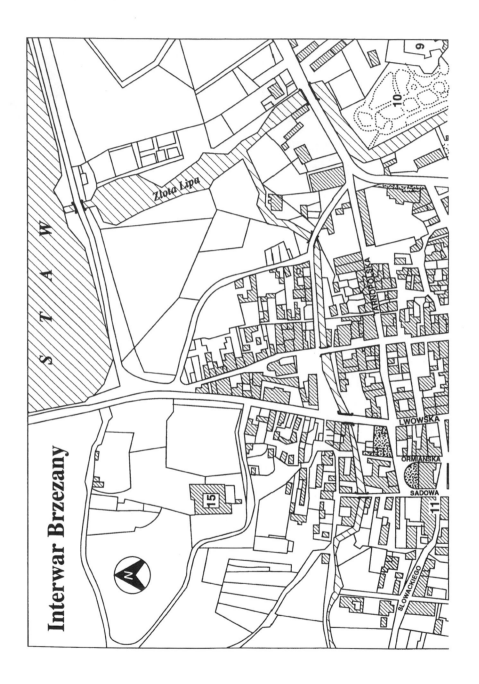

Interwar Brzezany

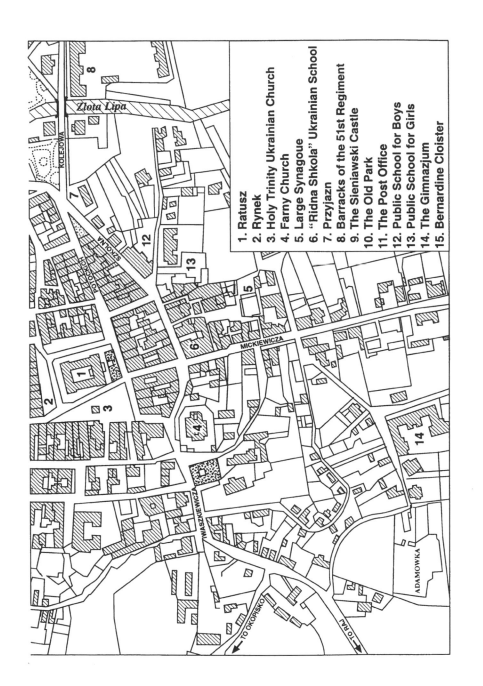

1. Ratusz
2. Rynek
3. Holy Trinity Ukrainian Church
4. Farny Church
5. Large Synagoue
6. "Ridna Shkola" Ukrainian School
7. Przyjazn
8. Barracks of the 51st Regiment
9. The Sieniawski Castle
10. The Old Park
11. The Post Office
12. Public School for Boys
13. Public School for Girls
14. The Gimnazjum
15. Bernardine Cloister

Zlota Lipa

KOLEJOWA

SZKOLNA

SLOWACKIEGO

MICKIEWICZA

IWASZKIEWICZA

ADAMOWKA

TO OKOPSKO

TO RAJ

THE "W" COMPOUND

TARNOPOLSKA

LWOWSKA

SADOWA

ORMIANSKA

RATUSZ

POTOCKICH

SZKOLNA

IWASZKIEWICZA

MICKIEWICZA

Brzezany Ghetto

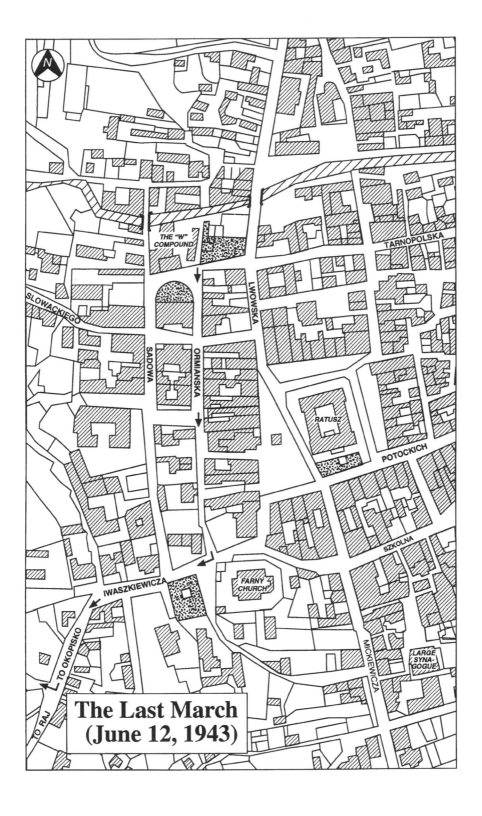

The Last March
(June 12, 1943)

Together and Apart in Brzezany

It was a sunny and hot afternoon in August 1991. We'd just landed at the tiny, shabby Lwow airport. I was returning to this part of the world after forty-six years. I had left it in August 1945, after which I lived in Lodz, Poland, for a number of years before emigrating to Israel, where I've been living ever since. I traveled to Lwow with my American-born wife, Judy, and my two sabra daughters, Shlomit and Efrat. Shlomit was named after my father, Shlomo, and Efrat was named after my grandfather, Efraim-Fishl. Both men were killed in Brzezany during the war.

The airport, which had seen better days, was my gateway to Brzezany, ninety kilometers southeast of Lwow. I had been chasing my past and my childhood for some time. I repeatedly examined the map of the town and old family photographs. I was both eager and scared to return. Luckily, my family agreed to accompany me. They've always been willing partners in my pursuit of the past. I needed their support. I was anticipating emotionally moving events, and I didn't want to be alone.

The first familiar face that I recognized was from a photo which I'd received from the Kontsevyches, the Ukrainian family who hid us during the war. It was that of beautiful Tania, Tanka's granddaughter. She told us that her old and ailing babushka had insisted on traveling the bumpy road all the way from Brzezany to greet us at the airport. Ania, Tanka's daughter and Tania's mother, hadn't been able to come and was waiting for us at home. Within minutes, Tanka and Tania and I were hugging and kissing. My wife was moved to tears. I tried to be more restrained. Tanka, whose physical appearance now made her a complete stranger to me, cried and kept calling me "my little boy." Although Tanka and Tania insisted that we join them and immediately travel to Brzezany, we apologized and told them that we would be coming the next morning. I hadn't known what to expect in provincial Brzezany and had decided to make Lwow, the big city where I had made some prearranged local connections, our temporary base. That same evening our 12-year-old, Efrat, had a high fever and a terrible sore throat. I was frustrated and even considered traveling alone to Brzezany. Judy convinced me that we should wait another day. Luckily, within a day, her condition started to improve.

I was very tense when we finally set out. As we approached Brzezany, I tried to recall the scenery and the architecture. I had a strong urge to find familiar objects. I was hoping to recapture certain moments which had lived on in my memory and imagination. We went first to Tanka's. When we approached her house I wondered whether I would recognize it. It turned out that they had built a new house where the old one used to be, the house where we hid for months in a narrow attic above a stable. During the war, Tanka's husband had been sent for forced labor to Germany, and she had remained there with two children, 9-year-old Ania and 5-year-old Henio.

Once young and full of energy, Tanka was now an old woman, hardly able to walk. I talked to her and tried to recover her memories of my past. She kept repeating her story in broken, rustic Ukrainian, which I barely understood. Tanka remembered carrying me on her back for miles on a cold and snowy night. She also recalled how some Jews she had hid before us were discovered and how she was nearly tried and punished for it. A miracle happened, as she maintained, and she was released. That's when my Aunt Malcia and Vovo appeared unexpectedly, and she didn't turn them down. How this simple peasant woman could once more put her own and her children's lives at risk is beyond my comprehension. Tanka insisted that we stay, but I was afraid to stay overnight. I didn't feel secure in this Ukrainian peasant neighborhood. I wasn't ready to take the slightest risk. The place where I felt so safe during those terrible times wasn't safe enough now. How could that be? Perhaps the answer to this question lies in the concept of relative security. After hiding in the attic, in the ghetto, Tanka's house was a shelter. Now, the big city seemed safer than provincial Brzezany. Or perhaps it was my undefined fear of Ukrainian peasants and the Ukrainian underground fighters of wartime, the *banderovtsi,* which subconsciously lurked somewhere in the background. We left for Lwow in the evening. I was overwhelmed and drained.

We returned to Brzezany the next morning. Only a few places really looked familiar. Perhaps the only site which I distinctly recognized was the town square, the Rynek, and the town hall building, the Ratusz. Nearby, on a slight elevation opposite the Ratusz, was the Ukrainian church with the carved statues on both sides of its entrance. Another slightly familiar sight was the dilapidated Brzezany synagogue, which had only vestiges of its former beauty. This is the place to which I had often walked with my father and Grandpa Fishl on Saturdays and holidays. In my mind, I vaguely pictured the *bimah,* the *aron hakodesh* with its silver lions, and felt the festive atmosphere.

What I was most eager to find was the house we had lived in before the war and the building inside the ghetto where we hid in the attic before moving to Tanka's. One minute I thought I had identified them, but the next minute

I wasn't sure. We were on Kolejowa Street, very close to the Ratusz. This used to be part of the ghetto. I looked toward a light-brown apartment building and was almost sure that we had lived there and hid in the attic. I went in and climbed the steps. The door to the attic was locked. I didn't dare knock on apartment doors and ask for the key. Then I was back on the street, not sure about anything anymore. I walked around and looked for familiar buildings and sights. It was impossible to pin them down. They seemed to have just disappeared. Whole sections in the center of town had been rebuilt. A garden was planted where houses used to be, trees were there instead of buildings. I wanted to fly back in time, but there was nothing to hold on to. I was chasing shadows. All I had were fragments of memory that never added up to something whole. My maps and drawings didn't help much. Names of streets had been changed several times, from Polish into German, then into Russian, and finally into Ukrainian. Polish Brzezany had become a Ukrainian town. Its former beauty still showed through the dilapidated facades of some old buildings around the Rynek. What used to be the Jewish cemetery on the Okopisko hillside on the way to the village of Raj was full of weeds and broken tombstones. This is where my father was shot and thrown into a mass grave during the last ghetto roundup, nearly half a century ago. We wandered around for a while, I said Kaddish, the prayer for the dead, and we left. My first return to Brzezany will always signify a major landmark in my mental and emotional journey back to the past.

* * *

The Poles called it Brzezany; the Ukrainians, Berezhany; and the Jews, Berezhan. These three ethnic groups had lived there for centuries. Brzezany, a village granted the status of town by the Polish King Sigismund the Old in the sixteenth century, became part of the Hapsburg Empire in 1772, following the partition of Poland. As a result of the disintegration of the Empire during the First World War and the emergence of independent Poland, Brzezany became part of Kresy, the eastern Polish borderlands that were not far from the Soviet border. The southeast region of Poland, where Brzezany was located, was usually referred to as eastern Galicia. The largest city in the region, less than 100 kilometers northwest of Brzezany, was Lwow. A somewhat closer large town, northeast of Brzezany, was Tarnopol. Brzezany was incorporated into the Soviet Ukrainian Republic in 1939 and became part of German-occupied "Distrikt Galizien" in 1941. In 1944, it again became part of Soviet Ukraine. With the collapse and disintegration of the Soviet Union in 1991, it has become part of independent Ukraine. Contemporary Berezhany is totally different from Brzezany of the interwar years. Almost all of its Polish inhabitants moved to Poland, and many of its Ukrainians fled to the west. Its Jewish population was annihilated. Today, Berezhany, a town of slightly more than 18,000, is almost completely Ukrainian.[1] Most of its inhabitants are Ukrainians who settled there after the war, having come from neighboring villages or other parts of Ukraine.

Whereas in the past the most common language in Brzezany was Polish, today one hears mainly Ukrainian and Russian in its streets. Most of the street names have been changed four times within half a century: first, during the short-lived Soviet rule between 1939 and 1941; then, during the German occupation in 1941; then again, after the return of the Soviets in 1944; and finally, after Ukrainian independence in 1991. Whereas during the interwar years the names of Polish military and cultural heroes, such as Pilsudski, Rydz-Smigly, Iwaszkiewicz, Mickiewicz, and Slowacki, were given to prominent Brzezany streets, during the second half of the century those same streets were given the names of Marx, Engels, and various Soviet leaders and generals. Today most of the street names reflect Ukrainian history and culture. Names such as Sheptyts'kyi, Bandera, and The Sich Riflemen, unthinkable under Polish or Soviet rule, are prominently displayed on its updated commercial map.[2] Contemporary Berezhany has very little in common with the multiethnic, multi-cultural, and multi-lingual community of old.

Interwar Brzezany was a neat, mid-sized town. Its population was about 11,000 before the First World War and about 13,000 on the eve of the Second World War.[3] Although the years 1914–1920 witnessed considerable demographic changes resulting from the war and the turmoil of the early postwar years, the basic size of its population wasn't seriously affected. The dominant group in Brzezany between the wars were the Poles. Every second person was Polish. The "Polishness" of Brzezany was enhanced by an army regiment of 1,000 soldiers and officers and their families, almost all of whom were Polish. Since Brzezany was a district town, many of its Polish inhabitants were employed by various administrative offices and institutions. The Poles were followed quite closely by the Jews: every third person in town was Jewish. Three out of every four stores in Brzezany were owned by Jews.[4] Ukrainians constituted less than a quarter of its population. But the surrounding countryside was predominantly Ukrainian. More than 60 percent of the peasants were Ukrainian, and about 30 percent were Polish.[5] Only a small number of Jews lived in the surrounding villages.

Various descriptions of Brzezany, as well as personal accounts of Brzezanyites, speak of the "Swiss" nature of the Brzezany landscape.[6] The town, located in a low-lying area, was surrounded by a number of gently sloped hills covered by forests: Storozysko in the north, Zwierzyniec in the northeast, Lysonia in the southeast, Ruryska in the south, and Babina Gora in the southwest. An impressive lake, the Brzezany Staw, through which flowed the Zlota Lipa River, was the striking feature of its northern edge. On a northwestern hill, overlooking the town, stood the centuries-old Bernardine Church and monastery. The town center, the Rynek, or the Ringplatz as it was called in Hapsburg times, was dominated by the Ratusz, the quadrangular town hall building with a belfry and clock on top. The Ratusz was surrounded on all four sides by buildings, some of which were constructed in a somewhat bombastic nineteenth-century style. Some were adorned with tall columns protruding from their front walls. On the ground floor of the Ratusz, as well as along the houses facing the Ratusz building, were numerous small shops, owned mostly by Jews. The space between the Ratusz and the block of houses to the north was used for weekly fairs, where peasants from nearby villages sold their produce. These were, naturally, the busiest days for the shop-owners. The open spaces around the Ratusz were also used for military parades and various festive occasions.

Opposite the western wall of the Ratusz, on a slight upgrade, was the Holy Trinity Tserkov, the Ukrainian church, with larger-than-life sculptures of Peter and Paul guarding the entrance. Not far from the Ratusz, on a slight elevation to the southwest, was the gothic Roman Catholic parish Farny Church, the largest place of worship in town. A few streets farther on, in the same direction, on a picturesque hill overlooking the town, was an impressive modern edifice, the Brzezany Gimnazjum. In the southern section of Brzezany, in the midst of the old and mostly poor Jewish quarter, was the Large Synagogue, constructed in a Renaissance style and modeled after the Synagogue of Livorno.[7] The short Potocki Street, leading eastward from the Ratusz, soon became Kolejowa, the Railroad Street, which ended at the local railroad station. On the northern side of Kolejowa, halfway between the town center and the railroad station, lay the grounds of the old, dilapidated Sieniawski Castle, surrounded by the Old Park. The Polish nobleman Nicholas of Sieniawa was the founder of the town of Brzezany. The castle was built as a massive fortress and included a church and a chapel, where the remains of its successive owners were interred. Along the southern side of Kolejowa, opposite the Sieniawski Castle, were the barracks of the 51st Army Regiment.

A 3-kilometer-long lane, shaded by tall linden trees, led from the southwestern suburb of Adamowka into the nearby village of Raj, which is Polish for "paradise." North of the lane, on a slope overlooking the town, lay the centuries-old Jewish cemetery, the Okopisko. Further toward Raj, south of the lane, was the extensive Christian cemetery where both Poles and Ukrainians buried their dead. At the far end of the linden lane, inside Raj, was the Potocki estate with its huge park and ponds and a beautiful Renaissance-style palace.

* * *

After leaving Brzezany in 1945, we resettled in Lodz, the "Polish Manchester," an industrial center and one of the few Polish cities which remained intact after the war. I spent five happy years there attending a Zionist Hebrew school. I was also a member of the Hashomer Hazair youth organization. By the time we finally emigrated to Israel, in the winter of 1950, I already spoke fluent Hebrew. Nevertheless, I went through a rather difficult "Israelization" process in one of the kibbutzim. Within a single year I became an Israeli, at least outwardly. I had to adapt to my sabra peers and must have paid a price for this. For years I bore a grudge against them. At the height of the Demjaniuk trial, in the course of a newspaper interview, I intentionally remarked that my memories of that simple Ukrainian peasant woman who saved me during the war were much more positive than the memories I carried from the kibbutz. I graduated from high school in a nearby town and was drafted into the army. The kibbutz, the army, and my studies at the Hebrew University in Jerusalem overshadowed my childhood in Brzezany. It gradually receded and dissolved into the distant past.

The first time I consciously started thinking about Brzezany was in the early 1960s. These were the long weeks of the Eichmann trial in Jerusalem. At the time I was studying history at the Hebrew University. One day, while browsing through some journals, I came across a short piece by Elie Wiesel, "The Last Return." Wiesel was telling the story of his first and last postwar visit to his hometown, Sighet. It moved me deeply. At that time I couldn't even dream about going back to Brzezany. I was totally immersed in my Israeli existence. The first time I traveled abroad was twelve years after coming to Israel. I was about to start my graduate studies at Harvard. I still recall the excitement and apprehension of returning to a non-Jewish world. It somehow reminded me of Lodz and Brzezany.

Although I had often heard ghetto and survival stories within the family, they didn't really affect me. I was busy with other things in my life. It was only in the mid-seventies, during my first sabbatical, while teaching at an American university, that I consciously started confronting my past. I was teaching a course on the Holocaust for the first time, and it was more difficult than I'd anticipated. I couldn't sleep well for a while. I struggled with the subject and with my personal involvement in it. I never revealed to my students that I was a survivor. During that American sabbatical, I met Ludwik and Jolka, a couple who were Polish scholars from Warsaw. In time, they would become very close friends. I'm sure that our friendship and the time we spent together influenced my attitudes toward Poles and Poland.

For years we hardly mentioned within the family Karol Codogni, his father, and Tanka Kontsevych. They were living, as far as we were concerned, on another planet. The reason must have been twofold: the issue of Righteous Gentiles was subdued for years in Israeli public discourse. And there was this wall between us in the West and Communist Eastern Europe. Perhaps it was also easier for us to suppress completely that part of our lives. Then, one day, following some casual remarks by my aging mother about remembrance and gratitude, I decided to try to find our Polish and Ukrainian rescuers. This was still the time when Poland and the Ukraine were the other side of the moon for the average Israeli. The last time we had seen these people was nearly forty years earlier. There had not been any contact during all that time. I had no updated addresses. The only way to try to locate them was to write to those places where they had lived back in the forties, Tanka in the village of Raj and Karol in Poland. I assumed that Karol would be living in Chojnow, a town in Silesia where many Poles who left Brzezany had settled. There were rumors among Brzezany survivors that Tanka had hidden some *banderovtsi* after we left Brzezany and was deported to Siberia. I didn't know what to expect. One morning, to my total surprise and excitement, I found an envelope with Soviet stamps on it in my mailbox. It was from Ania Kontsevych, Tanka's daughter, and the return address was Raj. It was short and personal. It spoke of the long-awaited letter which they had finally received from us. After my detective success with the Kontse-vyches, I decided to try to find Karol, whose family supplied us with food when we were hiding in the half-ruined Brzezany ghetto after the Judenrein. I was lucky for a second time. Although Karol didn't live in Chojnow any more, my letter got to him. A postal worker in Chojnow happened to be Karol's cousin and forwarded my letter. The renewed contacts with these Ukrainian and Polish families added a new dimension to my life. I had established a tangible link with a significant segment of my past. Now my ambition was to actually see these people again.

Another return of sorts was prompted by my research and teaching. They centered mainly on the war years, on Hitler's Germany and Stalin's Russia. The two leaders not only shaped the world of their times, they also affected my own life. Most of my work as a historian dealt with Jews in the Soviet Union during the war, primarily in territories not occupied by Nazi Germany. I was still incapable of doing direct work on any aspect of the "real thing." I was only walking around the edges of the Holocaust. But soon I started to make some forays into problematic territory. I spent a year at the Ukrainian Research Institute at Harvard University in the mid-eighties and started a project on Ukrainian-Jewish relations. This was already a small step toward my personal history. It was during that year, and completely by chance, that I was invited to participate in an international conference on Metropolitan Andrei Sheptyts'kyi, a leading Ukrainian clergyman in Lwow before and during the war. Sheptyts'kyi was an extremely complex and controversial personality. He was a prominent Ukrainian leader who saved Jews during the Holocaust. My presentation was on Sheptyts'kyi's relations with Jews. My interest in a Ukrainian who saved Jews was not accidental. I intended to show that not every Ukrainian was indifferent to the plight of the Jews. There was also a personal angle. My great-grandfather was one of the rabbis who greeted Sheptyts'kyi on his canonical visit to Brzezany before the First World War. At the Sheptyts'kyi conference, I was surrounded by dozens of Ukrainian priests from all over the world. They wore long black frocks and huge Orthodox crosses. This was both exciting and strange for me. At the Harvard Ukrainian Research Institute, I met young and old Ukrainian scholars. I was getting closer to a milieu that was both near and distant at the same time. By reading and talking, I attempted to grasp what made them tick. I tried to think "Ukrainian." My feelings were mixed.

My mind became preoccupied with Tanka, Karol, and Brzezany. I dreamed about them. In one dream I was in Brzezany with Tanka. Her daughter, Ania, took me for a walk. The sights were familiar; a street, a park. I spoke Polish in my dream. I tasted the food and fruits of my childhood. It was a good feeling. It evoked strong yearnings. In another dream I was with Karol in Poland. This was an anxiety dream. I'd lost my passport and visa. I was panicking and wanted to get out.

A short while after returning from my "Ukrainian" sabbatical, I finally met Karol for the first time since leaving Brzezany. He arrived in Israel in the spring of 1986 and was our guest for a month. He spoke only Polish, and I translated nonstop. In spite of the language barrier, an instantaneous friendship developed between Karol and my family. He kept talking about me as his "younger brother." He seemed like a real member of my family. He had known my Grandpa Fishl so well. I asked Karol to relive the war, the ghetto, the killings, and his family's assistance to us. What interested me most was their motivation. I couldn't get a clear-cut answer from him. I had requested Yad Vashem months earlier to recognize Karol as a Righteous Gentile and sent them my mother's and my own personal depositions describing the details of his and his father's assistance. Our request was granted, and a date had been set for the ceremony.

Karol received his Righteous Gentile award at Yad Vashem and met there with some of his boyhood friends from Brzezany, who arrived from all over Israel. This was a very emotional encounter. I also made an effort to bring our story into the public eye. We were interviewed on a popular live TV news program. I translated back and forth from Polish to Hebrew and was amazed that I could do it so easily. The interview with Karol centered on questions of survival and rescue. It showed that not everything was bleak, that humanity was not doomed. Not every Pole was an anti-Semite. For decades, the popular perception in Israel and among Jews elsewhere had been of a world totally hostile to Jews during the Holocaust. I kept trying for years to convey the message that the situation at that time and in those places was extremely complex and that, in spite of the tremendous obstacles, there were people who opened their doors to Jews. My survival story and Karol's part in it were tangible examples. My request for Tanka to be recognized as a Righteous Gentile was also approved and I intended to bring her over as well to receive her Righteous Gentile award, but she was in no condition to travel to Israel. Instead, Ania and Tania came to represent her. A friend, Harvey Sarner, a retired American Jewish lawyer who subsidized the visits to Israel of numerous Righteous Gentiles from Eastern Europe, helped out. They arrived from Kiev with the first group of Righteous Gentiles from Ukraine brought over by Sarner in the summer of 1992.

The momentous events in Eastern Europe in the late eighties and early nineties affected me both personally and professionally. The collapse of communism and the disintegration of the Soviet Union opened up possibilities which hadn't existed before. I could travel not only to Warsaw but also to Moscow, Kiev, Lwow, and Brzezany. Many Israelis who originated from Poland went back as tourists. I was part of that wave of nostalgia and return. But I differed from most Israelis and Jews in my perception of this "homecoming." Most Jews perceived Poland as an enormous Jewish cemetery and as basically enemy territory. They were not interested in contemporary Poland and things Polish. They traveled for one single purpose, to remember and to mourn. My thoughts and emotions were much more complex. Though I was fully aware of anti-Semitism and the wartime Jewish tragedy, I was also renewing contact with landscapes, languages, cultures, and people. The first physical encounter with my past, which I had been dreaming and thinking about for a long time, took place in the early spring of 1987. I returned to Poland after thirty-seven years. Although it wasn't easy for an Israeli to travel to Poland at that time, it was nearly impossible to travel to Soviet Ukraine, to Brzezany. My first visit to Brzezany would materialize only in 1991. My "Polish" return was, in a way, a step toward my journey to Brzezany.

The only way for an Israeli to travel to Poland was by joining a tourist group. I stayed with my group for only one day. We attended a ceremony at the Rapoport Monument for the heroes of the Warsaw ghetto uprising. Hundreds of young Israelis, with "Israel" on their sweatshirts, were holding blue-and-white flags. I noticed the blue shirts and white laces of Hashomer Hazair. I was deeply moved and excited. I had been here back in 1948, when we came to represent the Hashomer Hazair in Lodz at the unveiling of the monument. Our group also visited the old Warsaw Jewish Cemetery on Gesia Street. This was actually the only place in the city which remained completely intact. Here, in the land of the dead, I felt at home as a Jew, more so than in any other part of the city.

I spent the remaining days with Karol. We traveled together to Treblinka. I visited some other Jewish sites. But my visit to Poland was also a "Polish" one. I enjoyed hearing Polish spoken on the streets and being able to speak an almost fluent Polish myself. At least in the cultural sense, I felt at home. I wasn't on the lookout for Polish anti-Semitism and anti-Semites. And yet not everything went smoothly, at least in my own mind. One of Karol's younger relatives tried to convince me that it was the Jews who had helped Hitler rise to power. That upset me, and I tried to teach him a lesson in history. Then came the Lodz incident. I went to Lodz with Karol by train on Easter Monday. It was a gray, cold, and drizzly morning. I distinctly remembered the location of the house where we had lived in Lodz after arriving from Brzezany. I often thought about that building on the corner of Gdanska Street. The street was now completely deserted, nothing but dilapidated buildings and dark-gray courtyards. The sight was depressing. When I approached "my" house, I became dizzy and experienced an eerie sense of being catapulted back in time. I started checking the list of names at the entrance to the house, as if expecting to find somebody I had known there forty years earlier. I did the same thing in a neighboring house, where some of our acquaintances used to live. A group of teenagers was standing farther back in the courtyard. Suddenly, I was all wet. A bucketful of ice-cold water was running down my neck. I was instantly hurled back into postwar Lodz. I was being chased by Polish teenagers. Now and then, in the very same streets, I sensed fear and rage. Karol apologized and reminded me of the age-old Polish custom of "wet Easter Monday." Still, I couldn't overcome the sense of terror. My feelings and emotions concerning Poles and Poland were apparently much more complex than I would have liked to admit.

I flew to Warsaw again a year later, in the summer of 1988. One afternoon, while I was walking in the Lazienki Park with Ludwik, the Polish math professor whom I had met in Pittsburgh, distant memories of Polish landscapes came back to me. Something kept pulling me back to my childhood in Brzezany. Ludwik pointed out to me that a father was calling his young son by my Polish name, Szymek. The situation, the scenery, and the very casual sound of my name in Polish moved me. Indeed, throughout my stay in Poland I came to re-experience many long-forgotten sensations. The present was constantly intertwined with the past. Such was the case when I visited the historical sites of Krakow: Sukiennice, the old cloth halls, the Mariacki Church, the Wawel Citadel. Although I was seeing them for the first time, they were carved somewhere in my childhood memories. I must have heard and read about them. It was like returning to something distant and close at the same time. I recalled the children's story of the brave shoemaker boy and the dragon. The names of the famous Polish kings and queens echoed in my mind. From Krakow we went to Zakopane, a traditional and still very popular resort town at the foot of the Tatra Mountains, which we climbed day after day. Unlike many Jews, I experienced Poland as a place where one could also meet friends and go on a holiday.

A few days before my flight home, I was invited to lecture on Sheptyts'kyi at the Polish History Institute in the Old City Square of Warsaw. The Kosciuszko Auditorium on the second floor was full to the brim. Among the mostly Polish audience there were also a few Ukrainians. The furniture was dark and solemn. There was a bust of Kosciuszko, the legendary Polish national hero. A huge crystal-like chandelier in front of me was adorned with hundreds of little glistening Polish eagles. And here I was, a Jew and an Israeli, about to discuss a highly controversial Ukrainian personality who had been criticized at times by both Poles and Jews. On top of all this, I had decided to speak in Polish. I was both overwhelmed and nervous. As I lectured, I started sweating and felt faint. I took off my jacket and considered apologizing and stopping, but somehow I continued. When it was all over, I was completely drained. Why was this seemingly professional academic encounter so powerful and emotional for me? Perhaps it had to do with my complex and conflicting feelings about those triangular relations among Jews, Poles, and Ukrainians.

I flew to Moscow for the first time in December 1989, to participate in a conference. Next day I met Ania. I had arranged for her to stay with some Moscow friends of our Israeli acquaintances. Ania traveled all the way from Brzezany in Western Ukraine. She had never been to Moscow and was overwhelmed by the capital. She looked like a simple, good-natured woman. I asked her about her mother, who for health reasons couldn't join her. Ania told me time and again how Tanka wanted to see Szymek, her "little boy." I tried to elicit some details about their family. I wanted to understand why Tanka took us in when we were forced to leave the ghetto. Tanka, it turns out, was an orphan and had "lived with people," as the Ukrainian saying goes. Then, when she married, relations with her husband weren't the best. When he returned from forced labor in Germany after the war, he stayed in the house for only a short time and then left. Tanka's was a women's household most of the time. After we left Brzezany, they let a stranger who was looking for lodging stay overnight. The man stole whatever valuables they had and then left. This seemingly insignificant story was perhaps an answer to my question. The basic human qualities of such simple people as Tanka fascinated me: their naiveté, an almost childish behavior, their willingness to take risks without thinking about the consequences. All these qualities were part of the miracle which saved our lives.

I returned to Lwow and Brzezany, this time alone, in the summer of 1996. By then they were part of the new Ukrainian State. At the Okecie airport, flying out from Warsaw, I met a few elderly people who were about to visit their "old country" in Western Ukraine. I tried to communicate with them. My attempt was not very fruitful. These were Ukrainians who apparently had left during the war and settled in the West. Some were returning with their offspring—a Ukrainian "back to the roots" journey. When they heard that I was Jewish, our small talk just died. I didn't feel very comfortable with them, either. We were returning to the places of our past. But our return, though parallel, was separate. This time I was all alone in Lwow. Not only alone, but alone in run-down Lwow. I became depressed.

Like Brzezany, Lwow, which had been one of the most beautiful Hapsburg cities, was falling apart. In both cases, this was the result of Soviet-type neglect and poverty. I recalled reading or hearing somewhere about a Polish tourist who cried when he revisited his native Lwow years after resettling in Poland. Once a city of professionals, artists, and intellectuals, it now looked like an enormous drab provincial town. My mood didn't change much in Brzezany. The excitement of my first visit was gone. The Kontsevyches told me about the difficulties of everyday life. Although they had become "free," they didn't have enough money to buy food. Tanka was bedridden. She was ill and very thin. She recognized me immediately and told me that it was pure luck to be able to see me once more before the end. Ania was recuperating from a serious operation. Things didn't look good, and I promised to help.

When I came to Brzezany for the third time, in the summer of 1998, Tanka was gone. We visited her grave. They had become so poor that they couldn't afford a tombstone. I gave them money to cover the expenses. This was also the first time I stayed overnight in Brzezany. After my first two 1-day visits I had a strong urge to go to sleep and wake up there, as if this act could bring something back to me. Nothing in particular happened. I had some more time to walk around the city. It used to be my town, but now it was strange and distant. The material and architectural neglect and the human scenery made me both sad and angry. I still attempted to return to certain places. On a quiet and sunny Sunday morning, I again walked up the stairs of the light-brown house on Kolejowa. A tenant offered her keys to the attic. The place definitely reminded me of that wartime attic with its solid wooden beams. I lay down in the chicken droppings and looked out through a tiny opening in the roof, in the direction of the Ukrainian Church, the way I did more than half a century ago. I was trying to relive those moments.

While in Brzezany I met Stefan Dudar once again. He was a Ukrainian I had come to know back in 1991. At that time he had already retired from his post as director of the local ethnographic museum. Dudar is a pleasant and soft-spoken old-time gentleman. We conversed in both Polish and Ukrainian. His was a very unusual story. A native of Buczacz, not far from Brzezany, he had been friendly with Jewish students in the local Gimnazjum and fell in love with a Jewish girl, who was later saved by Dudar's family. They settled in Brzezany after the war, where his wife had died a few years earlier. Dudar, though always very helpful to Jewish tourists visiting Brzezany, has preferred not to talk about his family history. But this time he insisted that I come to his grandson's wedding, which took place in a local school auditorium that was very close to the Okopisko Jewish cemetery. It's quite possible that the school was built on the site of Jewish mass graves. As I waltzed with the groom's mother, who by Halakhic law is Jewish, I realized that I might be dancing on my father's grave.

A few hours before leaving Brzezany, I was introduced to Anna Lysak by Father Jakubczyk, the Polish priest of the minuscule Catholic congregation of Brzezany, whom I had met a year earlier at the reunion of Brzezany Poles at Ustron. It was raining heavily, and I interviewed her while riding around town with Volodia, a young historian from Lwow University whom I hired as my local driver. Volodia and my Polish friend Waclaw Wierzbieniec, a historian from Rzeszow, accompanied me to Brzezany this time. Anna was one of the two native Brzezany Jews who were still living there. Her father had fallen in love with a Polish girl and they had married back in the twenties. His family renounced him, but little Anna used to visit her Jewish grandparents. Anna's father was killed during the Yom Kippur roundup of 1941. The rest of her father's family moved to nearby Podhajce, and all perished there. Anna identified various prewar streets and buildings for me. She also pointed out a corner of the Christian cemetery, in back of the burial site of fallen Red Army soldiers. That was where the remains of those Brzezany Jews, including her father, who were killed at the quarry near Raj were re-interred in the seventies. Right opposite a monument commemorating Soviet soldiers there now stands a much more impressive monument commemorating the hundreds of Ukrainian nationalist partisans who were killed by the Soviets after the war. This unusual corner of the Brzezany cemetery portrays the essential aspects of a tragic past: Jewish victims of Nazi Germany, Soviet soldiers who liberated and occupied Brzezany, and Ukrainian nationalists who were killed by the Soviets.

When I returned to Lwow, there was a solemn celebration taking place on the main street. When I asked about the event, I was told that it was a requiem to commemorate the re-occupation of Western Ukraine by the Red Army in the summer of 1944. Strange. I remembered it as liberation.

* * *

I often considered writing my memoirs, particularly after I started my journey back into the past. But I finally concluded that what seemed to be my authentic memories were not really adequate for writing a personal memoir. On one hand, I envied those survivors who had a lot to tell. On the other hand, there were those who were babies or infants during the war and had even fewer recollections than I did. At times I thought that psychoanalysis, or perhaps hypnosis, could help me reconstruct the past. But the former was too expensive and the latter too frightening. The closest I came to writing my own story was my nearly obsessive reading of other Holocaust children's memoirs. I took part in several public meetings of such "children." My strongest impressions were physical. There was a surprising and shocking sense of aging that was strangely balanced by constant references to our identity as children and youths. Perhaps, in a sense, we remained children. The trauma of the war and the Holocaust didn't allow us to grow up normally.

I finally reached the conclusion that the only feasible way for me to return to my past was to integrate the bits and pieces of my personal memories into a study of my hometown. This would be not only a geographical and historical revisiting of the past but, more important for me, a way to revive and share the memories of others who lived in Brzezany; not only of the Jews but also of the Poles and the Ukrainians. I wanted to reconstruct Brzezany's past with the memories of its former inhabitants. I also expected them to fill in the gaps in my own memory. There were certain events, images, and impressions which I had carried for years in my mind and which I wanted to confirm as events that really happened. This would be a double experience for me—as fellow Brzezanyite and as a historian. I've used oral history in my research projects for years. Now I would use it in a much more personal and intimate manner. The interviewees would become a part of my reconstruction of the past.

FIGURE 1. Author with Tanka Kontsevych. Brzezany, August 1991.

FIGURE 2. From left to right: Ania, Tanka, and Tania Kontsevych, author, Judy Redlich. On the floor, from left to right: Shlomit and Efrat Redlich. Brzezany, August 1991.

FIGURE 3.   The Large Synagogue. Brzezany, August 1991.

FIGURE 4.   Vovo Szotenberg with
Ania and Tania Kontsevych during
their visit to Israel, April 1992.

FIGURE 5. Karol Codogni planting his Righteous Gentile tree. Yad Vashem, June 1986.

FIGURE 6. Annual reunion of Brzezany Poles. Ustron, June 1997. First row, third from right: Zbigniew Rusinski; fourth from right: author. Second row, fifth from right: Ryszard Brzezinski.

FIGURE 7.   With the Wanderer sisters. From left to right:
Rena, author, Ruth. Lakeview, New Jersey, September
1998.

FIGURE 8.   Author with Aleksandr Pankiv, overlooking the Okopisko
Jewish cemetery. Brzezany, July 1998.

FIGURE 9. Overview of Brzezany prior to the First World War (postcard). Courtesy of Ryszard Brzezinski.

FIGURE 10. Brzezany Rynek, prior to the First World War (postcard). Courtesy of Ryszard Brzezinski.

FIGURE 11.   Brzezany Rynek, prior to the First World War (postcard).
Courtesy of Ryszard Brzezinski.

FIGURE 12.   Israeli Brzezanyites, including Bela Feld and Natan Goldman,
visit Brzezany in the summer of 1997. In the background: the Ukrainian
Holy Trinity Church. Courtesy of Roni Ben-Ari.

2

CLOSE AND DISTANT NEIGHBORS

My first task, and the easiest, was reaching out to the surviving Brzezany Jews, some of whom had left the town before the war. Most of them lived now in Israel. First came the oldest, those born before the First World War.

Batya Bone-Prizand, born in Brzezany in 1911, described her childhood as "paradise." For some reason, I was happy to hear it. It reconfirmed, perhaps, my own childhood memories. I was also pleasantly surprised in a personal sense. It turned out that my Aunt Pnina was Batya's adored group leader in the Hashomer Hazair youth movement in Brzezany. Although Batya's family was orthodox and her father was a teacher of religion, a *melamed,* Batya attended the local Polish public grammar school for girls and at the age of 14 started her studies at the Brzezany Women Teachers' Seminary. She was 20 when she graduated in 1931 and was assigned a teaching position out of town. Less than a year later, she was on her way to Palestine.[1]

Bela Feld, a retired teacher, talked with me about her childhood and youth in Brzezany for the first time in many years. The Felds had three sons and two daughters. Bela, born in 1912, was the older sister. The Felds lived near Brzezany before the First World War. They fled to the Czech region of the Hapsburg Empire when the war started and resettled in Brzezany in 1918. Bela, like Batya, completed the public grammar school and studied at the teachers' seminary. She was also deeply involved with the local branch of the Hanoar Hatzioni Zionist youth movement. The long interview with Bela was permeated with a strong sense of loss. She kept returning to the tragic end of her family, particularly the end of her younger sister, Chanale. All perished in the Holocaust. Bela's older brother, Aryeh, the only radiologist in town, was shot during one of the earliest roundups. The others apparently perished in the Belzec death camp. Nevertheless, Bela was open-minded and fair when it came to judging Poles and Ukrainians. When she was studying in the Brzezany Women Teachers' Seminary, one of her closest friends was Hala Dydyk, a Ukrainian girl from a nearby village. For all those years, Bela had kept her graduation picture, in which the two of them stood near each other. After completing her seminary education, Bela lived and worked for a number of years in Lwow and emigrated to Palestine in 1935. She returned to Brzezany for a short visit in 1937. That was the last time she saw her family.[2]

Israel Ne'eman from Narajow, a small town north of Brzezany, had just returned from his first visit to his hometown in sixty-two years. Like many other Jewish families, the Neumanns fled the approaching front line during the First World War and reached Vienna, where they stayed until 1922. They were a strictly orthodox family. Israel's grandfather had been a rabbi in Narajow. Young Israel attended the local public school, where most of the students were Ukrainian. He was also an active member of the local Zionist youth organization and left for Palestine in 1935. Israel always speaks at our annual Brzezany commemoration meetings and usually fumes about Ukrainian and Polish anti-Semitism in his still deep and distinct baritone. Surprisingly, when he reminisced about his own childhood and youth in Narajow, he told me that he had had Ukrainian friends, and he even spoke about them with a certain affection.[3]

The younger interviewees, born after the First World War, were now in their 70s. Menachem Katz, or Munio Haber, as he was known in Brzezany, is an architect. He remains the "living memory" of our town. He was editor of the Brzezany Yizkor Book[4] and has published his Holocaust memoirs. Menachem drew designs of all the Brzezany synagogues from memory. He is also the man who now convenes our annual memorial get-togethers. Menachem is the only survivor of the "W" group. These Jews worked for the Wehrmacht during the German occupation and, contrary to expectations, were killed along with the other victims of the last Judenrein roundup. I hoped that Menachem would remember my father, who was one of them, but he didn't. Munio started his studies in the Brzezany Gimnazjum shortly before the war and continued in the Soviet-type *desiatiletka*—10-year school—in 1939–1941. When the Germans occupied Brzezany, he was a youngster of 16. During the last Judenrein roundup, in the summer of 1943, he was barely 18. Munio stayed with his stepfather in the "W" group barracks. His stepfather committed suicide shortly before the men were taken to the Okopisko cemetery. Munio survived with his mother and younger sister. After the war they settled in Israel.[5]

Natan Goldman, a retired educator, is tall and slightly stooped. He was the number-one Jewish sportsman in Brzezany before the war, and even now, close to 80, he persists in his daily swimming routine. One of Natan's feats was knocking out a Polish boxer who represented the army regiment stationed in Brzezany. Natan's was an unconventional Jewish family. His grandfather was a building contractor during the Hapsburg times. He and his brothers specialized in the construction of church copulas in the Ukrainian villages around Brzezany. The Goldmans opened a textile store near the Brzezany Rynek at the turn of the century. It soon became one of the most fashionable stores in town. A succession of maids did the housework while Natan's grandmother was running the store. One of them, according to Natan, was the mother of Edzio Rydz, the future commander-in-chief of the Polish army. Rydz was also a classmate of Natan's father, Leon. Both attended the Brzezany Gimnazjum before the First World War. In addition to running their store, the Goldmans acquired some farm land near Brzezany and went into the timber business. Young Natan went often to the farm and loved riding horses, something quite unusual for a Jewish youngster at that time.

Although Natan's father attended the Brzezany Synagogue from time to time, "he was almost an atheist," in Natan's words. Natan himself quit the *heder* at age 4 and remained a staunch atheist all his life. He was a student at the Gimnazjum in the thirties and a member of the Hanoar Hatzioni youth movement. Natan and his father traveled to Palestine, where the family owned some real estate, in the late summer of 1939. Natan's mother, Roza, and his sister, Bela, remained in Brzezany and survived the Holocaust. For years I have cherished a sweet childhood memory of playing with a beautiful sister and brother. It might have been Natan and his sister Bela.[6]

After meeting with Israeli Brzezanyites, I traveled to New York to interview my American *landsleit*. I had heard a lot about the Wanderer sisters, Rena and Ruth. They were both beautiful girls, growing up in a well-to-do and caring family who owned a store right opposite the Ratusz. It was run by their grandma, Fruma. Fruma was fluent in German and often traveled to Vienna to purchase merchandise. When I called Rena, the older one, and asked whether a young Polish historian, a colleague of mine who was doing research in New York, could interview her for my project on Brzezany, her reaction was curt and clear: "I hate all Polacks." When I spoke to her sister Ruth and told her that I'd recently been to Brzezany, she asked about the Staw, the Brzezany lake. She had heard that it didn't exist anymore. When I told her that it was there, though utterly neglected, her immediate reaction was, "I wish Brzezany would drown in that Staw." Rena advised me not to present the Poles in too favorable a way "for the sake of our martyrs." Still, during lunch in Ruth's suburban New Jersey house, she remarked, "I wonder what we would have done as potential rescuers." We didn't follow up this touchy subject. The Wanderers were among the luckiest Jewish families in town. Both parents and the girls survived the war. They were hidden successively by several Polish families. After the war, the Wanderers emigrated to America. I sent the Wanderer sisters information about the Regulas, one of the Polish families in whose house on the outskirts of Brzezany they had hid after the Judenrein roundup. I hoped that they would start the procedure of granting them the Righteous Gentiles award, but nothing came of it.[7]

Poldek was a retired medical doctor in his 80s. He lived in Queens, New York. Originally from Kozowa, a small town near Brzezany, he attended the Brzezany Gimnazjum before the war. When he graduated, in 1934, Poldek intended to study medicine in Lwow. He was turned down as a result of the prevailing anti-Jewish entrance regulations and went to study medicine in Vienna. After the Anschluss, in 1938, still short of completing his medical education, he was forced to return to Brzezany. Within a year, the Soviets gave him a chance to finally get his doctor's diploma from Lwow University.

Poldek's wartime story is very unusual. During the German occupation of Brzezany, he served as a physician with the Ukrainska Povstanska Armiia (UPA, Ukrainian Insurgent Army), the Ukrainian nationalist underground. Poldek was ready to talk about it on the condition that his full identity would never be revealed. He was convinced that being exposed would cause problems and might even be dangerous for him. He was still afraid of the Ukrainians, more than half a century later. Were other survivors, like Poldek, afraid of their gentile neighbors in America, especially those who reminded them of Poles and Ukrainians? I never encountered such fears among my Israeli interviewees. Poldek escaped from his Ukrainian partisan unit sometime in the summer of 1944 and returned to Soviet-occupied Brzezany, from where he went first to Poland, then to Germany, and finally to the United States, where he settled.[8]

From New York, I flew to Washington, D.C. to meet Dr. Stanislaw Skrzypek. He was living all alone in a slightly neglected suburban house, surrounded by Brzezany memorabilia. His family settled in Brzezany shortly after the First World War as part of the Polish settlement policy in the eastern borderlands. The Skrzypeks must have been a most patriotic and extremely nationalist Polish family. Stanislaw's father headed the Polish Settlers' Committee in the Brzezany region. They had a house and a farm near the Brzezany lake, the Staw. Young Staszek was very active in the local Polish Scouts, the Harcerstwo.[9] He graduated from the Gimnazjum in 1929 and left for university studies in Lwow. On the eve of the war he was an army officer and as such was arrested and interned in several Soviet prisons. Later on he succeeded in joining General Anders's Polish army, which was organized in the Soviet Union. After leaving Russia with Anders's army, Stanislaw arrived in Palestine sometime in 1943. Then he fought in Italy and reached England toward the end of the war. Stanislaw worked there for the Polish government-in-exile and eventually emigrated to America, where he worked for Radio Liberty.[10]

Mike Thaler is Professor Emeritus of Pediatrics at the University of California School of Medicine in San Francisco. For years he was president of the Holocaust Center of Northern California. He is also conducting research on medical ethics in Nazi Germany. For me he is also red-headed and quick-tempered little Manek, whom I used to play and fight with in Brzezany. He is one of the few Brzezany Jewish children who survived the Holocaust. An only child, he survived with both his parents. They went from Brzezany to Poland and then lived for a while in a displaced persons camp near Linz.

Young Manek attended the same *realschule* where Hitler once studied. From Germany, they emigrated to Toronto, Canada. Manek studied medicine in California and has been there ever since.

I met Mike for the first time since the liberation at the funeral of Dr. Wagszal-Shaklai in Haderah. I bumped into him a few years later at a Holocaust conference in Oxford, where we had a fierce argument about Ukrainians and Jews. Manek was convinced that all Ukrainians were, and still are, anti-Semites and that they murdered Jews in Brzezany and elsewhere during the war. Mike recently returned to Brzezany in the course of a professional consulting mission to Ukraine, more than half a century after he had left the town.[11] I called him several times to discuss his visit. When Mike was invited recently to speak at Ben-Gurion University, I suggested that we discuss publicly our Brzezany memories. One of Mike's remarks was that gentiles who assisted and saved Jews during the war were *meshuge* and that all the rest were anti-Semites.

Prof. Mati Shaklai is probably the youngest survivor from Brzezany. He is head of hematology in one of the largest medical centers in Israel. He is the son of Dr. Lipa Wagszal-Shaklai. His father wrote extensive memoirs of the war years and assisted Menachem Katz in preparing the Brzezany Yizkor Book. I remembered little Matus, who was the youngest of our bunch in the building on Kolejowa Street in the Brzezany ghetto. Mati's aunt, his father's sister Zlata, was married to my Uncle Yakov. Yakov was deported to Belzec, and Zlata was killed during one of the roundups in Brzezany. A few years ago I assisted Mati in locating Danek, the Polish doctor and his father's colleague and friend, who helped the Wagszals when they were hiding in the Brzezany countryside. Mati traveled to Poland with his older cousin Marek to meet with the 90-year-old Danek after fifty years. They presented him with a Righteous Gentile scroll and medal. After visiting Dr. Danek, Mati and Marek traveled to Brzezany.[12]

* * *

Zbigniew Rusinski was the first Brzezany Pole, besides Karol, with whom I had established contact. Rusinski is the Polish version of Menachem Katz. He collects every bit and piece of information about Brzezany and owns the largest collection of Brzezany memorabilia. He also published a book on Brzezany in the late nineties. It comprises only a small part of what he had amassed during the years. Rusinski, a teenager during the war, was a member of Szare Szeregi, the Polish underground Scout organization. He claimed that there was an organized effort by Polish Scouts to supply food to the Brzezany ghetto. Rusinski was shot and wounded by a local Ukrainian policeman during one such attempt. He had a close friend inside the ghetto, David, the son of Dr. Pomeranz. David had been one of the very few Jewish youngsters who belonged to the Polish youth movement in prewar Brzezany.

Dr. Pomeranz and his family were eventually killed by the Germans at the Okopisko cemetery.

The Rusinskis, like almost all Polish families, left the town after the war and resettled in Polish Silesia. Zbigniew became in time a military engineer and had been for decades a close friend and supporter of the Polish Scout movement. He was given the Righteous Gentile award for smuggling food into the Brzezany ghetto. I met him for the first time when I participated in a reunion of Polish Brzezanyites in Ustron, a picturesque resort site on the Polish-Czech border.[13]

I met Tolek Rapf and Tolek's younger sister, Halszka, during two successive visits to Poland. Natan Goldman had mentioned the Rapfs during his interview. Tolek was Natan's closest Polish friend in the Brzezany Gimnazjum. The Rapfs were one of the elite Polish families in prewar Brzezany. Their father, Jan Wilhelm Rapf, the town engineer of Brzezany, came from a completely Polonized Austrian family. Their mother's Polish family had been Brzezanyites for generations. The impressive Rapf villa, designed and built by their father, was across the street from the Farny Church, not far from the Rynek. It served as a meeting place for the local Polish intelligentsia. The Rapfs often hosted Father Lancucki, who was in charge of the Farny Church, and Dr. Bilinski, who was head of the Brzezany Hospital. Engineer Rapf, besides his official duties, was also a silent partner in some commercial enterprises owned by rich Jewish families who needed a Polish "facade." Both Tolek and Halszka studied at the Gimnazjum. Tolek was a classmate of Natan for a number of years and, like Natan, excelled in sport. He also belonged to the Polish Scout organization.

The peaceful and happy times ended for the Rapfs abruptly in the early fall of 1939, following the occupation of Brzezany by the Soviets. The father, who had been ailing for some time, died three months later. Then the family was forced out of their beautiful villa by Red Army officers and moved to Lwow. They returned to Brzezany shortly after the Soviet retreat and moved back into their house, which was requisitioned once more, this time by a high-ranking German official. During the German occupation of Brzezany, Tolek worked for the German firm Unduetsch, and Halszka worked at the local Kreishauptmannschaft. All that time Tolek was also active in the AK Home Army, the Polish underground. Mrs. Rapf, Halszka, and the rest of their family preferred to leave Brzezany before its reoccupation by the Soviets. Tolek had to stay, following AK orders. They were eventually reunited in Poland.[14] I looked up the Rapf villa on my latest visit to Brzezany. In spite of its shabby looks, it was still impressive.

Ludka Michorowska was a retired accountant who was active in ZBOWID, the Polish war veteran's association. Born in 1925, she was the daughter of Captain Lubelski, quartermaster with the 51st Infantry Regiment stationed in Brzezany. They lived in a 2-story, newly built house that was occupied by officers' families. After she graduated from the Brzezany public school for girls, she studied at the Gimnazjum for two years before the war. After the Germans occupied Brzezany, she worked in a small workshop producing little wooden boxes used for storing medical ointments. My father was in charge of that workshop for a while. Then she worked in a millinery run by Mrs. Wanderer, Rena and Ruth's mother. Ludka's father was a German POW during the war, and their family reunited only in 1948, in Poland.[15]

Ryszard Brzezinski was born in 1945, after his parents had left Brzezany and resettled in western Poland. Nevertheless, he insisted on being considered as a native Brzezanyite, since, as he kept repeating, he was conceived in Brzezany. Ryszard, like Rusinski, is also an avid collector of Brzezany memorabilia, and I sensed immediately the "competition" between the two. He dreams of establishing a Brzezany museum in his countryside house. Ryszard showed me some extraordinary old color postcards of the town. An enlarged copy of one such postcard now hangs in my study. Ryszard was one of the first Poles to return to Brzezany. His grandmother was allowed to visit her brother, one of the very few Poles who had stayed on in Brzezany. This was in the summer of 1953, a few months after Stalin's death. Ryszard went with her. Since then he has returned for family visits almost every summer.[16]

One of my last interviews in Poland was with Prof. Jozef Slotwinski, or, as his friends call him, Jozek. He was 90. I traveled to a sanatorium for privileged retirees near Warsaw, where he was staying at that time, and we chatted for a while. Slotwinski is not a native Brzezanyite. He arrived there in 1933 to teach Polish language and literature at the Gimnazjum after receiving a doctorate from Lwow University. He was 25 then, and he was the youngest and most popular professor in that respectable and conservative school. He was also an avid tennis player and belonged to that small group of Polish admirers of the "British sport" in provincial Brzezany.

Slotwinski would go often for visits to the Rapfs and soon fell in love with their oldest daughter, Lidka. Lidka was then an upper-grade student in the Gimnazjum who was talented, attractive, and an excellent athlete. They married a few years later. Slotwinski was one of the founders of Polish television after the war. He wrote and produced a number of television plays. There was something of the theater and of acting in him even now. His shirt and trousers matched perfectly. As he was talking and reminiscing, he gestured and actually acted out some Brzezany "types."[17]

My last interview in Poland was with "Anna Herzog." I was her guest for twenty-four hours. She explicitly asked me not to identify her for personal reasons. The Herzogs, an affluent Jewish family, owned a number of flour mills. Anna, born in 1922, remembered their comfortable 6-room apartment in the center of town. Theirs was one of the first houses to get electricity. The Herzogs also had a rented car at their disposal, a most unusual thing in prewar Brzezany. Unlike most Brzezany Jews, they were permeated with

26

Polish culture and were very close to the local Polish milieu. They hardly ever attended the synagogue. According to Anna, there were only a few assimilated Jewish families in Brzezany. Among them were the Grosmans and the Pomeranzs, close friends of the Herzogs. Young Anna was an excellent student at the Gimnazjum who also took piano lessons, swam, ice-skated, and played tennis. Her first love was Adas Goldschlag, who was also from an affluent and somewhat assimilated Jewish family.

Anna was assisted during the German occupation by a Polish priest; she married a Pole and converted to Catholicism. Both parents survived, left Brzezany, and lived as Catholics in postwar Poland. Anna became, apparently, the most devout Catholic in their family. Unexpectedly, I felt quite at home with her. What bound us together was probably the Polish language, literature, and culture in general. There was also a personal angle to our meeting. Anna's parents were close friends of Dr. Fredzio Redlich, a talented pediatrician and a distant cousin of mine. Fredzio, too, must have been one of those few assimilated Brzezany Jews. After leaving Brzezany, he settled in Lwow and married the divorcée of a Polish army officer. She hid him during the German occupation. I remember Dr. Redlich as a black-haired, middle-sized man who used to come to our apartment on Gdanska Street in Lodz, after the war, when I was sick.[18]

When Anna accompanied me to the railway station on my way back to Warsaw, she asked me to let her know the exact date of Yom Kippur, the Day of Atonement, so she could light a candle for her Jewish relatives who perished in Brzezany. She also gave me the telephone number of Adas Goldschlag in Florida.

After returning to Israel I called Adas, now Sam A. Goldschlag, and told him about my meeting with Anna. He was almost 80 and his health was poor, but his memories of prewar Brzezany were vivid. We spoke English interspersed with Polish, moving freely back and forth. Goldschlag's father, Dr. Pesah Goldschlag, was a prominent lawyer in interwar Brzezany. Theirs was one of the most respected Jewish families in town. Dr. Goldschlag was a public figure. He was chairman of the local chapter of the Hoover Commission for War Relief in Brzezany after the First World War and personally welcomed Herbert Hoover when he visited the town during his tour of Poland. Dr. Goldschlag also served at different times as city councilor, member of the Brzezany District Council, and head of the Jewish community. He was also friendly with Marshal Rydz-Smigly. They were friends when they studied in the Brzezany Gimnazjum before the First World War. Following Dr. Goldschlag's request, Rydz assisted his former classmate in getting his older son, Jozef, Adas's brother, into the medical school of Lwow University. Almost no Jews were accepted at that time to study medicine. Pesah and his son Adas were part of a delegation which traveled to Warsaw in March 1937 to bestow honorary Brzezany citizenship upon Rydz-Smigly.

Adas graduated from the Brzezany Gimnazjum and left for Palestine shortly before the war. He traveled there together with Natan Goldman. While in Palestine he served with the Jewish Settlers' Police. Then he got a job with British Airways, first in Eritrea and then in the United States. When I recently visited my cousin Ann in the Bronx she showed me a picture of Adas in New York back in 1946. He was sitting in a restaurant, surrounded by several young Brzezany *landsleit,* including Ann. Mr. Goldschlag became quite excited during the long-distance interview. He was more than glad to reminisce about Brzezany and tell me numerous Brzezany "vignettes," as he referred to them. He also sent me a whole pack of old Brzezany photographs.[19]

* * *

Finding the Ukrainians was the hardest nut to crack. In contrast to Brzezany Jews and Poles, I had absolutely no place to start from with them. Without the Ukrainian side of the Brzezany "triangle," I couldn't tell the whole story. I had to find a way. I got in touch with some young historians at Lwow University and, luckily, they were willing to help. This is how I finally got most of my Ukrainian interviews.

Iulian Pavliv, an engineer, was born in 1931 in the village of Narajow, north of Brzezany. His father, a shoemaker and an active member of the Prosvita Ukrainian cultural association in the interwar years, was arrested by the Soviets in 1940. Iulii started attending school in Narajow before the war. Then, during the German occupation, he was a student at the Brzezany Gimnazjum. He studied for a while in Lwow and finally graduated from the secondary school in Soviet Berezhany in 1947. He studied engineering in the Lwow Polytechnic.[20]

The oldest Ukrainian interviewee was Lev Rega, born in 1914 in the village of Dubszcze, southeast of Brzezany. His family always identified with Ukrainian nationalism. One of his uncles fought in the ranks of the Ukrainian Galician army, another was a Sich Rifleman. A third uncle was active in the Ukrainian nationalist underground in the interwar years. He was arrested and murdered by the Soviets in 1941. Lev studied first in the village school and then continued his education in the Brzezany Gimnazjum, from which he graduated in 1932. During his Gimnazjum years he was involved, as a member of the OUN, the Organization of Ukrainian Nationalists, in various illegal Ukrainian nationalist activities. Lev was arrested, interrogated, and tried in the Brzezany court. He was sentenced to five years of imprisonment in 1933. He started to serve his sentence in the Brzezany prison but was soon transferred to a prison in Drohobycz and ended up in the infamous Holy Cross prison near Kielce, where he was pardoned in 1936.

When the Soviets occupied the Brzezany region in September 1939, Lev fled westward into the German-occupied part of Poland. Like many young Ukrainian nationalists, he expected Hitler to grant them an independent

state, *samostiina Ukraina*. He joined one of the pro-German Ukrainian paramilitary units, *pokhidni hrupy*, and returned to his native village as a liberator
of sorts. He was then told that his parents had been deported by the Soviets.
At that time, Lev was part of the Brzezany regional OUN command. He was
arrested by the Germans, with other local OUN leaders, in mid-September
1941. They were taken first to the Tarnopol and later to the infamous Lacki
Street Prison in Lwow. In mid-November, Lev was transferred first to Krakow
and finally to a prison on the outskirts of Berlin. He was allowed to return to
his village in the summer of 1943. Lev's next arrest, this time by the Soviet
Ministerstvo Gosudarstvennoi Bezopasnosti (MGB, Ministry of State Security), was in February 1949. He was accused of Ukrainian nationalism and
sentenced to twenty-five years in labor camps, of which he served, luckily,
only seven years, in the ferocious Kolyma camps. He was released in 1956
and settled in Berezhany.[21]

Galina Skaskiv was born in 1925 in a Ukrainian village south of Brzezany
in an educated and nationally conscious family. Her father was a captain in
the Ukrainian National Republican Army in East Ukraine after the Bolshevik Revolution. After returning home he became very active in the "Prosvita"
Ukrainian cultural society and in the Ukrainian cooperative movement in
the region. He was also a member of the moderate UNDO, the Ukrainian
National Democratic Alliance. Galina's father was often harassed by the
Polish police. Galina's grandmother was severely hit and wounded by a
Polish policeman during the pacification campaign of the mid-thirties. She
died soon after that. Then, in 1938, when Galina was 13, her father was
murdered, apparently by OUN youngsters, who accused him of being too
soft on the Poles. Her mother was severely beaten up. Galina's two brothers
belonged to the OUN. One of them would be killed by the Germans in 1944.
Galina attended the Brzezany Gimnazjum during the last few years before
the war and continued her studies there under German occupation. When
the Gimnazjum was closed in early 1944, she returned to her village and
joined the Ukrainian underground, where she continued to be active after
the Soviet reoccupation of the region. She married in 1948, and soon after
that both she and her husband were arrested and accused of Ukrainian
nationalism. Other members of her family, including her mother, were also
imprisoned. When Galina was arrested she was pregnant, and she gave birth
to a baby girl in the Lacki Street Prison in Lwow. The girl died a year later in
a Kiev prison, to which Galina was transferred. She became utterly depressed
and considered suicide. Galina, her mother, and other members of her
family who survived the Gulag were released after Stalin's death. Galina then
studied classics, English, and German at Lwow University and subsequently
taught in local high schools. Galina's personal and family history reflects the
upheavals and tragedies of many Ukrainians under the Poles, Germans, and
Soviets.[22]

By a sheer stroke of luck, during a short visit to London, I succeeded in interviewing a few Ukrainians who originated from villages in the Brzezany countryside.

Marian Hajwa, a civil engineer by profession, has been active for years in the London Ukrainian Association. He was born in 1921 in Podhajce, thirty kilometers from Brzezany. As a young man, Marian's father had lived and worked in America and Canada. When he returned, he became active in the Ukrainian cooperative movement. Theirs was an educated Ukrainian family, and their father insisted that the children learn English. During most of his school years before the war, Marian was active in Prosvita, the Ukrainian cultural association. After completing public school in Podhajce in 1938, Marian started studying in the Brzezany Gimnazjum. When the Soviets arrived, he studied in a teachers' college and even started teaching in a village school. During the German occupation Marian got deeply involved in the Ukrainian underground, the UPA. When the Germans started retreating in 1944, he escaped westward with other Ukrainian partisans and joined a German-Ukrainian military unit. They ended up first in France and later in Italy, where Hajwa was recruited by the British. As a British soldier he was stationed after the war in mandatory Palestine, of all places, and even had a Jewish girlfriend for a while. As I interviewed Hajwa in his office on the second floor of the Ukrainian club, a man by the name of Hrabar arrived. Hajwa introduced me to him.[23]

Ivan Hrabar was slim and dark, and he stammered from time to time. Although he is Hajwa's age, he looked much younger. He spoke a quite unintelligible English, an unusual combination of London cockney and a strong Slavic accent. He was the least educated among my Ukrainian narrators, but somehow I felt much more at home with him than with the others. He reminded me of Tanka and Ania. Hrabar was born in the village of Posuchow, near Brzezany, in 1921; studied at the village school; and had been active in the Ukrainian youth movement before the war. After the Germans occupied Brzezany in the summer of 1941, he joined the local Ukrainian militia. At the same time, he was a member of the Ukrainian underground. Hrabar was arrested by the Germans in February 1942 and charged with smuggling weapons and ammunition to the UPA. He was repeatedly beaten and tortured, first in the Brzezany and then in the Tarnopol prison. Then he was taken for forced labor in Germany. He didn't return to his village after the war; he preferred to settle in England.[24]

Dmytro Bartkiw was an easygoing fellow with a good sense of humor. He worked for years as a librarian in the London University School of Slavonic Studies. He comes from Kotow, south of Brzezany. His family was one of the more affluent families in the village. Dmytro's father had worked in Germany for some time before the First World War and spoke German. When Dmytro was 11, his father enrolled him in the Brzezany public school for boys. When he was 14, Dmytro started attending the Brzezany Gimnazjum. He studied in the Soviet-style *desiatiletka* in Brzezany in 1939–1940 and in the Brzezany Ukrainian Gimnazjum during the German occupation. He lived at that time in the *bursa,* the Ukrainian student dormitory in the center of town, near the Ratusz. When the Gimnazjum was closed down, Dmytro joined the Ukrainian SS Halychyna Division and moved west. He took part in some battles in Austria and Italy. Finally he arrived in England, where he has been living ever since.[25]

Vasyl Oleskiw was director of the Ukrainian Information Service in London. He was tall, silver-haired, and soft-spoken. He was born in 1925 in Byszki, one of the poorest villages in the region, ten kilometers north of Brzezany. First he attended school in nearby Kuropatniki; during the German occupation he was a student at the Brzezany Ukrainian Gimnazjum. He and another out-of-town friend lived in a rented room near the Okopisko Jewish cemetery. They witnessed a number of executions at close hand. All that time he was a member of the Ukrainian underground. He insisted that the UPA was friendly toward Jews. Vasyl was arrested by the Germans in May 1944, a short while before the arrival of the Red Army, and taken to France. He settled in England after the war.[26]

My most unusual "Ukrainian" interview was with Aleksandr Pankiv. I met him at the wedding of Dudar's grandson, which was held in a school auditorium during my last visit to Brzezany. Pankiv was working as a custodian in the school, which was located right near the Okopisko Jewish cemetery. It was almost dusk on a pleasant summer day. We sat on a grassy hillside from which the whole cemetery was visible. Pankiv is just two years older than I am. He is short and sturdy. One can imagine how his fully gray crop of hair was once completely black. Pankiv told me an incredible story of his near-execution not far from the place where we sat. He was almost killed at the Okopisko by the Germans, who took him for a Jew. He also repeated a strange story that I had already heard from others in Brzezany: a number of children who studied at the Okopisko elementary school recently died from unknown causes. Some people in town believed that the school location, which was near or perhaps on top of Jewish mass graves, was the reason.[27]

* * *

I made some attempts to reach German eyewitnesses to what happened in Brzezany during the war, but I got nowhere. The next best thing was to examine interrogations and testimonies connected with trials of Nazi perpetrators in postwar Germany. First I contemplated traveling to Germany, but I wasn't sure whether I could sit in a German archive and read how Germans murdered Jews in Brzezany. I was lucky to find a German history student who was willing to help. In time I received from him hundreds of photocopied pages containing information on Brzezany during the Holocaust. Some of the names were familiar from the testimony of Brzezany survivors and from what I had heard once within my own family. It wasn't easy reading.

Hans Adolf Asbach arrived in Brzezany in the fall of 1941 after being appointed Kreishauptmann of the Brzezany region. He was born in 1904 in German Pomerania and graduated from a humanities gymnasium, after which he studied law and economics in Kiel. He joined the Nazi Party in 1934 and was appointed legal advisor at the Deutsche Arbeitsfront. In 1940, he volunteered to serve in the Generalgouvernement administration and held positions in several localities before arriving in Brzezany. During their stay in Brzezany, the Asbachs lived in a villa near the Farny Church. They also had a summer residence in the Kurzany estate, which was ten kilometers outside Brzezany.

On several occasions Asbach assisted the German security police in the roundups and deportations of Brzezany Jews. He left Brzezany before the last Judenrein roundup, when he volunteered for a transfer to the Wehrmacht in February 1943. He was apprehended by the Americans as a POW in April and was released in June 1945. After working as a mason for a short while, Asbach started a successful public career, the peak of which was his appointment as minister of labor and social welfare in the state of Schleswig-Holstein in the fifties. Proceedings against Asbach started in 1961 and were discontinued in 1976 at his death. A number of Brzezany Jews, such as Dr. Wagszal-Szaklai, Mrs. Roza Goldman (Natan's mother), and Munio Haber testified in the Asbach case.[28]

SS Sturmbahnfuehrer Herman Mueller was the highest-ranking German officer active in the roundups and killings of Jews in Brzezany. He was head of the Sicherheits-Dienst (SD), the Security Service in Tarnopol. Mueller was born in Essen in 1909. His father was a petty tradesman and he himself worked as a salesman for a while. He joined the Party in 1927 and the SS in 1931. He was also a member of the Sturm Abteilungen (SA) for a number of years. Mueller rose very fast in the Party ranks after the SA purge in 1934. Several court proceedings against him before Hitler's rise to power indicate that he must have been one of those "old-time" Nazi roughnecks who was prone to violence. He served in Tarnopol in the years 1941–1943 and was involved in numerous killings of Jews in the region. Mueller was arrested in 1961, sued, and sentenced to life imprisonment in 1966. He died in 1988.[29]

SS Scharfuehrer Willi Herrmann served with Mueller in the Tarnopol SD office. He was the same age as his boss. Herrmann was born in the Saar region. His father was a miner, and Willi himself, who barely completed a few grades at school, became a locksmith. When the Saar region was reunited with Germany in 1935, Willi joined both the Nazi Party and the SS. When the war started, he was mobilized into the Waffen SS and participated in the occupation of France. Since he had some health problems, he was dismissed from the army and went to serve in the Kripo, the criminal police. As such he was sent first to Lwow and later to Tarnopol, where he stayed until the German retreat in 1944. During his service in the Tarnopol SD, Herrmann participated in numerous roundups and killings of Jews in the region, including Brzezany. He was one of those who carried out the last Judenrein roundup in Brzezany, in June 1943. After returning to Germany, he was detained several times by the Americans and the French, after which he returned to his Saar hometown and resumed work as a locksmith. Proceedings against him were started in the early sixties; he was sentenced to ten years of imprisonment in 1966 and died two years later.[30]

Hubert Kohnen was head of the Brzezany branch of VoMi, the Volksdeutsche Mittelstelle; he was in charge of appropriating Jewish property for the Volksdeutsche, ethnic Germans residing outside the Reich. Kohnen, tall, blond, and blue-eyed, was born in Aachen in 1905, where he completed primary school. As a young man he worked in various jobs, and during the height of the economic crisis he traveled to Canada, where he stayed until the war. There, too, he lacked a steady job. He returned to Germany in 1939 and joined the Nazi Party. He served in the Wehrmacht for a while as a translator for Sonderkommando "R" and was stationed in Lwow. Kohnen was employed by the VoMi from the fall of 1941. He arrived in Brzezany in the summer of 1942 and stayed there until the last Judenrein roundup in June 1943. After the war he lived in Germany, where he was interrogated but never sentenced. Kohnen died in the early seventies.[31]

Hans-Hermann Mund was head of the Brzezany branch of Unduetsch, a German department-store chain with headquarters in Bremen. Born in Bremen, he specialized in export business. When the war broke out he was on a business trip to the Dominican Republic. After numerous adventures and delays, he finally got back to Germany in March 1941. He was sent by Unduetsch to establish a branch in Brzezany; he arrived there in October 1941. He stayed there until December 1943. In Brzezany he fell in love with Fraeulein Maria, one of Asbach's German employees, whom he eventually married. After leaving Brzezany, he worked for a few months in Drohobycz, then returned to Germany in the fall of 1944. He was one of the witnesses in the Asbach case.[32]

* * *

Besides interviews with Poles, Jews, and Ukrainians I also used German testimonies and depositions concerning Brzezany during the German occupation of the town. I also used a number of testimonies deposited at Yad Vashem and memoirs written by Dr. Eliezer Wagszal-Szaklai, Menachem Dul, and Janina Drobnicka-Oleksyn.

3

THE GOOD YEARS, 1919–1939

On my thirty-second birthday, which was also the day I got married, my in-laws presented me with a copy of the front page of the New York Herald Tribune *from April 2, 1935. The headlines gave a random glimpse of the world into which I'd been born. The boldest headline announced: "Britain Reported Ready to Give France Free Hand If Reich Attacks Russia." The ensuing article reported that British foreign minister Anthony Eden, who had held talks with Soviet leaders in Moscow, had just arrived in Warsaw and was about to meet "Poland's unofficial dictator," Marshal Jozef Pilsudski. Another article told the readers that "Pius XI Prays Inciters of War Be Destroyed." It reported the pope stating that "Despite the European horizon 'of dark clouds pierced with sinister flashes,' an armed conflict of the nations was morally unthinkable and materially and physically an impossibility." This was apparently how people all over the world, including those in my hometown of Brzezany, must have felt at the time.*

I was told many times by my mother and other members of the family that my coming to the world was like a miracle. This is also why I was named after my father's beloved rabbi, Shimon Babad, who had given him the appropriate blessing for fathering a son. Rabbi Babad died a few weeks before I was born. My mother, crippled from birth, had miscarried several times, but finally in her late 30s successfully gave birth. Since there were medical complications throughout her pregnancy, she went to deliver me in a hospital in Lwow. Decades later, my Aunt Pnina, who had left Brzezany in the early twenties to settle in Palestine, gave me a bunch of letters she had received from our family. I was amazed to discover my father's letter reporting the most important event in my life. The letter was written three weeks after my birth and was addressed, in Hebrew, to "my dearest brother-in-law Zeev and my sister-in-law Pnina." The rest of the letter was in Yiddish. My father went on to describe the happy and festive atmosphere in our house. It was spring, Passover, and the long-awaited child had arrived. "It's nearly impossible to describe our joy at having reached this happy moment, with God's help, to have dear Hana and our dear son with us at the Passover Seder." My father also described the moment he *had received the good news from Lwow. "I was alone in the store. I became so mixed up that I forgot to lock the door and ran home with the telegram. I was like a crazy man, 'meshuge,' as they say."*

As I read and reread these lines I was both happy and sad. They added a lot to my perception of myself as a welcomed and long-awaited child, but they also suggested an unrealized potential for a happy childhood and a normal life. Within a few years of my birth, our whole existence would be shattered by the war. My father, my beloved Grandpa Fishl, and almost all of my relatives would perish and disappear. The only normal and wholesome span of my life was those few years before the war.

What are my earliest memories? I remember growing up in Polish. Those around me must have spoken mostly Yiddish among themselves, but for some reason they insisted on speaking Polish to me. I distinctly recall a recurrent "question" addressed to me, perhaps at the age of 2 or 3. "What noise does an airplane make?" I was supposed to imitate it with a perfect "Polish" rolling sound of "rrrr." Yiddish speakers usually pronounced it in a guttural manner, which was ridiculed by Poles. My "Polish" pronunciation of the "r" sound is perfect to this day.

My earliest memories must be from age 3 or 4. Some of them are about women. I don't remember much about my mother, who was always busy in the store. I do remember her younger sister, Malcia, who spent time with me. She was then in her early 20s and a graduate of the local Polish Gimnazjum. I remember her singing contemporary Polish "hits" to me. I remember the words and tunes to this day. She would sometimes hum a Yiddish melody. I doubt whether I understood it at the time. Malcia would occasionally take me to the movies. I distinctly remember a film featuring a masked ball. I got so scared that we had to leave the movie theater. Another woman in my early life was a Ukrainian maid who used to walk me to the town park. A memory: she's holding me close to her lap. I touch her soft, warm breasts. We're inside a dark store packed with huge brown jute sacks with all kinds of goods. There's a strong smell of yeast and cinnamon. This might have been old Wagszal's store, on the corner not far from our store. Another woman is my Aunt Zlata, married to my mother's younger brother, Yakov. A memory: it's apparently Friday evening and I'm in bed. It's either late or I'm sick. Zlata is bending over me. I can still see her beautiful, gentle face, her dark-brown hair, and the décolletage of her dress. Another well-preserved memory: my little chubby cousin Matus and I are hiding behind a door. I press slightly against him and a delightful shudder spreads all over my body.

Another memory: I'm with my father at his parents' house, on the bank of the Brzezany lake, the Staw. It's a summer weekend, a Saturday or Sunday. The two of us are lying in the grass, very close to the water. It's extremely peaceful. I hear a continuous quiet hum in the air. It feels like bliss. I notice the stump of a missing finger on one of my father's hands. My grandparents, Yakov and Dvora Redlich, had a small garden full of sweet red currants and tart green gooseberries. I can still taste them. Grandma Dvora would insist on my drinking their goat's milk "straight from the udder." It was sweet, thick, and foamy. Perhaps the most delightful memory of taste and color are the little red wild strawberries, "poziomki." They usually came with sour cream and sugar.

Still another memory: some kind of official Polish holiday is being celebrated. Our balcony, looking out on the Rynek and the Ratusz, is decorated with a dark-red rug and small white and red flags. I hear a band playing and soldiers marching by. There's a sense of excitement and happiness all around. This is, perhaps, my first memory associated with a military parade. I would be preoccupied with parades, bands, banners, and soldiers throughout my childhood.

I have a vague recollection of our store facing the Rynek. One had to go up a few steps in order to enter a long, narrow, and dark interior. On the right side was a long wooden surface, on which cloth was measured and cut. Right behind it were shelves with large bales of cloth placed one on top of the other. A certain "clothy" smell permeated the air. Near the entrance to the store was a door which led into our cousin Yentale's dimly lit tavern. I remember her as an energetic and loud-mouthed woman who had two sons I played with from time to time.

It must have been early summer of 1939, a few months before the war, when my Aunt Malcia took me to the spa town of Iwonicz. I remember the mud baths she took, all black. It scared me. There were also many peaceful and happy moments. I recall lying on a soft blanket, being massaged by a blind man. He concentrated on massaging my flat feet. I can still feel the touch of his strong and gentle hands. A Victrola on a nearby stand was playing Polish hits. Years later, my Aunt Malcia told me that Manek Thaler and his mother were staying near us in Iwonicz at that time and that at one point Manek, a year older than me and quite a prankster, convinced me to spread butter all over my body, imitating the women who used ointment for their sunbaths. Another memory from Iwonicz: a Polish woman living nearby invited me to her house. She tried to teach me Christian prayers, which I faithfully repeated after her.

My last prewar memories were of my Aunt Pnina and her son Reuven coming for a visit from distant Palestine. Reuven, who was 8 when he came with his mother to Brzezany in the summer of 1939, has, of course, more detailed and distinct memories than mine. I spoke to him at his crowded laser lab in Haifa almost sixty years later. Reuven recalled arriving at the Brzezany railroad station and being taken to our house in a horse and buggy. He described our last prewar apartment on Szkolna Street and reinforced my own vague memories of the place. We both remembered the bed in my parents' room and a light-green tile stove in the corner. On winter days, a little pillow would be warmed up by the stove and wrapped around my cold feet. Reuven and I spent hours on weekend mornings jumping into huge, soft pillows filled with feathers.

The person Reuven remembered most was his uncle and my father, with whom he could communicate in Hebrew. They used to discuss all kinds of things, among them interpretations of dreams, which my father looked up in an old Hebrew book. "Grandpa Fishl, with his white beard, looked very impressive and very old and Grandma was always busy with pots in the kitchen. Malcia, your mother's younger sister, looked like a young 'shikse,' and people used to pinch her behind."

At the reunion of Brzezany Poles in Ustron, Natan Goldman gave me an old photo from late summer of 1939, just before he left for Palestine. Reuven remembered this picture being taken in the Old Park, near the Sieniawski Castle. "There was this man with a box, covered in black cloth. He told us not to move and took a picture. A number of curious children who just happened to be there joined in." According to Reuven, the photographed children were both Jewish and Polish. Looking at this photograph decades and worlds later, I was overcome with a unique sensation of pleasure and joy. Reuven was in the center. Behind him was Lusiek, a Jewish teenage neighbor of ours, who was adored by my Palestinian cousin. Happy and curious faces of children and youngsters of all ages were staring at the camera. A girl was holding a ball. A little boy, wearing a typical Polish schoolcap, was stepping into the frame. Another boy, with a closely shaved head, slightly older than myself, was kneeling in the front. And here was I, 4 years old, dressed in a white short-sleeved shirt and short black pants with suspenders. I was standing to the right of my cousin and a smiling teenage girl was holding her hand on my right shoulder. It seems to me that I can still feel the friendly and tender touch of her palm. I haven't the slightest idea who she was, but she seemed to know me. I was staring sideways with a frolicsome look. I must have spotted something funny and, unlike all the others, wasn't concentrating on the camera. This single little picture is the essence of a brief, happy childhood.

The realities of interwar Galicia were shaped by both the historical legacy of the Hapsburg Empire, of which that region was part for over a century, and the vicissitudes of the newly established Polish state. Although it had been quite backward for centuries in the socioeconomic sense, Galicia was granted a considerable measure of autonomy by the Hapsburg rulers and was considered to be one of the most politically liberal regions in that part of Europe.

Ukrainians and Jews were the two largest minorities in interwar Poland. More than 5 million Ukrainians constituted 16 percent, and more than 3 million Jews accounted for close to 10 percent of the overall population of the country in the thirties. The proportional share of the Ukrainians was much higher in the eastern borderlands. Three million Ukrainians, mostly peasants, constituted close to 60 percent of the population in eastern Galicia. The population of Tarnopol Province, where Brzezany was located, totaled about 1.6 million in the early thirties. Ukrainians here constituted 54.5 percent, Poles close to 37 percent, and Jews 8.4 percent.[1] Most Poles and Jews lived in cities and towns. The rural population was predominantly Ukrainian.

Eastern Galicia was at a crossroads of peoples, cultures, religions, and civilizations. A striking feature of the region was its multi-cultural, multi-lingual, and multi-religious character. Almost every educated person, re-gardless of their ethnic origin, knew German. The dominant language in the cities and towns was Polish. In the countryside, Ruthenian, or Ukrainian, as it was increasingly referred to, prevailed. Jews spoke mostly Yiddish at home and Polish outside. Most Poles were Roman Catholics and most Ukrainians belonged to the "Uniate," the Greek Catholic Church. Beyond the specific affiliations of culture, language, and religion within each one of these three ethnic groups, they also shared a tradition of "local" commonness. Mutual acceptance and tolerance among the various ethnic groups was encouraged under the benevolent rule of the Hapsburgs. However, nationalist, rightist, and semi-fascist ideologies, which were on the rise during the interwar years, exerted an increasingly negative impact on the common local identity of the "Galicians."

Although the east Galician village was mostly backward and poor, the cities and towns had a distinct Western orientation. Their models were Vienna and Prague, not Moscow and Kiev. Besides Lwow, the only major city in the region, most of the urban settlements were small and medium-size towns, like Brzezany. Many blended with the surrounding countryside. Their inhabitants were Poles, Jews, and Ukrainians, usually in that descending order. Most of the petty bureaucrats were Poles; most of the merchants and store-owners were Jews. Multi-ethnic local elites dominated the towns: a Polish estate owner, judge, and officer; a Ukrainian teacher or priest; a Jewish merchant, lawyer, or doctor. Numerous young Poles, Jews, and Ukrainians studied together in and graduated from classical secondary schools, the Gimnazjums. Graduation from a Gimnazjum and a successful matriculation exam, the *matura*, signified social advancement and becoming part of the local elite. The dominant culture and language in the Gimnazjum was Polish; however, most of the students, like the local elites in general, were also fluent in their own "ethnic" languages, such as Ukrainian and Yiddish.[2]

Interwar Poland in general and eastern Galicia in particular consisted of a multi-ethnic, multi-national, and multi-religious society, ruled by a succession of governments, which to a larger or lesser extent preached and conducted policies of "Polishness" and "Polonization." After almost 150 years of humiliating and frustrating foreign domination, and after vehement battles against Ukrainians and Bolsheviks during and after the First World War, the Poles and most of their political leaders were intent on turning their country into a distinctly national Polish state. "Polishness" became the touchstone of respectability.[3] Administration, education, language, and culture were supposed to be predominantly Polish. The large ethnic minorities, such as the Ukrainians and the Jews, were expected either to integrate and assimilate or to leave. The Polonization of the eastern Polish borderlands, of which eastern Galicia was part, was implemented by "colonization," the settling of ethnic Poles from other parts of Poland in these ethnically heterogeneous territories, and by police-military measures aimed at the local non-Polish population. The official Polish Roman Catholic church, with its distinctly Polish national traditions, was also granted a special status.[4] The Polish army, with its uniforms, flags, military bands, and parades, became a principal instrument for forging national unity and pride and a powerful symbol of the newborn Polish independence.

The first years of the Polish state witnessed a succession of political crises. The following period, that of 1926–1935, was marked by the charismatic and semi-autocratic leadership of Marshal Jozef Pilsudski, the legendary commander of the Polish Legionnaires, considered by many to be the founder of the Second Polish Republic. Poland was beset by a host of difficulties and unresolved problems in the economic, social, and ethno-national spheres. Yet most of its inhabitants led more normal lives than their neighbors in Soviet Russia or Nazi Germany. Polish culture and intellectual life were quite lively. The very fact of resurrected national independence generated a sense of pride and optimism. Pilsudski's death, in May 1935, resulted in an ideological and political turn to the right and in a growing right-wing Polish nationalism. The military, under the leadership of such high-ranking officers as Edward Rydz-Smigly, a native of Brzezany, dominated the so-called "government of the colonels." Minority problems, instead of being solved, became increasingly inflamed.[5]

Ukrainian nationalism, on the rise already before the First World War, assumed various organizational forms, mostly in the economic and cultural spheres. A network of Ukrainian cooperatives and credit unions as well as a number of cultural associations were active in the region. Prosvita, the most significant of the Ukrainian cultural frameworks, established and maintained Ukrainian schools, libraries, and reading rooms in villages and towns. Ridna Shkola ran a network of Ukrainian schools.[6] Plast, the leading Ukrainian Scout-type youth movement, attracted thousands. The First World War and the disintegration of the empires seemed to Ukrainian nationalists to be an opportunity to establish a Ukrainian state. The West Ukrainian National Republic, which lasted only eight months, gave the Ukrainians a foretaste of independence. The short-lived Ukrainian Galician Army became a significant point of reference in their national aspirations. The military struggle between the Polish and the Ukrainian armies in 1918–1919 and the subsequent Ukrainian defeat would leave a lasting imprint on Ukrainian-Polish relations. Unfulfilled hopes for the emergence of independent Ukraine resulted in disappointment and frustration.

Poland was torn between attempts to find political solutions and repressive policies vis-à-vis its minorities. Although some attempts were made to reach understanding and cooperation with Ukrainian moderates, recurring anti-Ukrainian policies increasingly antagonized the Ukrainian population. The largest and most influential political force among the Ukrainians in the interwar years, UNDO, the Ukrainian National Democratic Alliance, preached moderate nationalism and was willing to compromise with the state. Another influential force that supported moderate Ukrainian nationalism was the Ukrainian Uniate Church, which was headed by Metropolitan Andrei Sheptyts'kyi, the most revered Ukrainian spiritual leader in eastern Galicia. Sheptyts'kyi was constantly torn between his basically moral and humanistic attitudes and his Ukrainian national loyalties.[7]

Frustrated hopes and increasingly repressive Polish policies gave rise to a radical trend among the Ukrainians. Its leading representative was the OUN, the Organization of Ukrainian Nationalists. It drew its support from politically frustrated and increasingly nationalistic young men and women who had been influenced by integrationist Ukrainian ideologues. They were impressed by the emerging Nazi German state under the leadership of Hitler. Hitler's Germany was perceived by some Ukrainians, young Ukrainian nationalists in particular, to be a revisionist power bent on a complete rearrangement of European borders, according to nationalist/ethnic principles. This, in turn, signified a possibility for Ukrainian national independence. The wishful hopes they pinned on Hitler's Germany naively dismissed the Nazis' anti-Slavic racism and adversely affected Ukrainian attitudes toward Jews.[8] The OUN attracted numerous Ukrainian university and high school students, who formed illegal cells in schools and dormitories throughout eastern Galicia. These educated youngsters spread Ukrainian nationalist ideas within their native villages. Among their leaders were Stepan Bandera and Roman Shukhevych, both of whom would emerge as prominent leaders of the Ukrainian underground during the Second World War.[9]

The ever-brewing Polish-Ukrainian tensions peaked in the early fall of 1930. An extensive "pacification campaign" implemented by the Polish army and police affected thousands of Ukrainians in the eastern borderlands. It was marked by searches, demolition of buildings and property, and physical violence. Numerous Ukrainian organizations and institutions were closed. Those suspected of Ukrainian nationalist activities were arrested and tried. Attempts at reconciliation between the state and the Ukrainian minority were made in 1931, and some of the Ukrainian institutions were allowed to reopen. The basic conflict, however, between Polish etatism and nationalism and the national aspirations of the Ukrainians was never resolved. Violence and terror were increasingly applied on both sides. A repressive campaign against Ukrainian nationalists was conducted in the summer and early fall of 1934. It was partly caused by the assassination of Prof. Ivan Babii, director of the Ukrainian Gimnazjum in Lwow. Babii, a moderate Ukrainian nationalist who had formerly taught at the Brzezany Gimnazjum, was shot by a member of the OUN.

Polish nationalist attitudes increased after Pilsudski's death. Nationalist elements within the Polish population of the eastern borderlands, in eastern Galicia in particular, had a negative effect on Polish-Ukrainian relations. Fierce anti-Ukrainian attitudes were now advocated by the Polish National Democrats, the Endeks, and by the Polish military. This in turn weakened Ukrainian moderates and strengthened the influence of the OUN. The ever-growing tensions and successive crises in the international arena throughout the late thirties, the short-lived success of Ukrainian independence in Transcarpathia in 1938, and the supposed support of Ukrainian national aspirations by Hitler's Germany inflamed spirits in the eastern borderlands. Starting in the fall of 1938 and throughout the first months of 1939, a new wave of protest and terror, inspired and conducted by the OUN, spread all over eastern Galicia. It consisted of demonstrations, sabotage, and assassinations. Another anti-Ukrainian "pacification campaign," similar to that of 1930, followed. The Polish government, in which Rydz-Smigly now played a dominant role, decided on a new series of "Polonizatory" measures aimed at Ukrainian education and culture.[10] Polish-Ukrainian relations in eastern Galicia reached another point of crisis on the very eve of the Second World War.

Galician Jews, most of whom were quite backward in the economic sense, enjoyed the relatively liberal policies of the Hapsburgs. They were admitted to schools and universities and joined the free professions in growing numbers in the decades preceding the First World War. Although the majority of Galician Jews were still orthodox, there was a steady process of linguistic acculturation, first into German and later into Polish. Most of them still spoke Yiddish on the eve of the First World War, but Polish, which increasingly replaced German, was becoming the second language of the younger generation. It would become the mother tongue of many children born in Jewish middle-class families in the interwar years. Galician Jewry would eventually become the most Polonized part of the Jewish population in Poland before the Second World War.[11]

The First World War as well as the ensuing Polish-Ukrainian and Polish-Bolshevik conflicts severely affected the Jews of eastern Galicia. Shocked by the imminent defeat of the benevolent Hapsburgs and fearing Russian occupation, large numbers of Jewish refugees escaped westward, some to neighboring towns and others as far as Vienna, Prague, and Budapest. Those who remained suffered from wartime devastation and diseases.[12] The Jews found themselves in a precarious political situation as well. They were forced to maneuver among the competing forces in the region. They were often accused of siding with the "opponent," whoever that may have been at a given

41

moment. In November 1918, following the disintegration of the short-lived West Ukrainian National Republic and the occupation of Lwow by the Polish army, a Polish anti-Jewish pogrom resulted in dozens of Jewish deaths and injuries. This time Jews were accused of cooperating with the Ukrainians. Polish soldiers, mostly from General Haller's units, attacked and insulted Jews in various east Galician towns.[13] Acts of anti-Semitism perpetrated by Poles were also widespread during the Polish-Bolshevik war in 1920. They subsided in the subsequent years.

Pilsudski's takeover and his semi-autocratic rule were regarded by Polish Jews as a lesser evil, compared with the National-Democratic, semi-fascist alternative. They mourned his death in 1935. A distinct rise in both formal and popular anti-Semitism occurred in the latter part of the decade. Anti-Semitism became now more pronounced within Polish society at large as well as within the governing elite and the church. Anti-Semitic behavior, such as the infamous "ghetto benches" and outright physical attacks against Jewish students, became quite prevalent in Polish universities. The economic boycott of Jewish businesses and stores spread throughout Poland. A number of pogroms, in which hundreds of Jews were beaten and wounded, occurred in various Polish cities and towns in the years 1935–1937. Besides traditional "indigenous" Polish anti-Semitism, some sections of Polish society, particularly young Endek nationalists, were affected by extremist Nazi attitudes and policies against Jews. Surprisingly, however, anti-Semitism was more pronounced in the western regions of the country, which was less populated by Jews, than it was in its eastern borderlands.[14]

Ukrainian-Jewish relations in eastern Galicia were strongly affected by Ukrainian-Polish rivalry. The Jews were always culturally closer to the Poles than to the Ukrainians. The short-lived West Ukrainian National Republic promised the Jews civil equality and national autonomy. Ukrainians expected the other large minority of the region to side with them against a supposedly "common" enemy. However, in spite of the Polish anti-Jewish pogrom in Lwow and prevalent Polish anti-Semitism, east Galician Jews never committed themselves to a Ukrainian-Jewish alliance. They usually pleaded neutrality.[15] In fact, they were, for various reasons, much closer to the dominant Polish, urban, West-oriented majority than to the mostly peasant-oriented and politically weak Ukrainian minority. The Ukrainians, in turn, accused the Jews of "Polonizing" tendencies. The assassination of Simon Petliura, a Ukrainian nationalist military leader accused of acquiescing with anti-Jewish pogroms perpetrated by his soldiers in 1919–1920, by Shalom Schwarzbart and the subsequent Paris trial inflamed Ukrainian-Jewish relations. Economic rivalry and the growth of the Ukrainian cooperative movement resulted in anti-Jewish incidents in Ukrainian villages throughout eastern Galicia. Ukrainian integrationist nationalists, such as Dmytro Dontsov, propagated the image of the Jews as Bolsheviks and spread views about their detrimental effect on world politics. Then there was also the growing impact of racist Nazi anti-Semitism. Anti-Semitic opinions became increasingly explicit in the Ukrainian press of eastern Galicia in the years preceding the war.[16]

In spite of official and popular anti-Semitism, Jewish political and community life in interwar Poland presented a spectacle of abundance and variety. Parties, clubs, and organizations sprouted not only in major cities but also in the smaller towns and shtetls. This was also true for eastern Galicia. Divisiveness and factionalism were a trademark of Jewish politics here, as they were in Poland as a whole.[17] The leading force in Jewish politics in eastern Galicia was Zionism. The most vital and vibrant element within the Zionist movement was the various youth organizations, from the religious, orthodox Bnai Akiva on the right to the Zionist-Marxist Hashomer Hazair on the left. For young Jews, joining a youth movement was the norm, particularly in the thirties. Economic crises and anti-Semitism, along with the modernizing character of the Polish state, severely affected the authority of the orthodox Jewish home. Children increasingly rejected parental authority. The youth organization became an alternative family. It offered not only a new and exciting social environment but also a hope for a brighter future, by emigration, *aliyah,* to Palestine, Erez Israel. Those attracted to the youth movements in eastern Galicia were mostly the offspring of middle-class families, Gimnazjum students, already fluent in Polish, who had been influenced by both the local Polish and the national Ukrainian youth movements.[18]

Jewish emigration from Galicia, as from other parts of what would constitute independent Poland, was considerable in the decades preceding the First World War. More than a quarter million Jews emigrated from there in the years 1881–1910. Most emigrated to North America. Their reasons were mostly economic. A much more moderate rate of emigration ensued in the twenties and thirties. The causes were a mixture of economics, anti-Semitism, and Zionism, and the main target was Palestine. More than 100,000 Jews, including thousands of young Jewish men and women, emigrated from eastern Galicia to Palestine in the years 1923–1937. Many were members of the various Zionist youth movements.[19]

* * *

Brzezany suffered not only during the First World War but also during the turbulent postwar period which witnessed repeated Ukrainian attempts at independence and the Polish-Bolshevik conflict. It was only in the fall of 1920 that peacetime actually arrived in Brzezany.

Located in the eastern region of the Hapsburg Empire, not far from the Russian border, Brzezany witnessed continuous military operations during the war.[20] The front line moved back and forth, bringing devastation, misery, and suffering to the local population. Those who could do so fled with their families westward to places such as Vienna and Prague. The Russians occupied Brzezany during the first months of the war. They were forced out by the Austrians in late summer of 1915. Before leaving, they set fire to the Sieniawski Castle and to parts of the Rynek. The Russians reoccupied the region within less than a year, and fierce battles were waged near Brzezany in the summer of 1916, particularly around Lysonia Mountain, where Ukrainian units, which were part of the Austrian army, fought the Russians. This, as well as subsequent battles at Lysonia, turned the site into a symbol of nascent Ukrainian nationalism. A huge fire, resulting from war operations, turned a third of Brzezany into ashes in the summer of 1917.

The fall of 1918 saw the final collapse of the Hapsburg Empire and continuous Ukrainian attempts at independence. Brzezany was occupied by the Ukrainian Galician Army in early November. It was the first time that Ukrainian national colors flew over the Ratusz and the Holy Trinity Church. Ukrainian peasants in the surrounding countryside celebrated what seemed to them to be the long-hoped-for Ukrainian statehood. A new town administration, mostly Ukrainian, was established. Some Brzezany Poles were arrested, particularly those who were active in local Polish associations. There was an attempt to Ukrainize the schools. Ukrainian rule in Brzezany lasted for several months. The Ukrainians retreated eastward in late May 1919 and Polish units under General Haller, part of the emerging Polish army, marched into town. They were greeted enthusiastically by the local Polish population. Although Polish rule in eastern Galicia hadn't yet been finally established, May 1919 became, in the hearts and minds of the Poles, the beginning of a new era. Brzezany was now part of independent Poland.

The "Hallerczyki," General Haller's soldiers and officers, terrorized the local Ukrainian and Jewish population. A common practice was to cut off the beards and payess (sidecurls) of orthodox Jews. Battles continued in the region throughout the summer of 1919, and Lysonia once more became a battleground between Poles and Ukrainians. In June 1919, Brzezany was reoccupied for a week by the Ukrainian army. However, by July, Poles controlled the town as well as almost the whole of eastern Galicia. Bolshevik troops occupied Brzezany for a few weeks in early fall of 1920. It became the scene of a short-lived Bolshevik rule. Revolutionary committees were organized, and a Jewish "commissar" was nominated by the Bolsheviks. There were propaganda meetings and speeches in Polish, Ukrainian, and Yiddish. Goods were confiscated, particularly from the wealthiest Jewish and Polish shop-owners. The Poles recaptured Brzezany in mid-September and kept it under their rule for the next nineteen years.

* * *

The most urgent tasks in Brzezany, after years of instability and destruction, were its physical and architectural reconstruction. Attention was given first and foremost to Polish public buildings, such as the Farny Church and the Bernardine Cloister. Some houses around the Rynek were repaired in order to serve as town and district administrative offices. The military barracks opposite the Sieniawski Castle, as well as the two public schools, were renovated. The Gimnazjum moved to its new and spacious quarters. Situated on a hill overlooking the town center, it was a much more appropriate place of learning than its previous location in the Ratusz, where it was constantly subjected to the midtown hubbub and noises of the weekly fairs. Electricity, running water, and a modern sewage system were gradually introduced. By the mid-thirties, 1,000 Brzezany households had electricity.

Middle- and lower-middle-class families constituted a considerable part of Brzezany's population. Most of the affluent families in town were Polish landowners and high-ranking Polish officials, but there were also some rich Jews, such as the Loebls, who owned a modern flour mill. Jews were also prominent among local lawyers and physicians. Most of the stores were owned by Jews. There were a few small hotels and a number of restaurants. Martynowicz's restaurant offered meals and drinks and had an orchestra that performed in the evenings for entertainment. The best restaurant in town was in the Hotel Europejski, in the Rynek. Both were owned by Mr. Leon Berman. The Oasis coffeehouse advertised an "excellent jazz band." People danced at the Dancing Bar Raj.

Brzezany unquestionably joined the twentieth century with the opening of two cinemas, the first in the impressive Sokol, and the second in the newly constructed Przyjazn building. The Przyjazn cinema was owned by the Loebls. Polish and foreign films were screened in both places. Hollywood movies were the most popular. There were also a few local drama groups, and professional theaters would sometimes visit from Lwow and Krakow. People read newspapers in a number of languages. There were radios in 330 households in prewar Brzezany.[21] Brzezany had hardly any industry, but its economy benefited from its status as a district town. Inhabitants of smaller towns in the vicinity as well as peasants from nearby villages would arrive there for various services and shopping. Most of the stores in which these peasants would shop (usually on credit) were Jewish. The few local high-quality stores, which shipped their merchandise in from Lwow, Warsaw, and Vienna, catered to a clientele with higher-than-average incomes, such as landowners, senior government officials, doctors, lawyers, successful businessmen, and army officers.

The main school system in Brzezany had two large public schools, one for boys and the other for girls. More than 1,000 students attended these schools every year. Most of them were Poles, but there were also Jews and Ukrainians. Those who aspired to a high school education and succeeded in their entrance exams completed four years of study in one of the two public schools and at the age of 10 or 11 entered the Gimnazjum. They studied there for the next eight years. This system changed somewhat in the early thirties, when a student would graduate from the sixth grade of the public school and continue for another six years at the Gimnazjum. Students would usually graduate from the Gimnazjum and complete their matriculation exams, the *matura,* at the age of 18 or 19. Although the majority of the Gimnazjum students were sons and daughters of townspeople, a fairly large percentage were village boys and girls, both Polish and Ukrainian. There was also a women teachers' seminary in town, consisting mostly of Polish students, although there were also some Ukrainians and very few Jews. Out of 185 students in the school year of 1929–1930, 146 were Polish, 36 were Ukrainian, and 3 were Jewish. All in all, more than 2,500 students attended the various educational institutions in Brzezany on the eve of the Second World War.[22]

There were various sports activities in town, particularly among the young. The permanently stationed army regiment contributed considerably to the various athletic competitions. There were weekly matches and several championships during the year. The most popular sport was soccer, but there was also volleyball, gymnastics, water sports, and tennis. And there were, of course, the winter sports, such as skating and skiing. Even boxing arrived in Brzezany a few months before the war.

* * *

The predominantly Polish civil servants, along with the 51st Army Regiment, the Polish Scout organization, and the local Polish social, religious, and intellectual elite all contributed to the distinct "Polishness" of Brzezany. There was a great deal of enthusiasm in the way the various national Polish holidays were celebrated. Like Poles all over Poland, the Poles of Brzezany were very proud of their newly gained and extremely cherished independence.

The birthday of Marshal Jozef Pilsudski, the founding father of the Second Polish Republic, was a major event. The Brzezany newspaper reported on one such occasion that

> the town had assumed a festive appearance by the evening of March 18. Windows and balconies were decorated with Polish national colors and green garlands. At 6 p.m. a military band marched through the streets and played various marching tunes. It was warmly greeted by the crowds. The Brzezanyites woke up next morning to the tunes of a military reveille. By nine o'clock the streets were full of people hurrying to the various houses of prayer, to the Bernardine Cloister, the Tserkov and the Synagogue, where special prayers were held in the presence of town officials. In the meantime, the Rynek was filled with various detachments from the 51st Regiment. After a military review, a solemn mass was conducted by Father Lancucki at the nearby Farny Church. The stalls were occupied by representatives of the army, various government and town offices, and numerous associations and organizations. Banners and flags were placed at the

46

altar. After mass, a military parade marched through the Rynek. After that, a reception in honor of the Marshal's birthday was held in the Town Hall. The Mayor, Mr. Golczewski, received birthday greetings from representatives of various institutions. Among them was Dr. Pesah Goldschlag, representing the Lawyers' Chamber and the Jewish Community, and Father Adam Lancucki, representing the Roman Catholic parish. The Sokol movie theater screened a film, 'The Rebirth of the Polish State.' In the evening, the "Officers' Club," the "Kasyno," hosted the entire officers' corps as well as other invited guests. Following a number of speeches and recitations, the military band of the 51st Regiment closed the event. The Marshal's birthday was also celebrated in all Brzezany schools. Impressive programs were presented at the Gimnazjum and at the Women Teachers' Seminary.[23]

Other annual celebrations were Constitution Day on May 3 and Independence Day on November 11. Although they were celebrated as distinctly Polish events, the Jewish and Ukrainian communities also participated. Many Jews and even some Ukrainians identified with these state celebrations. Still another occasion was Regiment Day, celebrated every June, at which Brzezany honored the 51st Regiment. Glos Brzezanski announced on the tenth anniversary of the regiment's arrival in Brzezany that "Regiment Day is a holiday for the whole community." A mass for fallen regiment soldiers was conducted in the morning hours of that day at the Farny Church. At noontime the whole regiment and representatives of the Brzezany community filled the regiment stadium. A list of regiment soldiers who had fallen in the battles for Polish independence was read out. That day's celebrations were capped by a military band which marched through the streets.[24]

Like the rest of Poland, Brzezany was shocked by the death of Marshal Jozef Pilsudski in May 1935. Numerous commemorative events took place throughout the town on May 17 and 18, following the national mourning ceremonies in Warsaw and Krakow.[25] Portraits of Pilsudski adorned with Polish national colors and black crepe were displayed on all public buildings. Lights were dimmed in the evening. Crowds filled the streets. Mourning prayers were held in the Polish churches, in the Ukrainian Tserkov, and in the Large Synagogue. A military parade passed through the Rynek and the nearby streets. Pilsudski's death would be mourned annually in Brzezany until the outbreak of the war.

The Polish Scouts, the Harcerstwo, was a significant expression and symbol of Polish nationalism and independence. The Harcerstwo was founded in eastern Galicia within the framework of the Polish Sokol gymnastic association a few years before the First World War. It was permeated with a spirit of Polish nationalism and was closely connected with the emerging Polish military forces. Numerous Scouts joined the Polish Legions during the war and fought on various battlefields against Ukrainians and Bolsheviks. The first Scout group in Brzezany was organized as early as 1911. It wasn't active during the war and was revived in 1918. When General Haller's Polish units waged battles against the Ukrainians around Brzezany in the spring of 1919, a number of local Scouts somehow got hold of a few guns and assisted the Polish soldiers. Paramilitary training would become a major activity of the emerging Scout movement in Brzezany, as elsewhere in interwar Poland. Close ties were established between the Harcerstwo and the 51st Army Regiment.[26]

The local Polish Scouts, the Brzezany Hufiec, became the dominant official youth organization in town. Since it was distinctly Polish and Christian, it attracted hardly any Jewish or Ukrainian youths. Besides such common scouting activities as hikes and summer camps, the Scouts participated in various Polish national festivities and military parades. Uniforms, insignias, and banners became an extremely significant part of their lives. They also initiated humanitarian and community activities, such as assisting the poor. The Gimnazjum was a stronghold of Scout activities. Its headmaster and teachers, the Polish ones in particular, were staunch supporters of the movement. Harcerstwo also enjoyed the enthusiastic support of the entire Polish community. Most of the local VIPs, such as Olszewski, head of the Gimnazjum, and Rapf, the town engineer, were members of the local Association of Friends of the Scouts. The director of the Brzezany hospital, Dr. Stefan Bilinski, was chief physician of the Brzezany Hufiec. A large group of Scouts from Brzezany joined the Scout Youth Labor Brigades, which were sent to fortify the Polish-German border on the eve of the Second World War.

The Gimnazjum was a major landmark of "Polishness" and Polish identity in interwar Brzezany. It was closely connected with the local Polish youth movement, the Harcerstwo, and took a very active part in all state holidays and celebrations. At the same time, however, it also maintained its pre-independence classical humanist tradition; Greek and Latin were obligatory. Fairly good relations prevailed among its Polish, Ukrainian, and Jewish students and faculty. The three religions—Roman Catholicism, Greek Catholicism, and Judaism—were taught in separate groups to all Gimnazjum students. The Gimnazjum was established in the early nineteenth century as part of the Hapsburg educational system, and although German was always taught there, Polish was accepted as the primary language of instruction as early as the 1860s. Ukrainian subjects were taught in the so-called *utrakwistyczne* classes at the Gimnazjum, which were attended mostly by Ukrainians.[27] Each grade consisted of three levels, "A," "B," and "C." The Ukrainian-oriented "utraquistic" classes were the "C" classes, which had the lowest standards. The most advanced were the "A" classes, consisting mainly of Polish students. Jews studied in the "A" and "B" classes. Annual celebrations honoring the two respective national poets, the Pole Adam Mickiewicz and the Ukrainian Taras Shevchenko, were held there for decades. The Gimnazjum celebrated its hundredth anniversary in 1906. Many former graduates convened in Brzezany on that occasion. Special masses celebrating the anniversary were conducted in the Farny Church and in the Ukrainian Tserkov.[28] A long tradition of Gimnazjum graduate reunions continued throughout the interwar years.

The data available for 1936 quite accurately portray the ethnic and gender profile of the Gimnazjum in the interwar years. Out of 580 students, 293 were Poles, 176 were Ukrainians, and 111 were Jews. Among them were 339 males and 241 females. Whereas the first year consisted of 130 students, the last graduating class had only 40 students.[29] A roster of students reveals that Munio Haber had then just entered the Gimnazjum and was studying in "1B." Halszka, the younger daughter of town engineer Wilhelm Rapf, was a student in "2A," Anna Herzog was in "4A," and her boyfriend, Adas Goldschlag, was in the prestigious "8A." Natan Goldman and Tolek Rapf were in the newly introduced sixth-year-level humanities class. The faculty consisted of 23 male and 3 female teachers. Thirteen of them were Polish, 8 were Ukrainian, and 5 were Jewish.[30]

A look at one particular graduating class, that of 1934, reveals that of the 26 students who succeeded in their *matura* matriculation exams, 11 were males and 15 were females. Eleven were Jewish, 9 were Polish, and 6 were Ukrainian. Among them was Ludka, the older daughter of town engineer Wilhelm Rapf, and Poldek, a boy from a rather poor Jewish family.[31] An examination of the ethnic ratio of the Gimnazjum students and that of the successful *matura* graduates indicates that Jewish students were usually more successful than others in completing their course of studies.

In addition to the official and quite demanding curriculum, numerous extracurricular activities took place in the Gimnazjum. There were a number of voluntary study groups, such as those for Polish literature, Ukrainian literature, and philology. Several of the Polish teachers were very active in the Harcerstwo. The prevailing atmosphere in the Gimnazjum was that of serious scholarship and respect for the teachers. One of the very few unusual events was the Zawirski affair. Hipolit Zawirski, a youngish teacher of Polish literature who was quite a dandy, was sued by the Dorfmans, a Jewish Brzezany family. They accused him of taking bribes from Jewish students whom he would have otherwise failed, and they won the case.[32]

Interwar Brzezany wouldn't have been what it was without the 51st Infantry Regiment stationed permanently in town.[33] Its full name was "The 51st Infantry Regiment of the Borderlands Riflemen." Organized in Italy in 1919, it was co-opted into General Haller's army and took part in battles against the Ukrainians and in the Polish-Bolshevik war. The regiment arrived in Brzezany in the early twenties and stayed there until the Second World War. It promoted various sports, not only within its own ranks but in Brzezany at large. It had soccer, volleyball, and basketball teams. It constructed tennis courts at the barracks and water-sports facilities at the Brzezany lake, the Staw. Its officers and soldiers were instructors in paramilitary training in various Brzezany schools and in the Scouts. The regiment also conducted a wide range of educational activities with a distinctly Polish national patriotic flavor in Brzezany and in the surrounding countryside. The regimental library served not only the soldiers but the whole Polish community of Brzezany. The regimental officers' mess, the Kasyno, was a major venue and social gathering place for the town's Polish elite. People would come there to play billiards, listen to the radio, and dance.

The regiment, and its military band in particular, took part in all major celebrations and festivities. The return from summer maneuvers to Brzezany became a very special occasion, not only for the officers and the soldiers but for the whole Brzezany community. The local newspaper offered this report on one such occasion:

> The regiment was returning from its summer maneuvers. Large crowds gathered around a triumphal arch erected at the entrance to the railway station. Our beloved regiment had finally arrived. There were speeches and cheers. The military band was playing, appropriate to the occasion. The regiment marched to the barracks flanked on both sides of the street by cheering crowds throwing flowers at the soldiers.[34]

The most revered object of local admiration for the military was Edward Rydz-Smigly, regarded as a model Polish soldier and patriot. Rydz was born in the Brzezany suburb of Adamowka. His father died when he was 2 and his mother when he was 10. Young Edzio was then taken care of by his poor maternal grandparents. After entering the Gimnazjum he became friendly with the son of the town doctor, Uranowicz, and within two years he was invited to move into their house. Rydz was an excellent student and graduated in 1905 at the age of 19. At that time he was very interested in art, which he later studied in Krakow and Munich. Like numerous other Polish youngsters in Brzezany, Edzio joined a semi-legal Polish nationalist organization during his Gimnazjum years. During the First World War, he joined Pilsudski's Polish Legion.[35] In the interwar period, Rydz, who in the meantime had added the word Smigly to his name, became one of the leading officers in the Polish Army. After Pilsudski's death, Rydz-Smigly was appointed inspector general and marshal. He was also considered to be Pilsudski's heir and successor. Brzezany was, of course, immensely proud of its native son. Even when he became one of the most influential men in Poland, Rydz maintained friendly relations with his fellow Brzezanyites and assisted them in various ways.

The highlights of the marshal's affiliation with Brzezany were the celebrations of his fiftieth and fifty-first birthdays in 1936 and 1937. The Brzezany Gimnazjum was officially named "The Rydz-Smigly Gimnazjum." A delegation of 100 people from Brzezany and the vicinity went to meet Rydz-Smigly in Warsaw. It presented him with an honorary scroll and a pedigreed Arab

50

stallion named Tiger. The local newspaper reported that "in spite of the rainy weather, huge crowds took leave of the delegation traveling to Warsaw. Brzezany took on a festive appearance. Flags and pictures of the Leader were displayed all over town. Public buildings were illuminated. Festive services were conducted in the Farny Church, in the Tserkov and in the Synagogue. Celebrations took place in all schools."[36]

The Brzezany delegation stayed in the capital for three days. The highlight of the visit was, of course, the meeting with the marshal, in the "White House," Rydz-Smigly's official residence. The marshal was very moved by the occasion. He thanked his guests and shook hands with each one of them. "My memories of Brzezany have always accompanied me at the happiest and saddest moments of my life. Don't be surprised, therefore, that I'm so moved when I stand before you." He spoke of his childhood, when he liked to play war games in the Zwierzyniec forest, and recalled the Staw, Storozysko, and Raj. Rydz was particularly glad to meet the Gimnazjum students. The delegation's visit to Warsaw and meeting with Rydz-Smigly was the talk of the town for many weeks.[37]

The Brzezany town council was predominantly Polish. The council elected in the late twenties, for example, consisted of thirty-six councilors, most of whom were Poles. But there were also a number of Jews and a few Ukrainians. Among the Polish councilors were the head of the hospital, the director of the Gimnazjum, and the mayor of Brzezany. Among the Jewish councilors were lawyers and physicians. Among the Ukrainian councilors was a priest and a lawyer.[38]

* * *

The Jews were the second-largest ethnic group in Brzezany in the interwar period. They made up more than half of its population before the First World War. However, an insistent Polonization policy of the eastern borderlands in the twenties and thirties finally resulted in the numerical dominance of Poles. Still, Jews considerably outnumbered the Ukrainians. The First World War and the subsequent Ukrainian-Polish and Polish-Bolshevik conflicts had had a devastating economic effect on Brzezany Jews. Some left the region and never returned. There were also those who had emigrated to the United States before the war. A small diaspora of Brzezany Jews emerged, mainly in New York. They founded a Brzezany *landsmannschaft*, which existed until the early fifties. A "Berezhan" synagogue was active for decades on the Lower East Side.

As life started to stabilize in Brzezany in the twenties, so did the fortunes of its Jews. There were numerous Jewish artisans, and Jews dominated local commerce. Jews were also visible in the professions. There were a number of Jewish physicians and Jewish lawyers, most of whom had completed their studies in the Hapsburg times. As a result of Polish government restrictions on higher education during the thirties, some young Brzezany Jews were forced to study medicine abroad, and they faced difficulties getting positions after their return.

An overwhelming majority of Brzezany Jews, particularly the older generation, were religious. However, a considerable part of the younger generation studied in the Gimnazjum and belonged to various Zionist organizations. Thus, it was not uncommon for the offspring of orthodox parents to become secular. Significant changes took place with respect to language and culture. The parents spoke mostly Yiddish, though they knew Polish and some were fluent in German. Young Jewish men and women in interwar Brzezany increasingly used Polish. The mother tongue of most children born into Jewish middle-class families was Polish. Jewish religion, nevertheless, was thriving. Besides the Large Synagogue, which was filled to the brim on Friday evenings, Saturdays, and Jewish holidays, there was a large number of smaller prayer groups. Elderly Jews dressed in their Hasidic garb could be seen every Friday evening walking to their respective places of worship. The Large Synagogue not only served as the central venue for religious services, it also functioned as a public gathering place for the Jews.

The Jews of Brzezany led a very intense community life. Periodically they would elect their community leadership, which consisted mostly of educated professionals. There were dozens of Jewish associations, covering almost every aspect of community life in interwar Brzezany.[39] The most influential were the Zionist organizations, particularly the Zionist youth movements. The gamut ran from the religious Mizrachi to the socialist Hashomer Hazair. At one point there were three Hebrew schools. Most Jewish cultural activities in town took place in the "People's House," the Jewish equivalent of the impressive Polish Sokol building. Indeed, it served as a community center for the local Jewish population. Its most permanent feature was the Jewish Music and Drama Club. The club performed plays and operettas and even went on tour out of town. The club also owned one of the largest libraries in Brzezany.[40]

Most of the Zionist youth organizations in Brzezany were modeled after the world Scout movement founded by Baden-Powell. There were summer camps and many excursions "into nature." Ideologically, these organizations instructed Jewish youngsters in a "pioneering" spirit and prepared them for *aliyah,* emigration to Palestine. Although no statistics exist on the number of those who left Brzezany for Palestine in the interwar years, there must have been at least a few hundred. Thus, another Jewish Brzezany diaspora emerged in British Palestine. They would be joined after the war by those few who survived the Holocaust.

No detailed official accounts exist of the various Jewish public activities in interwar Brzezany. Some documentation, though, tells the story of two campaigns which took place in the thirties. One was a campaign against British restrictions on Jewish emigration to Palestine, and the other followed Hitler's rise to power. A mass meeting protesting British policy took place at the Large Synagogue on May 25, 1930. The main speakers were Dr. Willner, who spoke in Yiddish, and Dr. Pomeranz, who spoke in Polish. The third speaker spoke in Hebrew. A meeting of Brzezany Jewish youth at the People's House, at which British policy was criticized, followed on May 31. An anti-Nazi protest meeting was convened in the People's House on March 21, 1933. The speakers were Dr. Willner and Mr. Natan Loebl, the most affluent Jewish businessman in town. A year later, leaflets calling for a boycott of German products were distributed by Jewish youngsters in Brzezany, and a local Committee of Anti-Hitlerite Jewish Youth was established.[41]

It seems that a number of the same people were active in Jewish affairs and associations. The most conspicuous among them were Dr. Edmund Willner, a lawyer and head of the General Zionists' Organization and the Ezra Society; Dr. Pesah Goldschlag, a lawyer who was elected to the Brzezany town council several times; and Dr. Philip Pomeranz, who for some time headed both the Jewish Music and Drama Club and the Association of Jewish Veterans of Polish Wars for Independence. Most of the Jewish community leadership in Brzezany were people in their 50s and 60s. Majorko Thaler, Manek's father, represented the younger generation. He, too, was active in a number of organizations, such as the Jewish Music and Drama Club and the Achva Zionist youth movement. His correspondence with the Achva Center in Lwow shows how persistent Thaler was regarding the needs of the local branch in Brzezany.[42]

Although some young Jews suffered from the prevailing restrictions in higher education in Poland, and despite some instances of anti-Semitism, there was never a pogrom-like atmosphere in prewar Brzezany. Jewish religious and community life seemed to thrive. Middle-class Jews led quite comfortable lives. They dressed well, sent their children to the local public schools and to the Gimnazjum, and went for vacations to Krynica and Iwonicz, popular spas near the Tatra Mountains. In spite of what newspapers wrote about Hitler, the Nazis, and anti-Semitic legislation in Germany, there was hardly an inkling of the imminent upheavals and disasters which would soon affect the Jews of Brzezany.

* * *

The Ukrainians were less than a quarter of Brzezany's population, and their ties with the surrounding countryside were quite close, more than that of the Poles and the Jews. The short-lived Ukrainian rule in eastern Galicia during the First World War intensified the national identity of both the Brzezany Ukrainians and the Ukrainian peasants in the nearby villages. However, failed hopes for Ukrainian independence and the incorporation of the region in the newly established Polish state caused bitterness and frustration. This would turn over the years, following progressively suppressive Polish anti-Ukrainian policies, into outright hostility. In spite of the Polish rule and the prevailing Polish-Ukrainian tensions, various Ukrainian community organizations and associations, which ceased functioning during the war, were gradually revived in the early twenties. The most prominent among them were Prosvita, the most significant Ukrainian cultural association in eastern Galicia, which supported the establishment of Ukrainian schools, libraries, and reading rooms, and Ridna Shkola, the Ukrainian pedagogical society, which promoted Ukrainian education.

The Prosvita Center in Brzezany was headed intermittently by two local Ukrainian lawyers and included a number of Ukrainian Gimnazjum professors.[43] A breakdown of Prosvita members in Brzezany by profession shows that in 1927 it included 18 clergymen, 13 Gimnazjum professors, 28 teachers, and 65 farmers. The Prosvita Center in Brzezany supervised Prosvita branches in the neighboring villages. Prosvita reading rooms were much more than just places where one could read Ukrainian books and newspapers. Various Ukrainian cultural activities, such as choirs and drama clubs, were initiated and organized in these reading rooms. A successful performance of one such drama group took place in the village of Raj in December 1924. The drama club of the Brzezany Adamowka branch of Prosvita was so successful that it was invited to perform in a number of villages in the region.[44]

Almost 400 delegates participated in a regional Prosvita conference which convened in Brzezany in February 1927.[45] A regional Prosvita women's conference took place in March of that year. It was a big success. More than 500 Prosvita women filled the auditorium. Among them were representatives from Narajow, Kotow, Posuchow, Szybalin, and Raj. After a number of speeches and resolutions, the conference closed with the singing of the Polish and Ukrainian national anthems.[46]

The Polish administration started to interfere with Prosvita activities in the Brzezany region as early as 1934. All kinds of pretexts were used to close down reading rooms. Every announcement had to be translated from Ukrainian into Polish. The singing of "national" Ukrainian songs was severely forbidden. Every single poster announcing a public event had to get the approval of the Polish authorities. Such approval was denied when the name of a village was spelled in the Ukrainian rather than the Polish manner.[47] The village branches of Prosvita were, usually, more audacious than the Prosvita Center in Brzezany. Thus, the head of the Prosvita Center in Brzezany demanded in mid-1937 that those in charge of the village reading rooms abstain from "provocative" acts, remove controversial books, and prevent local youth from singing "illegal" Ukrainian songs and marching in formation.[48] He reported to the Prosvita Center in Lwow that "young people get together in the evenings at the Prosvita reading room in the village of Byszki, they sing noisily and yell up to twelve p.m. During festivities in the village of Kotow some young people marched in formation, wearing military style hats and uniforms."[49] Polish repressions against Prosvita culminated in the closing of all Prosvita branches in the Brzezany region in March 1937.[50]

A small Ukrainian school existed in Brzezany before the First World War, but it stopped functioning, like all other schools in town, during most of the war years. There was, indeed, a short-lived renaissance of Ukrainian education following the establishment of Ukrainian rule in the region in November 1918. Ukrainian became obligatory then in all Brzezany schools, and the Gimnazjum was renamed the "Ukrainian Gimnazjum." Almost all of its Polish students boycotted it and continued their studies in small informal groups. The situation changed drastically following the Polish "liberation" of Brzezany in the spring of 1919. All official education was now predominantly Polish. However, in spite of the negative Polish attitudes toward Ukrainian culture, a Ridna Shkola school opened in Brzezany sometime in the early twenties. It was first established as a four-grade school, and in time it became a six-grade school.[51] Its best graduates, as well as the best Ukrainian students from the village schools around Brzezany, usually continued their education in the local Gimnazjum.

The Ukrainian Ridna Shkola Association in Brzezany consisted of more than 200 members in the late twenties. Among them were 15 clergymen, 70 teachers, 27 state employees, 3 lawyers, and 1 doctor.[52] The association supported and supervised similar associations active in the villages throughout the region. Polish policies, which began to grow more restrictive and oppressive in the early thirties, also affected the Ukrainian school in Brzezany. A "pacification detachment" of the Polish state police raided the school building on September 22, 1930. A considerable part of the property was demolished. The major "crime" was two torn portraits, which were supposedly found in the school dustbin; one of President Moscicki and the other of Marshal Pilsudski. Dr. Bemko, head of the Ridna Shkola Association in Brzezany, was detained for a few days, and his office was severely demolished in the course of a police search.[53] The upshot was that the Brzezany Association of Ridna Shkola was closed for a while, but it was allowed to reopen following Bemko's repeated appeals to the authorities. The school itself, although harassed from time to time, continued functioning. It consisted of 165 students in the school year 1931–1932. About 100 were children from Ukrainian families living in the town. The others arrived daily from nearby villages. Most of the students' parents were either farmers or artisans. A Ukrainian drama club and a children's choir were active at school.[54]

The Ukrainian youth movement, the Plast, like the Polish Harcerstwo, was based on general Scouting principles; however, like its Polish counterpart, it also fostered a strong sense of patriotism and nationalism. It developed an extensive network of branches throughout eastern Galicia. Plast groups were mostly associated with primary and secondary schools. The height of its activities was during the twenties. The pacification campaign in 1930 resulted in the closing of all Plast branches. Illegal Ukrainian nationalist organizations, which grew throughout the thirties, mobilized some of its members among former Plast Scouts. The center of Plast activities in Brzezany, while the movement existed, was the local Gimnazjum, and the man in charge during its initial phase was Prof. Ivan Babii. He led an ongoing battle with Gimnazjum authorities to allow Plast activities. Shortly after Babii left for Lwow, in 1929, Plast activities in Brzezany were forbidden.[55] Prof. Babii, a moderate Ukrainian nationalist who had been appointed headmaster of the Ukrainian Gimnazjum in Lwow, was assassinated by Ukrainian extremists in the summer of 1934.

Radical Ukrainian nationalism in the Brzezany region was on the increase throughout the thirties. At times members of the OUN interfered with activities of the moderate UNDO. A mass UNDO meeting in Brzezany was stopped by Ukrainian Gimnazjum students affiliated with the OUN.[56] The Gimnazjum administration tried to curtail Ukrainian nationalist activities. Parents of Ukrainian students were convened for that purpose on one occasion by Headmaster Olszewski. His admonitions didn't help much, though. When the birthday of the Ukrainian poet Taras Shevchenko was officially celebrated in the Gimnazjum, some of the Ukrainian students provocatively intoned "*Shche ne vmerla Ukraina*" (Ukraine isn't dead yet)—the national anthem of Ukrainian radicals.[57] Anti-Polish events occurred intermittently in the villages around Brzezany. A newly appointed Polish teacher who replaced a Ukrainian in the Dubszcze village school was harassed. Ukrainian peasants were warned not to rent her a room, and after she succeeded in renting one, her window was smashed. A few weeks later, a shot was fired at that window.[58] In some village schools, OUN activists incited Ukrainian children against their Polish teachers. Ukrainian nationalists warned a number of Ukrainian women in Brzezany, wives of prominent local Ukrainian personalities, not to participate in charity events organized by the Polish Red Cross.[59]

Arrests of Ukrainian nationalists in Brzezany and vicinity started in the mid-twenties and increased in time. Numerous political trials in which Ukrainians were involved were held in the Brzezany court.[60] Ukrainians were arrested in Brzezany and in the neighboring villages in the fall of 1933 and accused of waging an anti-Polish campaign in schools. They were tried, and some of the punishments were quite severe. Mikola Zatsukhny, a Gimnazjum student and member of the OUN, was sentenced in early March 1934 to nine years of imprisonment for distributing anti-Polish leaflets. Lev Rega, from the village of Dubszcze, was sentenced to five years of imprisonment for a similar offense.[61] Several attempts were made by moderate Poles and Ukrainians to cool the spirits. In its editorial of September 1, 1935, *Glos Brzezanski* called for Polish-Ukrainian cooperation and understanding. A Polish-Ukrainian get-together was convened in the Sokol auditorium three weeks later, with the participation of the headmaster of the Brzezany Gimnazjum; the most respected local Ukrainian lawyer, Dr. Bemko; and the leading Ukrainian priest in Brzezany, Father Baczynski.[62]

Tensions and hostilities among Ukrainians and Poles continued. Ukrainian nationalists desecrated a number of Polish soldiers' and policemen's tombs at the Brzezany cemetery in May 1936.[63] There were a number of political assassinations. One of the first murders carried out by OUN nationalists in the Brzezany region was that of a Polish road supervisor. He was a member of the Polish Riflemen's Association and a noncommissioned reservist of the Polish army who lived in Taurow, a predominantly Ukrainian village east of Brzezany. A mass funeral lasting more than an hour took place in Brzezany on June 25, 1937. Representatives of all local Polish organizations and the local 51st Army Regiment participated. An editorial in the local Brzezany newspaper warned the Ukrainians that Polish "patience has been exhausted."[64]

A senior Polish forester with the Potocki estate was murdered near Brzezany on the second day of Christmas in December 1937. A mass funeral followed. The Brzezany newspaper called again for a staunch Polish stand against Ukrainian *hajdamaks*.[65] One of the two Polish priests officiating at the funeral was Jan Gach, who was from the village of Kotow. He would be turned in by Ukrainian peasants and killed by Soviet soldiers less than two years later. In some cases, moderate Ukrainians and mixed Polish-Ukrainian families were also affected. A Dubszcze household, which consisted of a Ukrainian married to a Polish woman and children who were raised as Poles, went up in fire in November 1938.[66] Dozens of OUN members were arrested as a result of the various incidents in Brzezany and vicinity. All branches of Prosvita, Ridna Shkola, and other Ukrainian organizations in the Brzezany region were closed in March 1939.[67] One of the last murders perpetrated by Ukrainian extremists before the outbreak of the Second World War was that of a Polish policeman who served in Plaucza Mala, a Ukrainian village that was northeast of Brzezany.[68]

The last prewar incident in Brzezany which reflected the ever-growing tensions between Poles and Ukrainians was the "funeral of Ukraine" in March 1939. A group of Poles, mostly Gimnazjum students, marched through the town with a coffin marked "Ukraine is dead." Windows were smashed in some Ukrainian houses. In a few days, bodies of two Poles, alleged participants in the "funeral of Ukraine," were found in the Zlota Lipa River, near Adamowka, a suburb of Brzezany.[69]

No detailed evidence exists concerning Communist sentiments and activities in Brzezany and vicinity in the twenties. A few documents and newspaper reports do reveal that the Komunistychna Partiia Zakhidmoi Ukrainy (KPZU, the Communist Party of Western Ukraine) conducted anti-government and pro-Soviet propaganda during the thirties. Communist leaflets were distributed in early 1932 in the village of Plotycza, east of Brzezany. They urged "Comrades Poles, Ukrainians and Jews" not to let fascism incite them against each other.[70] The centers of illegal Communist activities in eastern Galicia at that time were Lwow and Tarnopol. The most active branch of the KPZU in the Brzezany region was in the village of Potutory and was headed by one Herman Winter. A police report submitted in May 1932 claimed that Rachela Zukerbrot, a member of the Party Central Committee, had arrived at the Potutory railroad station and met with Winter. Zukerbrot and Winter, according to the report, sat in the bushes near the railroad bridge and "conducted a conference on organizational problems of the KPZU in the region."[71]

Though some Polish and Ukrainian names of local Communists were mentioned in a number of police reports and in the Brzezany newspaper, most of the names sounded Jewish. Extensive house searches were conducted by the police in Brzezany in May 1932, and a number of people were arrested. Among them were Zukerbrot, Winter, David Lang, Isaac Sauberberg, Kunio Grad, Fishl Reizer, David Weber, and Pawel Trauner.[72] They were tried in the Brzezany court in the spring of 1933 and given prison sentences that ranged from one to five years.[73] Some of those who were released after serving their sentence resumed illegal activities. For example, David Weber, who was released after serving eighteen months, was apprehended again in April 1936 and accused of distributing Communist leaflets. A subsequent trial was held in February and March 1937. Weber was sentenced to four years, Jacob Lapter to six, Fishl Reizer to four, and Usher Sauberberg, Isaac Sauberberg's brother, to half a year of imprisonment. Among the defending attorneys were two local Ukrainian lawyers, Bemko and Zakhidny.[74]

I spoke more than sixty years later to Mundek Harpaz, Isaac Sauberberg's younger brother. He told me that theirs was a rather poor Jewish family. There were three sons and a daughter. Their father was a tinsmith and worked most of the time in the villages near Brzezany. Both parents were orthodox Jews. Isaac, or, as they usually called him, Itschie, the firstborn, excelled at the Brzezany Gimnazjum, especially in math and physics. His gradual involvement in illegal Communist activities resulted in growing tensions within the family, and he moved out of the house. His prolonged imprisonments estranged him even more from his orthodox parents. During the short-lived Soviet rule in Brzezany, Itschie was appointed to several successive positions, and when the Soviets retreated in the summer of 1941, he and his family joined them. Both parents and his younger sister died of hunger and disease in faraway Samarkand. His younger brother, Usher, was murdered during the Soviet retreat. Itschie was killed during a German bombing raid near Stalingrad. The only one who survived the war was Itschie's younger brother, Mundek. He settled in Israel.[75]

The most prominent Jewish Communist in Brzezany was Elkana, or Kunio, Grad. His family too, like Itschie Sauberberg's, was a traditional Jewish family. Kunio completed public school in Brzezany and worked in various jobs. He also used to help out with his father's cows and horses. The peak of his career was his service as the first Soviet mayor of Brzezany in the fall of 1939, during the first weeks of the Soviet rule. He left Brzezany with the retreating Soviet administration in the summer of 1941. Kunio Grad was among the few Brzezany Jews who survived the war in Russia. Grad lived after the war in Poland and served as an officer with the Urzad Bezpieczenstwa (UB, the Polish Security). Eventually he emigrated to Canada and died there.[76]

* * *

Most of the interviewees, with the exception of the oldest, those who remembered the First World War and its immediate aftermath, nourished happy memories of their Brzezany childhood. Tolek Rapf spoke of his "beloved hometown." "I recall it with an enormous amount of feeling, since it was there that I spent the most wonderful years of my childhood."[77] His younger sister, Halszka, showed me her old family photo album. A picture which especially drew my attention was that of a house surrounded by a garden, with the members of the Rapf family posing in front of it. Under the photo was an inscription, summing it all up in a short, somewhat naive and nostalgic manner, "Czasy sielskie-anielskie. Brzezany, 1935" (Peaceful, angelic times. Brzezany, 1935). This old snapshot represented the essence of Halszka's prewar memories. She was sure that the Rapf villa, opposite the Farny Church, was one of the most beautiful houses in Brzezany.

At my request, Halszka took me on an imaginary tour of the villa and the garden. Most of the heavy, dark-colored furniture was brought from Vienna. The most impressive room in the house was engineer Rapf's study, with its books and its antique chiming clock, apparently one of four such clocks ever made. "For us, it was a kind of sanctuary. We seldom went inside," Halszka confided. "There was a beautiful garden in front of the house, tended by my mother and the gardener. A huge, beautiful maple tree grew there. There was a lawn and lots of flowers. Inside the garden, facing the street, stood a funny little dwarf figurine saluting those who passed by. Children walking up the street past our house returned his salute. That house, that time, those fifteen years before the war, are really the most significant period of my life. They are my life."[78]

Batya Prizand's childhood memories of Brzezany were pleasant and cheerful. "I clearly remember the house where I grew up and lived until leaving Poland. It was located on the edge of town, on a hill near the Bernardine Cloister. There were only three houses there, and ours, number one, was the most remote. It was a charming place. When I go back in time I realize that I spent my childhood in a paradise." Batya used the same Polish phrase I found in Halszka's photo album. She spoke of those distant "peaceful, angelic times" in Brzezany. She could recall almost every detail of their house: its design, its colors, its smells. The house bordered on a huge orchard of plum trees. "The path leading into that orchard was lined with currant and gooseberry bushes. At its very end was an alcove, surrounded by white and violet lilacs. I loved it. As a child I spent most of the time in that alcove, playing with friends. I had my own little flower garden in front of the house, where I grew pansies and sweet peas. In the winter, after a snowfall, we used to slide down the smooth, slippery Bernardine hill. We used to call it 'the glass mountain.' I had a very happy childhood."[79]

Vasyl Oleskiw, from the village of Byszki, recalled his early childhood. They lived in a thatched-roof house built of clay. "Most of the village houses were like that. Only two houses in the whole village had tin roofs. Most had soil-packed floors. Nevertheless, these poor village houses had a pleasant appearance. They were usually painted white with a tinge of blue, twice a year, in the spring and in the fall. There were orchards of apple, pear and cherry trees in between the houses."[80]

Most of my Polish and Jewish interviewees cherished their memories of the Brzezany landscape. The Brzezany lake, the Staw, and the hills around the town were frequently recalled. Tolek told me that "there were boats, canoes, people bathing and swimming. I have lots of memories of summer vacations at that lake. All around were hills, covered by thick forests. The location of Brzezany was charming, beautiful."[81] The Staw occupied an especially significant place in Dr. Skrzypek's memories. "We used to bathe and swim in the Staw. My future wife, Lidia, Dr. Danek's younger sister, once jumped off the diving board and didn't come up. She was apparently drowning. I pulled her out, and then we started going out together. I was 16 and she was 13."[82]

Brzezany neighborhoods were quite mixed and relations were correct, at the very least. Wladyslawa Cwynar, born in 1921, remembered her house as an "open house, where various people used to come and ask for assistance. We were in a neighborhood where three ethnic groups lived together, Ukrainians, Poles and Jews, rich and poor." One of her father's closest friends, she said, was Mr. Steinberg, a Jew, who owned one of the best stores in town. It was famous for its wines and chocolates. Her father and Mr. Steinberg had served together in the Austrian army during the First World War. "When I passed his store on my way to school, he always gave me chocolates," Wladyslawa recalled.[83]

Karol Codogni's family lived on the outskirts of Brzezany. His father, Stanislaw, was a blacksmith. They also owned some land and had a few cows and horses. Stanislaw did business with numerous Jewish craftsmen. "He needed them and they needed him. At times they quarreled and even went to court." Karol recalled that my Grandpa Fishl was friendly with his father and used to come to their house. Karol's father used to consult him on various business matters. Karol, actually, confirmed what I had heard within my own family. Grandpa Fishl and Stanislaw Codogni had been friends since the First World War. When my Uncle Wolcio and some other young Zionists from Brzezany decided to travel to Palestine, it was Karol's father, hired by Fishl, who took them in his horse carriage to Lwow. This was some time in 1920. Karol recalled how, as a young boy, he used to play with Jewish boys in his neighborhood. He even spoke some Yiddish at that time. When Karol was a teenager, two Jewish families rented rooms at their house and he became friendly with their boys. Living near and close to Jews was a perfectly normal thing for him.[84]

Almost all Ukrainian interviewees came from villages around Brzezany. Lev remembered his native Dubszcze as mostly Ukrainian with some Polish families and a few Jews. He didn't encounter any significant tension and conflict between Ukrainians and Poles until he started attending the Brzezany Gimnazjum. "There was no Jewish problem in our village. There was Faibish, there was Khaika, they sold things. Once a Ukrainian cooperative opened, people stopped buying from them and they moved to Kozowa." Although the village school was officially Polish, its Ukrainian teachers attempted to educate the children in a Ukrainian spirit. The local branch of Prosvita was very popular. Ukrainian study groups for the young were initiated. They read and discussed Ukrainian history, geography, and culture.[85]

Vasyl Oleskiw from Byszki recalled that there was a Ukrainian church in their village. The few Polish families who lived there had to walk to nearby Kuropatniki to pray in a Polish Catholic church. There was only one Jewish family in Byszki. "Moshko owned the local shop and Grandma used to send me there to buy salt, sugar, matches and kerosene. At school I studied with Moshko's oldest daughter, Berta." Almost all students were Ukrainian, and they didn't like studying Polish. At times the teacher spoke to them in Polish and they responded in Ukrainian. They were obliged to attend prayers in the local church on all official Polish holidays. "When we had to celebrate the 3rd of May, half of the kids disappeared on the way to the church."

Vasyl visited Brzezany for the first time when he was 7. "I accompanied my mother and father to Brzezany to sell onions, eggs, and chickens. As we approached the town we saw the Staw, the big lake. It was the first time I had ever seen so much water. It looked like an ocean to me. There were rows of beautiful small houses. I kept this image for many years. As soon as we reached the outskirts of the town, we were surrounded by merchants, mostly Jewish, who offered to buy our products. When we reached the center I realized that this was really a big town. I saw so many Poles and Jews for the first time. People spoke various languages: Polish, Ukrainian, Yiddish. There were lots of shops around the Ratusz and in the Ratusz building itself. Facing the Ratusz was a huge Ukrainian church. Up on a nearby hill was a Polish church."[86]

Dmytro Bartkiw remembered his native village, Kotow, as primarily Ukrainian with some Polish families. Nearby was a new agricultural settlement founded by Polish "settlers" from central Poland, whom they called *mazury*. There were no conflicts between them and the local Ukrainians, according to Dmytro. The village tavern was owned by a Jew named Miller. Jews from neighboring villages used to come and pray in his house on Jewish holidays. A Ukrainian campaign against alcoholism in the mid-thirties forced Miller to close shop. The small village school was run by a Polish principal, a woman. The majority of the students in Dmytro's class were Ukrainians, but there were also a few Polish kids from the village and some children from the *mazury* families. The Ukrainians kept to themselves most of the time. They were taught Polish patriotic poems and songs and had to celebrate Polish holidays. "We boys used to arrive early at school, sit on the windowsills, and sing Ukrainian songs," Dmytro recalled. He also remembered some cheerful events in his village: "Young people from the vicinity would gather at the village commons for singing and dancing. Everyone was dressed in embroidered Ukrainian folk costumes. Boys wore those wide, red-colored Cossack trousers and the girls wore their colored kerchiefs."

When Dmytro was 11, his father enrolled him in the Brzezany public school for boys. "We went there by horse cart and arrived in Adamowka, where we met some Jews who knew my father. He told them that he was taking me to school in order to make a *pan*, a gentleman, out of me." Dmytro used to travel daily to Brzezany by train to attend school. The morning train was crowded with village children traveling to study in Brzezany. Dmytro recalled walking daily from the railway station to the boys' public school; he passed the Sieniawski Castle on the right and the army barracks on the left.[87]

Vasyl Fanga, from Szybalin, recalled that a few poor Jewish families lived in his village. "There was this Khaika or Surka. She had a small shop. When people bought on credit she would write it on the wall. Sometimes the boys would come there and lean on the wall, so that whatever was written there was wiped off, and Surka didn't remember who owed what." Young Vasyl knew some Jewish boys in Brzezany and once, out of curiosity, he even went into the Brzezany Synagogue. He also used to light matches for some Jews on the Sabbath. Some boys from his neighborhood in Szybalin organized a group which would meet from time to time and discuss Ukrainian history. Their "instructors" were Ukrainian teenagers, students at the Brzezany Gimnazjum. "On one occasion we collected some used metal, glass, and barbed wire. We sold it, and with the money we earned we bought yellow and blue paper and made a Ukrainian flag. We all got together on a Ukrainian holiday, each one holding his little flag. Suddenly, we saw a Polish policeman riding a bike from the direction of Brzezany. We broke up and ran away."[88]

Israel Ne'eman recalled his school years in the townlet of Narajow. Most of the students were Ukrainian. "There were, on the average, two Jews in each grade, and the relations were good. A Ukrainian boy whose father was a plasterer and a Communist was my close friend. He warned the other boys not to touch me." Israel had very fond memories of his Narajow school.[89]

The Brzezany Gimnazjum lives on quite distinctly in the memories of its graduates, even after decades. Those were apparently the years when their identities, ideas, tastes, and opinions were shaped. For the young Poles, the Gimnazjum was the embodiment of new, independent Poland. Tolek clearly remembered his years at the Gimnazjum, from which he graduated just before the Second World War. As far as interethnic relations were concerned, Jewish students, according to Tolek, usually teamed up with their Polish classmates against the Ukrainians. He remembered that during the late thirties, when Polish-Ukrainian relations flared up, Polish students would assist the local police in their anti-Ukrainian pacification campaigns. As for social life of the students, "Poles usually associated with Poles. We were quite friendly with Jews, but there were no intimate relations among us." Sporting events were, perhaps, an exception.

Tolek recalled in detail a boxing match, the first of its kind in Brzezany, in which the Gimnazjum team competed with a team representing the 51st Infantry Regiment. "Our heavyweight was Natan Goldman. His opponent was a huge monster with the looks of a gorilla. We were sure that he'd wipe the floor with Natan. At a certain moment Natan managed to deliver a precise blow to his head and the guy became completely disoriented. Natan took advantage of the situation and started to 'massacre' him. The man was carried out of the ring. It was a knockout. The Gimnazjum crowd went wild. Natan was the hero of the day."[90]

Halszka, Tolek's younger sister, became a student at the Gimnazjum in 1936, when she was 12. "Those were wonderful years. We were close to each other and there was a sense of complete freedom." Halszka's closest friends were Polish girls, but she also fondly recalled some of her Jewish classmates, such as Bela Goldman, Natan's younger sister; little blond Hermina Glazer; and Anna Herzog, who "played the piano like a professional." Halszka also remembered some of her Jewish teachers, such as Prof. Schleicher, who taught Greek, Latin, and German, and Prof. Schoechterowna.

She didn't recall any anti-Semitism at school and vaguely remembered some tensions between Poles and Ukrainians. Halszka recalled the various Polish state holidays celebrated at school and the military parades. "Kazik's father led the military band of the 51st Regiment, turning and twisting his golden baton. Behind the band marched the various units of the regiment. I loved it."[91]

Relations among Polish and Jewish students at the Brzezany Gimnazjum were, according to Dr. Skrzypek, considerably better than in Lwow schools. He recalled anti-Semitic incidents during his student days at Lwow University. "Jewish students were caught and beaten up in the corridors. They were sometimes forced to open their flies in order to check whether they were circumcised. But, generally speaking, there were no murders."[92]

Poldek's family lived in Kozowa, a small town southeast of Brzezany. After completing elementary school in Kozowa, Poldek started his high school education at the Brzezany Gimnazjum. There were only three Jewish boys in his class. They spoke to each other in Yiddish and Polish. Poldek distinctly remembered one of his Polish teachers, Kowalski. "That Kowalski, who looked like a *szlachcic* [nobleman] with a mustache, was a terrible anti-Semite. He hated his Jewish students, and each year he selected a different victim. I was one of them." Poldek recalled the Zawirski affair. Prof. Zawirski, who taught Polish, was known for taking bribes, especially from Jews. They even had a rhyme for it: "*Zawirski, krol lapowek, piedzdziesieciu dolarowek*" (Zawirski, the king of bribes, of 50-dollar bills). He was sued for failing Jewish students whose parents refused to bribe him. For Poldek, as apparently for other Brzezany Jews, the fact that Zawirski had been exposed, tried, and sentenced was a source of satisfaction. "It was sensational, really sensational."[93] Jozek Slotwinski remembered Zawirski as "tall and elegant, and a terrible womanizer."[94] When I interviewed Dr. Skrzypek, he showed me a photo of his wife's class at the Gimnazjum. Zawirski, young, good-looking, and self-assured, was surrounded by nine young women. Five were standing behind him, two were seated on either side of him, and two reclined on the floor in front of him. Zawirski, dressed in an immaculate three-piece suit, looked like a rooster in a chicken coop. The girl standing on the far left was Lidka Danek, Skrzypek's future wife. One of the two girls sitting on the floor at Zawirski's feet was my Aunt Malcia.

Natan Goldman was known at the Gimnazjum as a prankster and a trouble-maker. He excelled in practical jokes. Unlike most of the Jewish students, Natan was an outstanding athlete. Tall, strong, and good-looking, Natan was the bane of the Jew-baiters at school. He beat up some of them in defense of his Jewish classmates. He became most famous for the boxing match. "One of my best friends at the Gimnazjum was Tolek Rapf," Natan recalled. "He, too, was an excellent athlete. I often went to their house."[95]

Adas Goldschlag had numerous Polish friends at the Gimnazjum. One of them was the son of the hospital director, and another was the daughter of the commander of the 51st Regiment. He mixed easily with the local Polish "elite" and was, apparently, the only Jewish youth in town who played tennis. He recalled some anti-Semitic incidents. "Two new students arrived from out of town in the mid-thirties and they started the whole thing. They convinced the class that Jews should be seated in separate benches. The frightening thing was how two hooligans could, without any difficulty, terrorize all the others. I became a 'ghost' to my Polish friends. They didn't see me, didn't greet me, didn't talk to me." However, as the *matura* exams approached, Adas, an excellent student, whose help was always welcome, "all of a sudden ceased being a shadow and became a person again."[96]

Anna described her Gimnazjum years with great affection. She was an excellent student. "I passed all exams with straight A's." Most of her friends were Polish girls from the "best" families in town. Her most admired teacher was Jozek Slotwinski. "He arrived in the mid-thirties and took over our class. He was of medium height, thin, athletic, and good-looking. He was the most pleasant and most wonderful teacher we ever had. He was quite aware about the girls' crushes and would advise the boys how to approach their prospective girlfriends. However, the minute he decided to start teaching, we became completely quiet. He could teach us in twenty minutes what others couldn't in an hour." Anna took piano lessons, swam, ice-skated, and played tennis. One of her partners was Adas Goldschlag. When she was 15 and Adas was 17, they started going out steadily. "Adas used to come to our house on Saturday afternoons or on Sundays. My mother would join us for the movies. She would also escort us to the tennis courts and to the lake. At times, the Gimnazjum headmaster would arrive there to supervise the students." During the day I spent with Anna, I heard a lot about her friendship with Adas. It sounded like a real love story.[97] Mr. Goldschlag commented in the course of our long telephone conversation, rather laconically, "I was in love with her and she was in love with me. That's how it started and that's how it ended." He left Brzezany for Palestine shortly before the war. He would meet Anna again years later. By then she was a staunch Catholic, married to a Pole.[98]

Lev Rega, from the village of Dubszcze, maintained that he didn't encounter significant conflicts between Ukrainians and Poles until he started attending the Gimnazjum. "It wasn't easy there for Ukrainian village boys. And besides, they considered us inferior." The Ukrainian teachers attempted to help them. Lev recalled one of them, Prof. Shipailo, with great affection. Shipailo was in charge of the local Ukrainian students' dormitory. "He took very good care of us, made us feel equal to the Poles and lifted our spirits. He was murdered by the Soviets in 1941."[99]

Galina Skaskiv attended the Gimnazjum during the last few years before the war. "Students in all A-level classes came from the local Polish elite. They were the sons and daughters of the military. Poorer Poles and the Jews studied in B-level classes. C-level classes, where Ukrainian was taught, consisted of Ukrainian students. The Ukrainians kept to themselves." Galina mentioned a number of her Ukrainian teachers. It was Prof. Boikovych, a teacher of Latin and French, who particularly impressed his Ukrainian students. Besides being a respected teacher, he was also an ex-colonel of the Ukrainian Galician Army. Galina spoke of growing tensions and outright hostility between Poles and Ukrainians. "The Polish Scouts, the Harcerstwo, hated Ukrainians. They persecuted us and prevented us from speaking Ukrainian."[100]

Jozek Slotwinski, the only Gimnazjum "professor" I succeeded in reaching, was only 25 when he arrived in Brzezany in the winter of 1933, after receiving his doctorate at Lwow University. He taught "Polonistyka," Polish language and literature. "This was a solid, old-style classical Gimnazjum, with Greek and Latin. It was a dignified and respected institution." Slotwinski recalled his success with the Gimnazjum teenagers with great verve and enthusiasm. Unlike most of the other teachers, he was quite close to them in age and had his special way, even with the wildest. "When I stepped into that class I was utterly frightened. Then, after a couple of weeks I had them feeding from my hand. Some of the boys even imitated my hairstyle." When he left Brzezany for a position in Lwow in the fall of 1937, Slotwinski was carried to the train by his admiring students.

At my request, Slotwinski tried to relive the social milieu of his Brzezany years. "First of all, there were the officers from the 51st Regiment and their wives. They were the most prominent at the various social events. Then there were the town officials and their wives and daughters, as well as judges and lawyers. Most of them were Poles." His memories of Brzezany were definitely positive. "I recall it as a place of decent people. In spite of the mixture of Poles, Jews, and Ukrainians, the atmosphere was rather peaceful. Brzezany is always a source of pleasant memories."[101]

Batya Prizand and Bela Feld studied at the Brzezany Women Teachers' Seminary. Before graduating from the girls' public school, Batya was already set on becoming a teacher. It wasn't easy for a girl from a rather poor and orthodox Jewish family to be accepted at the seminary. When she asked Mr. Olszewski, the director, whether she had any chance, he demanded to know in advance whether she would write on Saturdays. "I couldn't decide for myself and talked it over with my mother. We went for a long walk and she said 'Go and tell him you will, since this is your future.'" Batya's father was hardly aware of the fact that his daughter was entering a world completely alien to him.

Batya, or Basia, as she was called in Polish, was 14 and spoke excellent Polish when she started her studies at the seminary. Most of the few Jewish girls who studied there came from the richest families in town, and the fact that she was accepted "caused a sensation in town." Basia made a number of Polish friends at the seminary. The closest was a village girl, Wikta Jakielanka. They were both 16 at the time. "She loved me. She could have been suspected of being a lesbian by today's standards. Once, when we went to the movies, she told me 'Basia, you are like the very best man for me.' Wikta was unusual. She wrote poems and was extremely sensitive and quite moody at times. Once, at wintertime, she sent us a note from her village about her intention to commit suicide. A few of us from Hashomer Hazair hired a sled with horses, rode to her house, and talked her out of it."[102]

Bela Feld, too, remembered her seminary years quite well. At that time she was already deeply involved with Hanoar Hatzioni, one of the Zionist youth organizations in town, and was committed to settling in Palestine.

That was perhaps why she could sympathize with the national sentiments of her Ukrainian classmates. "I actually preferred Ukrainian to Polish girls. They understood that I, too, had my national identity. One of my closest friends at the Seminary was Halyna Dydyk, from the village of Kotow. She was tall and sang well. I really liked her. We had lots of things in common. We used to study for finals in my house. We also used to sing together. She knew that I was involved with Hanoar Hatzioni and I knew that she was a member of Plast. Neither of us, because we were seminary students, was officially allowed to belong to these organizations. Halyna couldn't comprehend why Jews, another minority in Poland, didn't join the Ukrainians in their struggle against the Poles. I spoke about our differing objectives and we had a fight. 'There will come a time,' she said, 'when we shall take revenge.' And still, I respected her for her convictions. I often wondered how she behaved during the war."[103]

The various youth movements occupied a central place in the lives of young Poles, Jews, and Ukrainians in interwar Brzezany. Tolek was a member of the Polish Scouts, the Harcerstwo. "There was an extremely patriotic Polish atmosphere there. Meetings, lectures, discussions. We were greatly impressed by national holidays, celebrations, uniforms."[104]

Batya vividly recalled the *ken*, the Hashomer Hazair meeting place in Brzezany. "We used to meet there in the evenings. It was like a second home. We used to sing for hours on end. Then we danced endless horas, polkas, and mazurkas. Some of us nearly fainted from exhaustion. Those were wonderful, unforgettable evenings." One of her counselors was Aryeh Feld, Bela's brother, who taught them Hebrew poems and songs. "I was living in three different, and at times conflicting, worlds. There was my orthodox family, the Polish school, and the Zionist youth movement."[105]

If there was anti-Semitism in interwar Brzezany it usually assumed quite mild forms. Michal Kaminski, a teenager in the thirties, recalled that "if there was a Polish and a Jewish bookstore, an Endek would place himself in front of the Jewish store and demand that Poles buy books in the Polish store only. Some of the prospective buyers would tell him to get lost and went straight into the Jewish bookstore, since the merchandise there was a penny cheaper."[106]

Although relations between Ukrainians and Jews in Narajow were peaceful most of the time, Israel recalled an event which he described as a "pogrom." "It was a Friday evening during the summer. A Ukrainian youngster, Chernyi, climbed through a window into Milshtok's house and stole something. After a chase and a fight, Chernyi was shot dead by a Polish policeman. Within an hour or two, throngs of Ukrainians started milling around in the center of town. The Jews ran into their houses and locked themselves in. Ukrainians started robbing Jewish stores. Some Jews were wounded, but there were no fatalities. Dr. Grinfeld pulled out his gun and stopped the mob for a while. Then soldiers of the 51st Regiment arrived from Brzezany and things calmed down."[107]

Motek Majblum, a Gimnazjum student at the time, recalled that anti-Jewish sentiments increased in Brzezany in 1936–1937. "The severe discipline in the Gimnazjum prevented acts of outright anti-Semitism there. Hostility showed up, though, after school. I personally went through a scary experience. There was an attempt to drown me while I was swimming in the lake."[108]

After graduating from the Brzezany Gimnazjum, Poldek went to Lwow in order to find out whether he would be accepted to study medicine at Lwow University. He was attacked by Polish students on the university grounds. "They used to walk around holding sticks with razor blades attached to them. A young guy with a stick approached me. He didn't talk to me at all. And suddenly—boom! He cut open my head. I was bleeding like a pig. A fellow Jew pulled me out of there."[109]

Polish-Ukrainian relations in Brzezany and in the surrounding countryside deteriorated considerably throughout the thirties. This is amply reflected in the memories of the Ukrainian interviewees.

Lev, a Gimnazjum student at the time, lived in the Brzezany Ukrainian dormitory, the *bursa*. He recalled an incident in the fall of 1930. "It was November 11, a Polish national holiday. They took us to the Brzezany municipality early in the morning. When we returned to our dormitory, everything was topsy-turvy. Our quilts and pillows were torn. Pictures of Shevchenko, of our saints, and even of Jesus were ripped up. Windows in some Ukrainian houses in town were smashed. They broke into Ukrainian shops and poured kerosene over the sacks of flour and rice. They ruined our libraries. It was pure vandalism. That's how our hatred towards the Poles started and that's why we answered the OUN call. It was our response to stupid Polish chauvinism."[110]

Marian, who lived on the outskirts of Podhajce, recalled a traumatic event which occurred when he was 10. "For us children, soldiers were always an attraction. One day, four cavalry men, Polish Uhlans mounted on horses, appeared in front of our house. One of them charged directly at me and almost knocked me down. I fell unconscious and mother took me into the house. Then they caught my father and hit him again and again. It was terrible. They tore down our roof, ran into our storage room, and destroyed the sacks of grain and cabbage. It was sheer barbarism."[111]

Vasyl Oleskiw, from the village of Byszki, remembered a pacification campaign sometime in the thirties. "About a hundred mounted Uhlans rode into the village. They had a list of people who fought for Ukrainian independence in 1918 and 1919, and they beat up those people. I remember them, riding those horses, dressed in very impressive uniforms, holding swords and lances. In a neighboring house they hit a man repeatedly until he died. He had been an officer in the Ukrainian army during the First World War."[112]

Dmytro Bartkiw, from Kotow, recalled an incident which occurred in his village. "Some *srakobyitsi*—ass-hitters, as we called them—arrived in our village. It was late at night. There was a shriek of a siren and I woke up. I was sleeping in the attic then. There was screaming and yelling everywhere. They dragged out a young man, one of the Ukrainian cooperative movement activists, and threw him into a roadside ditch. Then two of them started beating him with sticks. He was yelling and his mother was running around and shouting. I backed away from the little attic window. I was scared."[113]

Galina's story was, perhaps, the most tragic. It dwelt not only on Polish but also on internal Ukrainian violence. Her grandmother died a few weeks after being hit by a Polish policeman during the pacification campaign of the mid-thirties. Then her father was murdered. Galina was 13 at that time. "They ran into the house and started to hit my father and my mother with huge sticks. My father tried to escape, and that's when they shot him in the back. Mother managed to run away. It was a sad and painful event for us, especially when it turned out that these weren't only common bandits. Some of them were members of the OUN. A day or two earlier, young OUN people had torn a Polish flag hanging at the entrance to the school building and had thrown it into the toilet. My father said that this wasn't the right thing to do. He called them *barany*—lambheads. That very evening there were rumors in the village that my father would be killed. Nobody believed it, but in a day or two he was murdered."[114]

Vasyl Fanga, from Szybalin, remembered the mid-thirties as a watershed in Ukrainian-Polish relations. "One time five military trucks arrived in the village with their sirens screaming. There was panic. They started beating up people. They would go from house to house, saying nothing, just beating. The Polish police took some young men from our village to Lysonia, where they ordered them to dig up the graves of the Ukrainian Sich Riflemen who had been buried there. Then the remains were taken somewhere. Our boys managed to bring four of them back to the village, and they were reburied in the village cemetery." Vasyl also recalled how Ukrainian-Polish relations deteriorated in Brzezany. "One time they prepared a casket, wrote 'Ukraine' on it and went to the Staw, the Brzezany lake, to drown it there. They also tried to force a Ukrainian priest, Father Baczynski, to say a prayer for the 'deceased' Ukraine. It was dreadful." Vasyl admitted, however, that Polish anti-Ukrainian acts were child's play compared to what would happen later under the Soviets.[115]

* * *

The interwar period is remembered by the Poles who lived in Brzezany as the best of times. Not only did Poles occupy the highest administrative posts and constitute the town's social elite, they also nurtured satisfaction and pride in Poland's independence and in their town's "Polishness." Child-hood and youth in Brzezany epitomized the happiest years in their lives. Some Brzezany Jews, too, had very pleasant childhood memories; Halszka Rapf and Batya Prizand used identical language to describe those memories.

Most Brzezany Jews, although aware of Polish anti-Semitism and discrimina-tion, didn't experience, on the whole, outright hostility. The Jewish middle class became increasingly acculturated into Polish language and culture. There were, however, only a small number of Jewish families which became assimilated into the Polish milieu. Some close friendships were shaped among Polish and Jewish adolescents in the Gimnazjum and in the women teachers' seminary, but mostly each group kept to itself. Social distancing between Jews and Ukrainians was more pronounced, although there were some unusual friendships, such as that between Bela Feld and Halyna Dydyk.

Polish-Ukrainian relations, at least in the twenties, weren't too bad. How-ever, the gradual suppression of Ukrainian culture and a certain amount of violence used against Ukrainians by the state and the military during the thirties caused increased frustration and hostility. The Polish pacification campaigns became a significant component of the memories of the Ukrai-nian interviewees. The tense Ukrainian-Polish relations resulted in some cases of Ukrainian terrorism around Brzezany in the late thirties. Both Pol-ish and Ukrainian interviewees vividly recalled the symbolic act of the "fu-neral of Ukraine" in Brzezany. Were these events a direct preamble to what would transpire between Poles and Ukrainians during the war? As bad as they were, they still seemed a far cry from the horrendous and tragic times of war, occupation, and suffering which would commence in the fall of 1939.

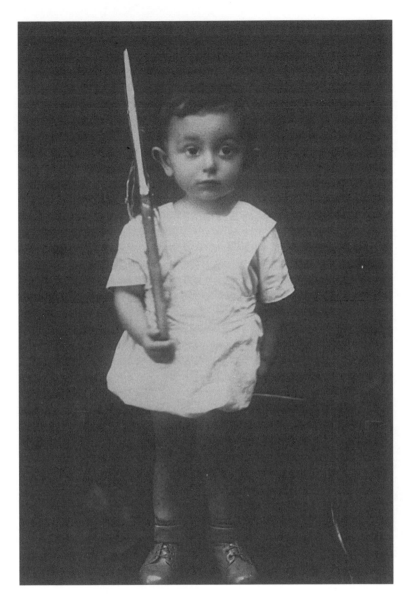

FIGURE 13.　Author, age 3.

FIGURE 14.   Author's parents: Chana Redlich (née Bomze) and Shlomo Redlich. Brzezany, 1930s.

FIGURE 15.   Author's maternal grandparents: Efraim-Fishl Bomze and Rivka Bomze (née Schwarz).

FIGURE 16. A group of Brzezany children in the Old Park, near the Sieniawski Castle, summer 1939. First row standing, left to right: author, cousin Reuven Nir. Courtesy of Natan Goldman.

FIGURE 17. The Brzezany lake, the Staw. Courtesy of Sam Goldschlag.

FIGURE 18. The Brzezany Gimnazjum. Courtesy of Ephraim Schmidt.

FIGURE 19. Gimnazjum boys' class with Prof. Staettner, early 1930s. Second row, fourth from left: Tolek Rapf; sixth from left: Natan Goldman. Courtesy of Tolek Rapf.

FIGURE 20. Gimnazjum girls' class 5A, 1928, with Prof. Zawirski. Top left: Lidia Danek; top right: Rozia Schwadron. Bottom left: Malcia Bomze. Courtesy of Dr. Stanislaw Skrzypek.

FIGURE 21. Girls' Hashomer Hazair group in the 1920s. Top row, second from right: Nuska Oberlender. Middle row, second from left: Basia Prizand; third from left: Pnina Bomze; far right: Malcia Bomze. Bottom row, second from left: Esterka Halperin; on right: Chancia Dorfman. Courtesy of Batya Prizand-Bone.

FIGURE 22.   Young Jewish men and women in Brzezany, near the Rynek, late 1930s. Left to right: Natan Goldman, Renia Has, Mundek Hamer, a girl from Rohatyn, Munio Ornstein, Sylka Finkelstein. Courtesy of Natan Goldman.

FIGURE 23.   Graduating class of the Brzezany Women Teachers' Seminary, 1930. Second row from top, second from right: Halyna Dydyk; third from right: Bela Feld. Courtesy of Bela Feld-Danieli.

FIGURE 24. The Rapf villa, 1935. Courtesy of Halszka Rapp-Wierzbicka.

FIGURE 25. A delegation from Brzezany and the Brzezany District presents Edward Rydz-Smigly with Tiger, a pedigreed Arab stallion, March 18, 1937, on the occasion of his 51st birthday. Courtesy of Sam Goldschlag.

4

THE SOVIET INTERLUDE, 1939–1941

The Red Army entered Brzezany six months after my fourth birthday. As far as I can recall from my fragmented memories, nothing really changed. My carefree childhood seemed to continue as usual. But there was a relative novelty: some Russian words and songs. I must have attended a Soviet kindergarten. I have a vague memory of learning an ode to Stalin, reciting Russian poems, and seeing a picture of Stalin and Voroshilov, applauding. A Red Army officer, apparently Jewish, used to visit our house. I adored his smart appearance, the shining dark-red star on his cap, and the fragrance of the brown leather belt and straps on his chest. I apparently encountered my first radio around that time. A Russian woman who lived close by invited me to her apartment, and I peeked curiously into the back of the dimly lit box, wondering whether some little man was producing all those sounds. Przyjazn, the movie theater, was around the corner. I don't remember whether I actually watched any films there. I do distinctly recall standing in front of a small magic box in which films were being previewed.

Life must have changed. Our cloth store must have been closed down. I assume that it was around that time that my father started working in a small state-owned workshop which produced little round wooden boxes used for storing medical ointments. A postcard with a Soviet stamp, written in Hebrew, dated April or May 1940, was sent by my father to my mother's sister in Palestine, announcing that our family was fine. My aunt and her 8-year-old son had visited us in Brzezany less than a year earlier, just before the war. My father was eager to know whether Reuven remembered his younger cousin and his uncle. My mother, he wrote, had recovered from a gall bladder attack and an eye inflammation, and my Grandma Rivka was suffering, as usual, from recurring headaches.

It must have been during this time that a young and good-looking blond man in his early 20s started visiting our house. His name was Vovo Szotenberg. He and his father had escaped from Brzeziny, near Lodz, through bomb-ridden Warsaw and had arrived in Brzezany along with the thousands of refugees flooding the town. Theirs was a quite rich Jewish family from Rostov-on-Don; they had left Russia after the October Revolution and settled in Poland. His father now worked as an accountant in one of the state-owned enterprises. Vovo, who had studied auto mechanics before the war, passed his driving test and started working at the same firm. It was my Aunt Malcia, my mother's youngest sister, who, although she was not a great beauty, succeeded in snatching away Vovo from her local competitors. Vovo appreciated finding a "home" in our house. There were differences in background and upbringing. The Szotenbergs were much less Jewish, religious, and traditional than our family. Grandpa Fishl used to say, half-jokingly, "Those blond locks will kill me one day." The irony was that those locks and Vovo's good looks would eventually save at least part of our family. When, in later years, I discussed his Brzezany days with Vovo, he did not seem to remember much but kept repeating that our family were "wonderful people." "Your father was very concerned with the house and the family. He was always running out and bringing things." My mother, according to Vovo, was mostly at home after the store was closed down, and she used to help Grandma cook and prepare meals.

My last memory of the Soviet years is that of our family staying for a day or two on the outskirts of town and of myself standing next to half-drawn window curtains, watching endless convoys of soldiers, carts, horses, and cannons. I was apparently witnessing the Red Army retreat.

The twenty-one months between September 1939 and June 1941, a relatively short span of time, was an extremely significant, dynamic, and, at times, tragic period in the lives of the millions of Poles, Jews, and Ukrainians who inhabited eastern Poland. The Soviet occupation, its initial and final stages in particular, generated animosity and acts of violence among the population. The Soviet "revolution from abroad" brought terror and suffering to many during this seemingly peaceful prelude to the "real" war and German occupation.[1]

Poland, which was paralyzed by the German blitzkrieg in the West and surprised by the Soviet invasion in the East, was incapable of organized resistance. Confusion and chaos marked the first two weeks of the war and became even more pronounced during the second half of September, following the Soviet invasion. A temporary power vacuum emerged as the Polish army and administration disintegrated and Soviet rule had not yet been consolidated. In some places, voluntary and highly patriotic Polish Citizens' Guards were formed. Some Ukrainian peasants and Communist sympathizers, including Jews, formed anti-Polish voluntary militias. An interethnic civil war was brewing.[2] The population of the eastern Polish territories was confused. Some Soviet leaflets stated that the Red Army would assist Poland in its fight against Germany. At the same time, other leaflets urged ethnic minorities, such as Ukrainians and Belorussians, to fight against their Polish landlords. Mutual suspicions and outright hatred among the various nationalities had already been on the rise in the prewar years. This short interim period of instability and chaos resulted in destruction and death, mainly in the countryside.[3] The situation started to stabilize, particularly in the cities and towns, following the Soviet occupation.

The Red Army, which occupied eastern Galicia during the second half of September 1939, was welcomed by friendly crowds composed mainly of young Jews and Ukrainians. The Polish population, subdued and frightened, generally remained aloof and suspicious. Although full-scale Nazi Holocaust policies were to be initiated only in the summer of 1941, atrocities committed against Jews by the Germans were known, at least in part, by the local Jewish population; that knowledge was supplemented by information from incoming Jewish refugees. Moreover, the power vacuum that followed the disintegration of the Polish state was ripe for potential anti-Jewish pogroms. Some Jews, particularly the young and the educated, harbored a grudge against the Polish state because of its discriminatory policies in education and employment. The presence of Jewish officers and soldiers in the ranks of the Red Army evoked feelings of relief and solidarity. For the relatively few Jewish Communists, the arrival of the Soviets seemed like a dream come true. Many Ukrainians who had suffered from discriminatory Polish attitudes and policies throughout the thirties seemed to welcome any change. The Poles' reaction was mixed. They preferred any rule to a power vacuum, which particularly threatened those Poles who lived in the countryside, where they were exposed to Ukrainian vengeance and terror. At the same time, Russia and Bolshevism were perceived as the perennial enemies from the East. The Poles were, therefore, equally antagonistic to Hitler's Germany, which had invaded half their country, and to Bolshevik Russia, which now occupied the other.[4]

Citizens' militias and committees, which had been formed during the Polish retreat, often acted as welcoming hosts to the arriving Red Army units. But they were first controlled and then replaced by completely loyal Soviet elements. A rapid rotation of personnel occurred at the local level during the initial weeks of the occupation. In many places, the first Soviet-appointed institutions contained a very high proportion of Jews. However, after the Soviets consolidated their rule and appointed Soviet personnel to the most significant positions, local Jews were relegated to inferior posts or removed altogether.[5]

All former public organizations and institutions, whether Polish, Jewish, or Ukrainian, were dissolved. Former loyalties and commitments were now under suspicion. The Soviet administration called on the population to "unmask" and turn in hostile elements.[6] At the same time, there was a massive propaganda campaign that emphasized liberation from Polish nationalist and economic oppression. Critical remarks against anti-Semitism appeared from time to time in local Soviet newspapers. A special effort was made to impress the Ukrainian population with the new regime's "Ukrainianism." Much was done to Ukrainize the educational system.[7] Soviet-Ukrainian newspapers and books were published. Some of the Ukrainian intelligentsia were offered opportunities for work and advancement that had not existed under Polish rule. At the same time, Ukrainian nationalists were mercilessly repressed. Those OUN leaders who had not been arrested maintained contacts with the Ukrainian underground and hoped for the German invasion.

Significant economic changes occurred. Wide-ranging confiscations took place. Members of the upper and middle layers of society, such as landowners, industrialists, and merchants, suffered the most. These were primarily Poles and Jews. The new Soviet regime actually liquidated Jewish commerce. It first affected large Jewish businesses, but in time, all retail trade was affected. Jewish shop-owners and traders sought ways to integrate into the state-owned shops and cooperatives. A similar process affected Jewish artisans. There was a gradual transition from independent work to labor in small factories and cooperatives. Jews in the liberal professions, such as lawyers, had to change their occupation and became state employees in various branches of the Soviet administration. Jewish doctors were employed in the government's medical services and could occupy positions unattainable before the war, and Jewish doctors who had completed their studies abroad and had not been given licenses by the Polish authorities were now granted the right to work without any restrictions. Some illegal private practice still existed. The situation of Jewish engineers also improved. There was free access to higher education, teachers' colleges, and vocational courses for Jewish students. They moved from small towns to larger cities, where educational opportunities became available. New social strata rose to prominence. Small artisans and people of "proletarian" origin or background became "important" people. There was now more contact and mingling among Poles, Jews, and Ukrainians. Soviet-style cultural affairs and entertainment brought young people of all three ethnic groups together.[8]

The countryside was greatly affected by the changes. Starting in October 1939, land and livestock were confiscated from landowners and monasteries. Land was distributed among poor peasants. However, this redistribution, which benefited primarily poor Ukrainian peasants, was only an interim step. A collectivization policy was initiated in the spring of 1940. It evoked strong opposition and caused upheaval in some villages. The process, which might have resulted in more serious clashes between the regime and the local peasantry, was cut short by the Soviet retreat in the summer of 1941.[9]

Within a few months of the Soviet occupation, drastic shortages developed. Very little could be bought in the state-owned retail stores. People had to sell personal belongings in order to buy food. Long lines in front of shops became a frequent sight. Red Army soldiers, who came from a backward consumer economy, bought up large quantities of whatever they could lay their hands on. Living space became scarce. Some of the better apartments and houses were confiscated for state, army, and Narodnyi Komissariat Vnutrennykh Del (NKVD, People's Commissariat of Internal Affairs) personnel.[10] Hundreds of thousands of refugees, fleeing from western and central Poland, rented rooms or stayed with friends and relatives. There was a substantial deterioration in the quality of life.

A visual change affecting the aesthetics of public space was taking place. Symbols of Polish culture, statehood, and nationalism, which had been so important and visible in the interwar years, rapidly disappeared. Street names were changed. Inscriptions were altered from the Latin alphabet to the Cyrillic. Portraits of Soviet leaders, Soviet banners, and Soviet posters appeared everywhere. Red stars replaced eagles and crosses. Loudspeakers were installed on the streets. In many towns, the new Soviet administration cleaned streets, repaired sidewalks, and planted public gardens. Soviet holidays and festivals, accompanied by music and parades, enlivened the otherwise drab everyday existence.[11]

Within a few months, a uniform system of Soviet-style education replaced former schools. The programs and language of instruction were changed. The schools were de-Polonized and secularized. Ukrainian and Russian acquired a preferential status. Some Yiddish-language schools were established, but they did not last long. Atheism was propagated in all schools. Teachers had to undergo rapid re-education. Some were replaced by new personnel who arrived from the Soviet interior. An atmosphere of constant action and excitement was maintained by way of competitions, celebrations, and cultural activities.[12]

Within a few weeks after the annexation, the NKVD established control over all areas of life. Massive arrests were conducted as early as the second half of October 1939, and they increased in 1940. They included primarily Polish army officers, landowners, businessmen, policemen, and members of prewar Polish organizations, such as the Scouts and the Riflemen's Association. At times people were arrested arbitrarily. Thousands were held in jails in big cities and in small towns.[13] The NKVD arrested Ukrainian political leaders and members of the Ukrainian nationalist underground. Thousands of Ukrainian activists fled to German-occupied Poland. On the whole, Ukrainians found their exposure to Soviet rule to be a negative experience.[14]

Demographic changes in Soviet-occupied eastern Poland were fast and dramatic. Enormous waves of refugees from western and central Poland, which was occupied by the Germans, flowed into the eastern territories. More than half a million of these newcomers arrived there in the fall of 1939. The refugees had an especially significant impact on the size of the local

Jewish population. Every fourth Jew at this point in time was a refugee. Although voluntary and informal assistance was offered by local Jews, tension and friction between indigenous Jews and the Jewish refugees were visible at times. Large-scale deportations into the Soviet interior were conducted forcibly from early 1940 through June 1941. They included Polish army officers, members of the middle class, and people previously active in community and public life. Most of them were Poles. However, the wave of deportations in the summer of 1940, which included refugees from German-occupied Poland, included large numbers of Jews as well. A total of about 1,500,000 people were thus uprooted and sent East.[15]

* * *

There was an atmosphere of tension and uncertainty in Brzezany during the first half of September 1939.[16] The German army was steadily advancing eastward. False air-raid sirens made people nervous and jumpy. One day a large Luftwaffe plane with black crosses on its wings appeared in the sky and dropped thousands of leaflets containing anti-Soviet propaganda. It also dropped a bomb, which luckily did not explode. Groups of people would gather daily in the central square, the Rynek, to discuss the situation and argue about the future. Thousands of refugees, both military and civilian, moved through the city southward, in the direction of Zaleszczyki and the Polish-Rumanian border. Main thoroughfares were constantly blocked by horsecarts, wagons, cars, trucks, and motorcycles. Some local Jews tried to cross the Rumanian border, but very few succeeded. Food became scarce. Money lost its value. The 51st Regiment left Brzezany for the Polish-German front in early September. Some of its units encountered heavy German bombardment.[17] Local order in town was kept by the National Guard and a temporary city militia composed of Poles and Ukrainians. This militia was headed by a local Ukrainian lawyer. The local administration, to the extent that it functioned in those days of panic and disorder, was in the Ratusz, where people were frantically running up and down the stairs. A temporary town committee consisting of Polish, Ukrainian, and Jewish representatives was established. It was headed by Dr. Bemko, a respected Ukrainian lawyer and well-known public figure. His deputy was Dr. Bilinski, head of the Brzezany hospital and a prominent local Polish personality.

On September 15, at the request of Dr. Bemko, political prisoners, mostly Ukrainian nationalists, were released from the Brzezany prison. This release of hundreds of Ukrainian prisoners led to increased acts of terror in the countryside around Brzezany. Polish households in Narajow, Kuropatniki, and other villages were burned. Some Polish peasants, mainly "settlers" (peasants from other parts of Poland, who were encouraged by the government to settle along Poland's eastern borders in the twenties and thirties), were murdered. Close to 100 Poles were killed by Ukrainians in the vicinity of the villages of Potutory and Koniuchy. Contacts were established between the Ukrainian underground and Ukrainian members of the temporary militia. A large quantity of weapons and ammunition quickly passed into the hands of Ukrainian nationalists in the surrounding villages. Individual Polish soldiers marauding through the area were apprehended and killed by Ukrainian nationalists. Polish policemen and retreating Polish army units were attacked. At the same time, Polish detachments set fire to Ukrainian farms in Raj, Narajow, Lesniki, and Koniuchy.

The first Soviet tanks rolled into Brzezany from Adamowka in the morning hours of September 20. They were greeted by a small crowd at an arch that had been hastily prepared the night before. The Red Army presence was soon felt everywhere. The town committee was disbanded in a matter of days and a new administration, set up by the Soviets, was installed. The regional Soviet commissar appointed a new city council. The first Soviet mayor of Brzezany was Kunio Grad, a Jew who had been a Communist and a political prisoner before the war. Dr. Bemko was appointed his deputy. Most other positions were occupied by Ukrainians and Jews. Isaac Sauberberg, a Jewish ex-political prisoner who was one of the most active members of the KPZU, the Communist Party of Western Ukraine in the area, was appointed head of the Financial Department. His deputy was a Pole who had served as head of that department before the war. The secretary of the new city council was Volodymyr Prishliak, a Ukrainian and former legal clerk. Kuba Winter, a Jew who had been active in the KPZU distributing illegal Communist propaganda and who had been sentenced twice during the thirties, became head of the Brzezany post office.

Almost all of the new Jewish appointees had been active in the KPZU and had served sentences for political activities in the thirties. They were mostly young people in their 20s without any previous administrative experience. Some of them would be replaced in a matter of weeks by Soviet officials. The Soviet practice during this initial phase was to appoint local Communists and sympathizers to top positions and leave some of the prewar Polish personnel as their deputies and assistants. The most important positions were manned, in time, by new personnel from the Soviet Union. The initial appointees were then given second- and third-rate jobs. Kunio Grad, for example, became head of a local carpenters' cooperative.

Medical services, though reorganized according to the Soviet system, were hardly affected by personnel changes. The local hospital was still headed by Dr. Bilinski, and it employed Polish and Jewish staff. Dr. Lipa Wagszal, a young Jewish physician, was appointed head of the Brzezany polyclinic. He couldn't have dreamed of such a position before the war. The polyclinic wasn't spared the run-of-the-mill Soviet-style propaganda meetings. During one such gathering, Dr. Wagszal called upon the staff to contribute generously to a government loan.[18] In time, a few doctors and nurses arrived in

Brzezany from the Soviet interior. Several local Jewish women who attended a course for nurses joined the Red Army and survived the war in its ranks.[19] They returned to Brzezany after the liberation.

All schools in Brzezany were "Ukrainized." The Gimnazjum turned into a Soviet-style *desiatiletka,* a ten-grade school. A Yiddish elementary school was opened, but it lasted only a few months. Initially, local teachers were appointed to administrative positions in the Brzezany schools. In time, they were replaced by personnel brought in "from the East." The Komsomol and Pioneer youth movements were introduced. Children and young people were encouraged to spy on, and turn in, members of their families. Soviet-style propaganda meetings became the order of the day. They usually took place outdoors in the Rynek or, when the weather was bad, in the Sokol auditorium. This was a novelty for the Brzezanyites, and many went to hear the speakers out of sheer curiosity. The official language at these affairs was Ukrainian, and it was only natural that most speakers were Ukrainian, although some were Jewish. The most impressive public celebrations were those of May 1 and the anniversary of the October Revolution.

Various kinds of restrictions and harassment now affected local churches and synagogues. Of all the synagogues only two, the Large Synagogue and Rabbi Yudel's synagogue, continued to function under the Soviets. The others became residential quarters for Jewish refugees. The main entrances to Polish churches and to the Ukrainian church in the center of Brzezany were closed. People had to enter through back doors. Services were severely limited and electricity was cut off to some churches during midnight Christmas prayers.

All stores, which were predominantly Jewish, were nationalized. Some of the Soviet officials used this opportunity to stock up on various goods. Consumer products became increasingly scarce. The few coffeehouses and music and dancing places that had enlivened the social life of the town in the prewar years were closed. In their place, drab Soviet-style restaurants with very little to offer opened up. At the same time, however, the two cinemas were playing to packed houses, and a Ukrainian theater and choir, as well as a light-music orchestra, were performing in the Sokol. Sports competitions were also held. All this, together with the numerous propaganda meetings, created a semblance of constant activity and excitement.

Soviet security services became very active in Brzezany and in the surrounding villages. The local Soviet newspaper called on its readers to be on the lookout for "hostile elements" and "turn them in to the security organs." Ukrainian "bandits and nationalists" were mentioned in particular. In early October 1939, the newspaper reported that a Ukrainian nationalist group in the village of Koniuchy, headed by one Vasilii Protsyk, had organized an anti-Jewish pogrom, during which an old man and a 6-year-old child were burned alive.[20] The man was apparently the owner of a local tavern. Arrests among the Ukrainian population started in December. It was mainly the Ukrainian intelligentsia, such as lawyers, teachers, and school principals, who were apprehended. Some of their families were deported. Massive arrests and deportations, mainly of Polish "settlers," started in February 1940. Some of the wealthiest Jewish families were also deported. Another wave of deportations started in May 1941 but was not completed due to the German invasion. An atmosphere of constant fear prevailed in the town and countryside. Arrests and deportations increased the hostility among the local population toward the new regime, and anti-Soviet partisan groups, both Ukrainian and Polish, became active around Brzezany.

Brzezany went through an unprecedented demographic upheaval during the short-lived Soviet occupation. A deluge of refugees, predominantly Jewish, arrived and settled in town. Their number is estimated in the thousands. They seemed to double or even triple the local prewar Jewish population. Some of them returned west when it became possible. Some were deported to the Soviet interior. Nevertheless, they still formed a considerable part of Brzezany's Jewish population. Numerous Poles and Ukrainians from Brzezany and the vicinity were deported to the Soviet interior. The population profile of the town on the eve of the German occupation differed considerably from that of the prewar years.

* * *

The expectations of and the reactions to the arrival of the Soviets among Poles, Jews, and Ukrainians in Brzezany and its vicinity varied. They depended a great deal on the conditions and perceptions of everyday life during both the years before the war and those few confused and at times dangerous weeks of interregnum preceding the appearance of the Red Army.

The first three weeks of September 1939, when Polish authority and administration in and around Brzezany started to disintegrate, were marked by a sense of insecurity and by acts of violence, mostly in the countryside. Tolek, the 18-year-old son of town engineer Jan Wilhelm, recalled that the mood in Brzezany was tense. The 51st Army Regiment had left for the front, and Poles were afraid of Ukrainian raids.[21] Sima Ehre, whose family lived in the small town of Narajow, northwest of Brzezany, recalled that local Jews feared a Ukrainian pogrom. "The Ukrainians had a list of fifty Jews who they wanted to get. We were lucky. The Russians came that night."[22]

Most of the violence, though, occurred among Poles and Ukrainians. Iulian Pavliv, who was only 8 at the time, recalled stories repeated for years within his family that there were attempts by the Ukrainian underground, the OUN, to attack Polish policemen and soldiers. "One day, the principal of the local Polish school, who headed the Narajow branch of the Polish Riflemen's Association, grabbed a machine gun and started shooting at a group of Ukrainians from a second-floor window of the school building.

These were people from a nearby village who were armed with pitchforks, axes, and a few rifles. They were marching in the direction of the police station."[23] It's quite evident that the Ukrainians were on their way to kill Polish policemen.

Myroslav Labunka, a Ukrainian from the village of Kotow, south of Brzezany, recalled that when the Polish military started retreating, a number of young Ukrainians armed with scythes and knives demanded that his father join them in killing Polish "settlers." His father was almost killed by them when he refused their "offer." Labunka remembered another incident. "A day before the Bolsheviks arrived, a Polish sergeant riding a bicycle started shooting at Ukrainian peasants and encouraging Poles to kill Ukrainians. His bike was turned over by a young Ukrainian woman and the gun slipped from his hand. Then some Ukrainian peasants attacked him with axes and he was slaughtered instantly."

Still another incident related by Labunka involved not only Ukrainians and Poles but also the newly arrived Bolsheviks. A shot was fired while Soviet soldiers were passing through his village. Somebody remarked, as was quite customary among Ukrainians, that the culprit was "the Polish priest." Upon hearing this, one of the soldiers went into the local church, grabbed the priest, and shot him. The priest was left wounded along the roadside, and every passing soldier used him for target practice. He died at the end of the day. That priest was Jan Gach, a staunch Polish nationalist, known in Kotow for his persistent efforts to "Polonize" Ukrainian children.[24]

The arrival of the Red Army in Brzezany signified for its Polish population more than the disintegration of Polish statehood. It also portended subjugation to the feared and hated Bolshevik empire, whose ideology and values were believed to be completely alien and threatening. Tolek Rapf spoke of the mood prevailing at that time among his Polish neighbors and acquaintances. "The Russians were barbarians, rabble, Asians, another world. When the Bolsheviks entered Brzezany, terrible times started for us Poles. They arrived as our diehard enemies."[25] Tolek's 15-year-old sister, Halszka, recalled hearing faraway shots. Together with her ailing father, she stepped out of the house into the front garden of their villa. Soon they spotted a Soviet tank. "Holy God! I remember how this Bolshevik tank, rolling along Iwaszkiewicza Street, approached our house. The turret and the barrel seemed to aim directly at us, and then it stopped. It only aimed, it didn't fire."[26]

The mood of Brzezany Jews prior to the Soviet occupation of the town was ambivalent. Some apprehensions prevailed, mostly among older people, orthodox Jews, and the prosperous. However, quite a number of younger Jews, those who harbored a grudge toward the Polish state because of its anti-Jewish discriminatory policies in higher education and employment and the few Jewish Communists in particular, experienced a sense of relief. A vague fear of the German alternative had also some effect.

87

Munio Haber, a youngster of 14 at the time, recalled that "the Polish army was retreating. Many Jewish soldiers took off their Polish uniforms and donned civilian clothes. There was an air of panic. Then one day, quite peacefully, Soviet tanks covered with flowers entered the city along Tarnopolska Street. Some Brzezany Jews greeted them enthusiastically. The atmosphere, at least among Jews, became more relaxed."[27]

Froyko Schmidt, the red-headed son of a Jewish glazier who had left the socialist-Zionist Hashomer Hazair youth movement and joined a small illegal group of local Communists a few years earlier, remembered the arrival of the Red Army as an utterly joyful event. "I felt good, very good." He recalled that those who greeted the Soviet tanks in Brzezany were mostly Jews.[28] Rozka Majblum, a young Jewish woman in her mid-20s, reacted rather differently. She was standing at her window and watching Red Army infantrymen marching into Brzezany. "They had no real shoes. They looked miserable in those long shabby coats."[29]

For many Ukrainians, the very prospect of a change from Polish rule and domination seemed to promise a measure of relief. Polish-Ukrainian tensions in eastern Galicia and in the Brzezany region intensified in the late thirties. Ukrainian community and cultural activities were being increasingly suppressed by the Polish administration. In spite of Stalin's oppressive policies in Soviet Ukraine, some Ukrainians, especially the poorly informed peasants in villages around Brzezany, hoped for better days.

According to Iulian Pavliv, Ukrainian peasants knew very little about Soviet intentions. "They were confused. There were high expectations of meeting the Red Army. There was talk of our brother Ukrainians coming to liberate us." OUN people took over the Narajow police station when the Poles retreated and hoisted the blue-and-yellow Ukrainian national flag. A triumphal arch was erected and adorned with flowers. "Next day, when the first Soviet soldiers arrived in Narajow, things became clearer. The Ukrainian flag was torn down and replaced by a red banner."[30]

Vasyl Fanga, from the village of Szybalin, recalled that "people erected an arch made of green pine trees and waited for the Soviet Ukrainian army, which was supposed to arrive from Tarnopol. Those people didn't really know what kind of an army this would be." The first Soviet soldiers and officers who arrived in the village were greeted with the traditional bread and salt. "We were hoping that a Star had come to us from the East. People had tears in their eyes, they were happy."[31]

Galina Skaskiv, from Bozhyki, remembered how the first Soviet soldiers arrived in her village at midnight. People expected "Cossacks from the Ukraine" and were heartbroken when instead some "strange-looking fellows on horses, wearing funny triangular hats, appeared in front of the church." Arrests started within a week, and it became quite clear that "a dreadful army" had arrived.[32]

Vasyl Oleskiw, from Byszki, a village northeast of Brzezany, was 15. He remembered his first encounter with the Red Army as a rather enjoyable event. A small Soviet aircraft landed on the outskirts of his village as a result of some mechanical problem. Vasyl was among the local youths who ran to see the unexpected attraction. The young pilot spoke excellent Ukrainian and was very friendly.[33]

As everywhere else, life in Brzezany changed considerably, mostly for the worse. Confiscation of property, the closing of stores, and the requisition of houses and apartments affected mostly the upper and middle layers of the population, regardless of ethnic affiliation. Still, it was the Brzezany Poles, who formed the social and economic elite of the town, who suffered most.

Ludka, the Polish captain's daughter, recalled that Soviet soldiers appeared in Brzezany a day after her sixteenth birthday. Within a few days, her family was told to leave their apartment. It was taken over by Soviet military personnel. Within a few weeks, food was in short supply and long lines formed in front of the stores. People sold jewelry and even clothing in order to sustain themselves.[34] Halszka vividly recalled the appropriation of her family's beautiful villa opposite the Farny Church in the summer of 1940. "When I approached our house, I saw my mother outside, in the garden, in tears. The door was shut and sealed and nobody could go inside. Mother was sitting and crying."[35] Rozka Majblum maintained that life in Brzezany had changed completely. Their family's prospering confectionery store, known for its excellent chocolates, was closed down, and they were forced to start selling whatever they owned in order to buy food.[36]

Arbitrariness and terror became quite common. Most of it was directed from above, but there were also some provocations and retaliations against the Soviets. Arrests and deportations conducted by the NKVD, the Soviet security police, affected mainly Poles and Ukrainians. Tolek traveled to Lwow sometime in November 1939 and was staying with his crippled uncle, an ex-colonel of the Polish army. He recalled a traumatic event. "Two NKVD officers, accompanied by three young Jews wearing red armbands, came at night and arrested my uncle. They made offensive and disgracing remarks, pointing to a painting of Jesus and a picture of Pilsudski." Wladyslawa recalled that several Polish students in her class just disappeared. "They were deported with their families to Siberia and Kazakhstan. We lived in constant fear. We knew that this could happen to anyone."[37]

Vasyl Oleskiw from Byszki, who was attending school at nearby Kuropatniki, recalled the first deportations. "A Polish girl from Kuropatniki was in my class, and one day she just didn't come to school. Their whole family was deported to Siberia."[38] Vasyl Fanga from Szybalin recalled that in the early summer of 1941, two NKVD officers from Brzezany were attacked on the main street of the village by young Ukrainian nationalists, apparently members of the OUN underground. One was killed on the spot and the other wounded. A number of local Ukrainians were then arrested and executed in the forest.[39]

The Grossfelds, a Jewish family, lived on a farm near Brzezany. Their son, Sewek, studied engineering at the Lwow polytechnic and used to visit his parents from time to time. During one such visit, on an early winter morning, Soviet policemen knocked on their door and informed them that they were being deported. As far as Sewek recalled, they were the only Jewish family on the cattle train used for deportation. Since they lived on a farm, they were apparently assumed to be Polish, like all others in their vicinity. This mistake actually saved their lives. They survived the war in Siberia.[40]

Poles and Ukrainians from Brzezany and the surrounding villages both tended to accuse Jews of collaboration with the Bolshevik regime. The fact that some Brzezany Jews welcomed the Soviets and were appointed temporarily to positions of authority generated an image of "traitors." Poles and Ukrainians perceived the Jew in his traditional role of petty merchant and store-owner. The new functions that some of them began to perform under the Soviets gave rise to resentment.

Tolek Rapf remembered how "crowds of young Jews with red armbands and flowers in their hands greeted a Soviet tank approaching from the direction of Adamowka. There were also a few Ukrainians among them, but no Poles, absolutely none."[41] Tolek's sister Halszka recalled one of the Soviet propaganda meetings in the center of town. "There were many Jews in the crowd. I remember some who threatened my father and myself with their fists, calling him a bourgeois capitalist. On another occasion a man with Semitic features stood on a balcony near the Ratusz, addressing a crowd in broken Polish. He told them that the time of the capitalists was over."[42]

In Iulian Pavliv's family, they often talked about Jews as Soviet collaborators. "The Jews were expecting the Soviets." It was assumed that Jews acted as outposts for Soviet intelligence and maintained close contacts with Bolshevik Russia even prior to the war. Stories repeated within the family had it that the thriving Jewish Zionist youth organizations in Narajow before the war were subsidized and guided "from the East." The Jews, he argued, collaborated openly with the Soviets in the years 1939–1941. A number of his relatives were arrested by the NKVD, and these arrests, according to Iulian, were facilitated by Jews. He also recalled that "a malicious Jew" was in charge of his father's arrest.[43]

In spite of economic difficulties, arrests, and deportations, some interviewees had cheerful memories. The new Soviet administration made an effort to prove to the locals, especially to the young, that "life became happier and merrier." Ludka recalled frequent celebrations and festivals. There were many sporting events and competitions of all sorts. Russian films were being screened at the Przyjazn cinema. Soviet songs, such as "Katiusha," became very popular, even among her Polish friends.[44]

The Brzezany Gimnazjum went through a quite thorough change. From an elitist, explicitly Polish school, it turned into a Soviet *desiatiletka*. Standards of admission were lowered in order to admit more students of "proletarian" and peasant origin. The curriculum changed. Some subjects, such as religion, disappeared completely. Many former professors were replaced by Soviet teachers who came from the East.

According to Wladyslawa, there were many Soviet propaganda meetings at school. One of them was convened on Christmas Day, which was a regular school day under the Soviets. A Soviet official spoke to the students, who were assembled in the gym. He told the mostly Christian crowd of Polish and Ukrainian students that Jesus was never born and that the Polish girls shouldn't wait for the return of their local boyfriends. Instead, they should marry Red Army soldiers.[45]

Munio Haber had rather pleasant memories from his studies at the *desiatiletka*. He liked some of the new Soviet teachers, especially his young, dark, and good-looking biology teacher. Munio and two other boys his age, a Pole and a Ukrainian, formed a threesome and used to spend long hours together. Sometimes they would go out and drink vodka. Such socializing among Polish, Jewish, and Ukrainian students wasn't very common in prewar Brzezany.[46]

Some young Brzezany Jews, whose prospects for higher education had not been too bright in interwar Poland, were now given a new chance. Poldek had applied to medical school at Lwow University in the mid-thirties but went to study medicine in Vienna instead due to discriminatory anti-Jewish policies in prewar Poland. After the Anschluss in March 1938, he left Vienna and returned to Brzezany, where he was idle most of the time. Now, under the Soviets, he was offered an opportunity to complete his education at Lwow University. He was even granted a scholarship. "They didn't care whether I was a Jew or anything else. They gave me a chance to finish my studies."[47]

Chanale, Bela Feld's younger sister, had graduated the Brzezany Gimnazjum shortly before the war and had no way of earning a living. Under the Soviets she was accepted into an accounting program in Lwow and received a scholarship to cover her living expenses. In a letter she wrote Bela, who had emigrated earlier to Palestine, Chanale was optimistic about her future. "For young people in general and for young Jews in particular," she wrote, "a new world has opened up. Everybody has a chance to study. Everybody is eager to learn." The letter reached Bela in a roundabout way some forty years after it was written. Chanale, like the rest of the Feld family, didn't survive.[48]

Thousands of refugees from German-occupied Poland, mostly Jews, swarmed into Brzezany. They were assisted to some extent by local Jews, but their sheer number and everyday difficulties resulted in problems and tensions. Munio told me that "relations between Brzezany Jews and Jewish refugees were very satisfactory."[49] Joseph Soski, originally from Krakow, one of those refugees who arrived in Brzezany, had slightly different recollections. "A small minority went out of their way to help. The majority kept to themselves."[50]

* * *

Although everyday life in Brzezany and the region seemed quite peaceful in the prewar years, relations among Poles, Ukrainians, and Jews weren't that normal. Polish nationalism was on the rise. Ukrainians were frustrated after the continuous curtailment of their cultural and national activities as well as the frequent arrests and trials. This in turn bred some acts of violence against the Poles. Some Jews, especially the young, were frustrated about anti-Jewish educational and employment policies.

On the whole, the two years of Soviet rule in Brzezany intensified uneasiness, frustration, and outright hostility among its three ethnic communities; the Soviets provided a significant point of reference. The fact that both Poles and Ukrainians feared and hated the Bolsheviks didn't ameliorate their tense bilateral attitudes. Each group focused on its own particular suffering and victimization. The few weeks of instability and chaos preceding the arrival of the Soviets in the early fall of 1939 sparked acts of outright violence between the Poles and the Ukrainians. The fact that some Brzezany Jews welcomed the Red Army and that some of them were appointed to positions of authority intensified anti-Jewish feelings among both Poles and Ukrainians. The relatively peaceful prewar coexistence among the three ethnic groups was badly affected by the Soviet interlude. All this was to have a significant impact on interethnic attitudes and behavior under the German occupation.

5

THE GERMAN OCCUPATION, 1941–1944

For me, the war began on a peaceful summer afternoon a few months after my sixth birthday. We had just finished our Sabbath meal. We sat around our dinner table, humming Sabbath songs. Suddenly, we heard a powerful explosion, followed by the sound of broken glass. Later I would learn that a bomb had demolished the Przyjazn movie theater on the street corner. In a few moments everybody was running downstairs into the cellar. I recall hearing the terrifying sequence of whining sounds followed by heavy thumps all through that dreadful night. The split second of silence between the end of each whining sound and the ensuing thump filled me with terror. From time to time we peeked out of the cellar to watch the flames reflected in the dark skies above us. My father and my mother's younger sister Malcia left the cellar for a few hours and ran to the Okopisko Jewish cemetery on the outskirts of town. It was considered to be safer during the night bombings. They returned at dawn. A nauseating stench emanating from the scorched ruins filled the air for days and weeks.

Nothing dramatic happened in the following months. We must have moved from the small apartment house near Przyjazn to a much larger one in the newly established Brzezany ghetto. Before the war it had been a hotel. There was a long, dark corridor along our floor with doors leading off into a number of small rooms. Several families occupied the floor. There were also some children in that house, and we had fun playing together. We used to meet once a week, on Saturdays. Each child would bring some candy or a piece of cake. We sang, played games, and recited poems. I remember Matus, Dr. Wagszal's little son. Dr. Wagszal's sister, Zlata, was married to my Uncle Yakov. Matus recited children's poems in Polish, one about an elephant and another about a locomotive. These are definitely cheerful memories. I also remember sitting for hours in the kitchen, drawing columns of marching soldiers with airplanes circling over their heads. They had black crosses on their wings. I remember one day sitting at our kitchen table holding a tiny metal hacksaw, the kind used by Jews to escape from sealed railway cars on their way to the death camps. I don't recall fear, only fascination and a sense of curiosity. When we played on the street, we liked to frighten old Jewish ladies, yelling at them in German. Another game was "Germans and Jews." From that time inside the ghetto I also remember a roomful of men wrapped in prayer shawls. It might have been Yom Kippur.

The most frightening moments occurred during the "actions," the roundups. Each house had its "bunkers," the hideouts. Once, when we hid in a small space behind a closet, loud footsteps and shrill German voices were nearly on top of us. Somehow, my mother remained outside, and a German kicked her right in the chest. Luckily, she wasn't carted away. During another roundup my father hid us in his workshop, which was outside the ghetto. Years later, at a reunion of Polish Brzezanyites in Ustron, an elderly lady recalled that during the German occupation she worked in a workshop which produced small round wooden boxes. She didn't remember the name of the Jew who was in charge, but I bore a striking resemblance to that man. "He spoke correct Polish, was always cheerful and joked. It was very pleasant to work with him. One day he brought a little boy with him, wearing short, dark pants. It must have been you."

I have a distinct recollection of the last action, the Judenrein roundup. It was in the middle of the summer heat. We were hiding in an elaborate hideout with many other people from our building. This was a well-camouflaged double attic next to the hot tin roof. My father was not with us. He had gone the previous evening to join a group of Jews who worked for the Germans outside the ghetto, whose clothes were marked with a "W" sign. Therefore, in the attic with me were only my mother and my grandparents. The tin sheets so close to us radiated unbearable heat.

Through a crevice in the roof I enviously observed some youngsters splashing themselves with water from a nearby well. I remember my mother, stripped to the waist, crying. She must have received the horrible news. The "W" people, who were supposed to last longer than anyone else, were among the first victims of the last roundup. The news about my father's death must have reached us on Monday, following Saturday's roundup. Monday has been an "evil day" for me ever since.

I often wondered why my memories of my father are so scarce and why I remember Grandpa Fishl rather well. Is the reason the fact that Fishl stayed with me in the attic while my father "disappeared"? Was I suppressing the memory of my father's death to try to erase the shock of becoming an orphan? My mother hardly ever mentioned him in our conversations. Although he died and we survived, I bore a grudge against my father, whom I must have subconsciously accused of "abandoning" us. Only decades later when I used a Gestalt technique was I able to have a meaningful "dialogue" with him, listening to his side of the story. This was the first time that I really mourned and came to terms with him.

People were gradually leaving the attic, looking for better hiding places. One night my mother took me by the hand and we walked into a neighboring village. The stalks in the wheatfield were high, smelling with the ripeness of summer. We knocked on a few doors, but nobody wanted to let us in. We returned to the attic and stayed there. Years later I read in Dr. Wagszal's memoirs that his young relative, Hermina, was with us in that attic. This girl went downstairs one day and was intercepted by people who came to loot the deserted house. She bribed them and they let her go. It's a miracle that we weren't turned in by all those who left the attic and were probably caught by the Germans.

Remaining in the attic now was our foursome, another boy my age with his grandmother, and a single old lady. Our immediate problem was finding food. Grandpa Fishl decided that the only way to survive was to contact an old acquaintance, Polish locksmith Stanislaw Codogni. Codogni's son, Karol, recounted fifty years later: "It was nasty weather, late at night. Fishl and a woman knocked on our door. My mother gave them hot milk and they told me to go fetch some potatoes. We also gave them a freshly baked bread and some onions. Fishl put everything into a sack, which he carried on his back. He resembled Santa Claus."

From then on, according to Karol, Fishl would appear at their doorstep at night, sometimes accompanied by my mother, and collect a sack of food prepared in advance. The Codognis lived in constant fear that Grandpa might be caught by the Germans. In a letter Karol wrote me forty years later, he recalled: "Our house wasn't far from the ghetto and we were watched at all times. Still, we were able to help a few people who escaped from the ghetto. During the day they would hide in our place and at night continue on their way. I don't know how many survived." In spite of the mounting danger, the Codognis continued to supply us with food. Karol told me that during one of those forays Grandpa Fishl asked for some string to tie the food to the attic's ceiling to prevent it from being nibbled away by rats. This reminded me of a "rat game" I used to play in the attic. I would hold a piece of bread in my stretched hand, and a rat would run very fast from one side of the attic to the other, trying to snatch it away from me.

I do not recall severe hunger. Most of the time we ate well-baked dark bread, prepared by the Codognis. Grandpa Fishl used to save the crust for me, which I considered a delicacy. When we ran out of bread, we subsisted on raw beets and raw potatoes. Their taste was revolting. All in all, my sojourn in the attic was at times scary but at other times pleasant. From time to time, usually in the late afternoon, we would hear the rhythmic click of marching boots accompanied by a rather cheerful melodic German song. I can hum it to this day. Grandpa Fishl was my most constant companion. We would lie side by side and talk for hours on end. He taught me how to read, in Polish, of course, and told me all about our family. Both his brothers had emigrated to America. One of them I would meet years later in New York. He resembled my beloved grandpa.

I'll never forget the first death I witnessed. The old woman who was living with us in the attic became sick—most likely with pneumonia—and it appeared that she was dying. I can still hear the sound of her groaning and wheezing. After she died, Grandpa and Mother tied the body onto a ladder and carried it down to the basement. This must have been an arduous feat for old Fishl and for my short and limping mother. Another frightening sight was Grandpa Fishl suffering a severe hernia attack. He was lying there, groaning softly, a dark-blue mark on his exposed belly. Luckily, he got better in a day or two. On a more mundane level were our daily hunts for lice and fleas. I can still recall that special click that followed each "execution." Throughout our daily routine one thought kept recurring in my mind: What happens if we are caught? What shall I do then? So I promised myself that no matter what, if we were caught by the Germans, I should try to escape.

For a number of months luck was on our side. Nobody moved into the vacant house beneath us. But as winter came, our luck ran out. New tenants started fixing up an apartment just a floor below us. When Grandpa and Mother went down the stairs on their way to the Codognis, a woman appeared in a door and warned them that if we didn't leave within a day or two, she would report us to the police. We had to get out, and fast. At that time, my mother's younger sister Malcia and Vovo, her young and good-looking husband, were hiding in Raj, a village near Brzezany. Tanka Kontsevych, a young Ukrainian woman and a mother of two whose husband was sent for compulsory labor in Germany, had been keeping them in her house since the Judenrein roundup. Tanka used to visit the Codognis and carry messages between us and Malcia. A few hours after the new tenant demanded that we leave, Grandpa Fishl, disguised as an old woman, went to the Codognis and asked them to convey an urgent note to Malcia in Raj. My aunt persuaded Tanka to take us all in. The following evening my mother and I descended from the attic. The street was covered with snow. On the corner was a lone figure, the Codogni's young son Karol. When we approached him, he whispered "Follow me and pray to God."

A woman waited for us farther up the street. It was Tanka. Karol left and we started walking behind the Ukrainian woman. By now my limping mother could hardly walk. My own muscles must have atrophied in the attic and I could hardly move my legs. Tanka ended up carrying me on her back while holding on to my mother's hand. Slowly we trudged through thick, crisp snow toward Raj. From time to time mother swallowed a handful of snow. When I asked Tanka half a century later what she remembered about that night, she told me that I was small and my legs hurt. She also recalled that the walking took several hours, since she preferred a roundabout track through the fields. We must have reached her house at dawn. I can still taste the freshly baked white bread and hot milk. I couldn't believe my luck when I was promised that

*from then on I could have all the bread and milk I wanted. After we had
eaten, we had our first warm bath in months.*

*The following evening Tanka was supposed to meet my grandparents at the
Codognis. To our dismay, she returned very late, and alone. My grandparents
had not turned up. Later Karol heard that they were discovered hiding in a
cellar, turned in to the police, and driven off to the prison on a sleigh. "For us
this was like a blow from an ax," Karol told me years later. "The question now
was, should we leave everything and run away?" They stayed. A prison
warden told Karol a few days later that Fishl and his wife had been shot. He
didn't know whether they had been interrogated or tortured. Only years later I
realized the courage of those two old people and the mortal danger that faced
us all, including Tanka and the Codognis.*

*Our lives at Tanka's settled into a daily routine. We told stories and played
cards. Apparently I wasn't much of a sport, because any time I'd lose at remi
(a card game) I would cry. But even if I didn't, I would cry too. I accused
them of letting me win on purpose. Nothing pleased me. We had several hiding
places at Tanka's. The one I remember best was a tiny attic over a barn,
occupied by a lone, skinny cow. Some pleasant memories are still lodged in my
brain. I'm looking out into the garden on a sunny morning. I see grass and
trees and I can feel the warmth of the sunshine. I try to imagine how pleasant
it would be when the war is over. I am totally happy. There were also those
pleasurable moments at night, pressing closely against my young aunt. I was
almost 9. Sex must have started to be significant for me. Tanka was another
object of my sexual fantasies. Soon after our arrival at her house I must have
become aware that a love affair was going on between the young Ukrainian
woman and my Uncle Vovo. Perhaps this was the reason she had taken us in.
Vovo promised Tanka that after the war he would divorce Malcia, marry her,
and take her to his hometown in Poland, where his family owned a big
apartment building.*

*Tanka, though illiterate and rather plain, must have been a provocative
woman in other ways. I remember German soldiers coming into the house quite
often to tease Tanka while she was cooking. Whether I witnessed these scenes
myself or merely heard about them from the adults, they had imprinted Tanka
in my mind as an object of desire. There was also a dark and tragic side to the
complex relationship between my uncle and the two women. When Vovo and
Malcia came to stay in Raj, Malcia was already pregnant. When she went
into labor, Tanka left the house and stayed away for many hours. When she
returned, the infant was dead. All this had happened before we came.*

*There were some frightening moments. On one occasion as German soldiers
horsed around with Tanka downstairs, we sat just above them with baited
breath. The tiniest creak could be fatal. I went in my pants, right there, in
utter silence, like an animal. One afternoon while Tanka was out, two
German soldiers walked in and started yelling for straw. The straw was with*

us, in the attic. Ania, Tanka's 10-year-old daughter, remembered the event fifty years later: "The Germans started to climb to the attic. I knew that up there was this little boy and if they found them they would take them away and kill them. So I grabbed one German by his pantleg and started pulling him off the ladder. Then I pulled the ladder itself. We had a sort of tug-of-war. Then my mother returned, quickly went up to the attic, and started throwing down the straw. At the same time she covered up with straw the people who were hiding up there. And then the Germans finally left."

I cannot precisely identify the moment the war was over for us. But I do remember the nights before our liberation, the persistent shelling on some faraway horizon. Occasionally, a bright flare dropped from a Soviet airplane would eerily illuminate the darkness of the night. The adults whispered gleefully that the Germans were retreating. Then it was over, and we returned to Brzezany.

On Sunday, June 22, 1941, Nazi Germany launched a surprise attack against Soviet Russia. The German army started to advance along a 2,000-mile front. The German air force, the Luftwaffe, conducted massive bombardments of cities and towns throughout the region. The speed of the German advance was unprecedented. All of eastern Galicia was occupied within two weeks. Various SS and police units followed behind the Wehrmacht. Among them were the notorious Einsatzgruppen and the mobile units of the Gestapo. The first short-lived phase of the German military administration lasted from late June until early August, when eastern Galicia was incorporated into the Generalgouvernement. From then on it was administered by German civilian authorities. At the core of this administration were the heads of districts, the Kreishauptmaenner. These were mostly ambitious ideological Nazis. The top layer of the German administration consisted of people who arrived from Germany, the Reichsdeutsche, who quite often brought along their families. They formed a closed society far from home that was quite separate from the indigenous population.[1] At the same time, however, certain social contacts did exist. Some Germans had Polish and Ukrainian acquaintances and even used Jews for various services. There were also the Volksdeutsche, ethnic Germans who resided outside of Germany. They were highly favored and used by the Nazi regime in the occupied territories. In addition to the German civilian administration, regular German police units, the Sipo (the Security Police), and the SD (the Security Service), were stationed throughout eastern Galicia. They implemented a rule of intimidation and terror which affected the local population. The Jews, however, constituted a particular target. The Nazi security apparatus was more active in eastern Galicia than in other parts of the Generalgouvernement.

Eastern Galicia, like other German-occupied territories in eastern Europe, was targeted for massive German settlement in the long run. Short-term objectives primarily involved economic exploitation. It seems that German policies here were less severe than in other parts of eastern Europe. A certain effort was made to win the goodwill and cooperation of the local population. The fact that eastern Galicia had been a sphere of German culture during the Hapsburg era was apparently relevant in this context. Although the German occupation adversely affected the whole population, the various ethnic groups suffered and reacted in different ways. Poles and Ukrainians were exploited economically and were affected by the Nazi rule of terror. Among the most severe German policies were the arbitrary confiscation of property and foodstuffs and the appropriation of the labor of millions of Poles and Ukrainians, who were sporadically sent to Germany. This resulted in the increasing pauperization of the population, at times even in periods of famine. The Jewish population was not only economically exploited; it was also systematically persecuted and almost totally annihilated.

The Polish population, which was mostly urban, was severely affected. First came the extensive German bombing of the cities and towns, and then, within days, the German conquest. Polish property was confiscated and part of the Polish upper strata of society, particularly the intelligentsia, were imprisoned and murdered during the first weeks of the occupation. On the whole, however, the antagonism between Poles and Germans was less pronounced here than in central Poland. Some Poles residing in the countryside actually gained from the re-privatization of land, which had formerly been collectivized by the Soviets. The German occupation of eastern Galicia came in the wake of the disastrous Soviet rule. Moreover, the growing tensions between Poles and Ukrainians overshadowed the Polish-German conflict. The Germans allowed a modest Polish cooperative system and a network of social support, the Polish Welfare Committees. The Germans applied a policy of cultural suppression against the Poles, but a modest official Polish school system, supervised by the Germans, was allowed to exist. A parallel illegal system of education, which emphasized Polish culture and Polish national values, was established. It even granted illegal high school diplomas and conducted university-level instruction. In some towns of eastern Galicia, close to half of the local Polish youth took advantage of this illegal education.

The Polish underground, primarily the Armia Krayowa (AK), the Home Army, was active in eastern Galicia, as it was in the rest of occupied Poland. Its primary objective in this region was to defend the Poles from the Ukrainians rather than fight the Germans. Some direct anti-German acts did take place, particularly in the latter period of the occupation, when the Wehrmacht started its retreat. The prewar Polish Scout movement, the Harcerstwo, which was referred to as Szare Szeregi during the German occupation, continued to function illegally and maintain strong ties with the AK. Some

Poles, however, joined auxiliary German-supervised police units. Unlike the Ukrainian militiamen, many of whom had strong ties with the national Ukrainian underground, these were mostly the dregs of society, and they were treated as such by their fellow nationals.[2]

Most Ukrainians welcomed any change which might occur following the retreat of the Soviets. Acts of terror perpetrated by the NKVD during the last days of Soviet rule increased Ukrainian hatred of the Bolsheviks. The Soviet withdrawal was unexpected and was conducted in a disorderly manner. It also affected tens of thousands of prisoners. Some were released. Most of the political prisoners, however, had either been deported eastward or killed in the prisons.[3] Thousands of them, mostly Ukrainians, were murdered by Soviet security personnel during the last week of June. Major massacres occurred in such cities as Lwow and Stanislawow, but prisoners were also executed in numerous smaller towns. There was widespread evidence of torture. After the Soviet retreat, mutilated corpses were found both inside and outside the prisons. These murders had a shocking effect on the Ukrainian population.

The emotional shock of the Soviet killings, intensive Nazi propaganda about the dangers of Judeo-Bolshevism, and the prevailing stereotype of the pro-Soviet Jew resulted in anti-Jewish pogroms in territories recently occupied by the Germans that had been formerly annexed by the Soviets. Some of the murders were committed by the local Polish population. Such was the case in Radzilow and Jedwabne. Most of the pogroms, however, were perpetrated by Ukrainians, mostly by Ukrainian peasants. Jews were murdered in Lwow, Tarnopol, Drohobycz, Zloczow, Buczacz, and other eastern Galician towns.[4]

Most Ukrainians in eastern Galicia, Ukrainian nationalists in particular, responded enthusiastically to the momentous changes. They rejoiced over their liberation from the hated Soviet regime as well as over the prospect of some form of Ukrainian independence. The Organization of Ukrainian Nationalists, headed by Stepan Bandera and known as OUN-B, proclaimed the establishment of a Ukrainian state. The head of the Ukrainian Uniate Church, Metropolitan Andrei Sheptyts'kyi, issued a statement of support. Ukrainian "expeditionary detachments," the *pokhidny hrupy*, followed the Wehrmacht into the Ukraine, hoping to ensure the realization of Ukrainian interests. All these seemingly momentous events were warmly greeted by the Ukrainian population in the cities, towns, and villages.

Within days, however, Bandera and his closest associates were arrested. Hitler was unequivocally opposed to Ukrainian independence. The Germans were, at best, ready to use the Ukrainians as temporary collaborators. They were also interested in using them as a counterweight to the local Polish population. The incorporation of eastern Galicia into the General-gouvernement and the arrival of a permanent German civilian and security administration clearly demonstrated Nazi intentions. In September 1941, numerous Ukrainian nationalists, mostly supporters of Bandera, were arrested. Many Ukrainian nationalists went underground, and the high point of the honeymoon between the Germans and the Ukrainians seemed to be over.[5] At the same time, however, parts of the Ukrainian underground continued to maintain contacts with German authorities, and various Ukrainian administrative structures and organizations were tolerated. Local Ukrainian militias, which served the Germans in various ways, were organized throughout the region. The existence of Ukrainian militias resulted in a feeling of relative security among the Ukrainian population, at least until the fall of 1943, when German acts of terror were increasingly directed against the Ukrainian underground. When German-Ukrainian relations deteriorated in the course of 1943, almost half of the Ukrainian militiamen deserted and joined the underground.[6]

Ukrainians, unlike Poles, were assigned to administrative, judiciary, and labor administration posts in many eastern Galician towns. Most of the mayors and village bailiffs were Ukrainian. More Ukrainian schools than ever before offered Ukrainian youth a nationally oriented education. A network of official Ukrainian cultural societies and youth organizations was established. Town and village cooperatives attempted to support the economic needs of the Ukrainian population. This effort had rather limited results because of the prevailing conditions. Some Ukrainians benefited from the expropriation of Jewish businesses and from the confiscation of Jewish property.[7] The active participation of Ukrainians in the German administration exacerbated Polish animosities. As far as the Ukrainians were concerned, they had a strong desire to take up posts and responsibilities which had been consistently denied to them in prewar Poland. Ukrainians also served in German military units, such as the SS Halychyna Division. The primary objective of both the leadership of the Ukrainian underground and most Ukrainian public figures was to ensure the existence of a significant Ukrainian military force, which would eventually facilitate the establishment of a Ukrainian state.

The Ukrainian underground, the UPA, consisted of tens of thousands of partisans. Its commander-in-chief was Roman Shukhevych, alias *chuprynka*. The UPA enjoyed wide popular support and was considered the core of a future Ukrainian state. The demarcation line between the German-supervised Ukrainian auxiliary militias, Ukrainians serving in the German army, and the Ukrainian underground was ever so thin. What bound most Ukrainians and Germans together was their mutual hatred of Soviet Russia. The primary objective of the Ukrainians, however, was *samostiina Ukraina*, independent Ukraine. This, in turn, was tightly interwoven with Ukrainian enmity toward the Poles and with Ukrainian hopes for a Pole-free Ukraine. Hostilities against Ukrainian peasants, which were perpetrated by the Polish underground in the Kholm region north of eastern Galicia, added to the volatile situation. Numerous UPA units moved from the Kholm region southward into eastern Galicia in the first half of 1944. This, in turn, resulted in a wave of anti-Polish terror throughout the region. Murders of Poles were particularly brutal. The Polish underground responded with a series of revenge campaigns. Some Poles started escaping westward, fleeing Ukrainian nationalists as well as the advancing Soviet army.

German policies of terror as well as the intensifying Ukrainian-Polish conflict affected ordinary people, the youth in particular. This led, at times, to outright banditry. Society as a whole became increasingly demoralized and brutalized.[8] At the same time, however, there were also instances of assistance and life-saving acts among Poles and Ukrainians that extended across the lines of national and ethnic affiliation.[9]

The Jews suffered the most. A wave of anti-Jewish pogroms erupted in the cities, towns, and villages of eastern Galicia during the first days of the German occupation. The initiation and conduct of the pogroms weren't identical in the various localities. Whereas in the larger cities there was organized collaboration between the German Einsatz and security units and various Ukrainian organizations, in smaller towns and in the countryside the killing of Jews was more spontaneous. It was usually organized with the assistance of local Ukrainian militias and OUN groups. The position of the German regular army, the Wehrmacht, was somewhat ambivalent. In most cases, the humiliation and murder of Jews by Ukrainians were linked to the NKVD executions. Both German and Ukrainian nationalist propaganda widely used the theme of Judeo-Bolshevism and alleged Jewish participation in the Soviet terror machine.[10]

The fate of the Jews in eastern Galicia, as elsewhere, was determined by Hitler's Final Solution. Mass murder started there comparatively early in the German occupation. Whereas Jews in the remaining parts of Poland lived their miserable lives in the ghettos for more than two years before the onset of mass murder, the Jews of eastern Galicia faced roundups and murder relatively soon after the arrival of the Germans. Mass killings started there as early as October 1941. Many murderous acts, unlike in the rest of occupied Poland, where Jews were deported to labor and death camps, took place on the outskirts of towns, in nearby forests, and in local Jewish cemeteries. The Ukrainian Labor Service, the Baudienst, and sometimes the Ukrainian police, in coordination with the German civilian administration, were in charge of preparing the death pits. The victims were usually shot on the edge of these pits. Most of the executions were organized and conducted by the German security police, the Sipo, assisted at times by the local German police, the Gendarmerie. Acts of brutality on the part of the executioners were quite common. Drinking of alcohol before, during, and after the executions was widespread. The victims were usually forced to undress before being shot.

VoMi, the Volksdeutsche Mittelstelle, which functioned as part of the SS, was in charge of confiscating and collecting Jewish property, including victims' clothing, for redistribution among the Volksdeutsche. Its representatives in the various localities made sure that Jewish property was taken from the living and the dead alike. VoMi personnel usually accompanied the executions.[11]

Ghettoization in eastern Galicia started in the fall of 1941 and continued throughout 1942. Jewish Councils, the Judenraete, were established by the Germans in order to assist them in their anti-Jewish policies. At times the Judenraete attempted to alleviate the plight of the Jews.[12] Mass deportations of Jews to the closest death camp, Belzec, started in the early spring of 1942. Oppression, economic exploitation, and the murder of Jews in the various localities continued. Although the explicit perpetrators were officers and soldiers of the German security apparatus, the German civilian administration was also deeply involved. It extended its assistance in organizational and administrative matters. The Kreishauptmaenner usually insisted on participating in all anti-Jewish activities.[13]

The *aktionen,* or "actions," the periodical roundups which first took place throughout the towns and later within the closed ghettos, became the nightmare of the Jewish population. They were usually supervised by the German security police and were carried out by the local German, Ukrainian, and Jewish police. The roundups resulted either in deportations to Belzec and labor camps or in local executions. Jews attempted to avoid both by hiding in "bunkers," hideouts prepared in advance within the ghettos, or by staying out of town, if that was possible. As a result of the deportations and local executions, the Jewish population of eastern Galicia shrank from 500,000 in the summer of 1941 to about 150,000 in early 1943.[14] A series of roundups in the spring of that year hastened the implementation of the Final Solution in the region. The last remnants of the Jewish population, who were living in the remaining ghettos and labor camps, were annihilated in the summer of 1943. Only an extremely small fraction of eastern Galician Jews survived the war.

The wartime attitudes and behavior of Poles and Ukrainians toward Jews varied. Poles, mostly urban dwellers, had had more intensive social contacts with Jews than the predominantly Ukrainian peasant population. Polish anti-Semitism was somewhat less pronounced in the region than in other parts of occupied Poland.[15] Attitudes within the major Polish underground, the AK, were either indifferent or explicitly hostile. The Jews could expect very little assistance, if any. The rightist nationalist Polish partisan groups were openly anti-Semitic. Only socialist- and Communist-oriented Polish partisan units, which represented a small minority in the region, were friendly to Jews. It seems that the majority of that small percentage of the local Jewish population which survived the Holocaust was either assisted or hidden by Polish families. In some cases this was done for money and valuables; in others, out of a moral or humanitarian motivation.[16] When hidden Jews were discovered, the Germans severely punished the assisting families. In some cases, the families were executed. Denunciations of both Jews and those who hid them were common occurrences. Willingness to assist and hide Jews increased in the latter part of 1943, as a result of the growing hostility of the Germans toward the non-Jewish population and the changing military situation.[17] But very few Jews were still alive by that time.

The Ukrainian population was either indifferent or anti-Jewish. Some Ukrainians did, however, assist and save Jews. The Ukrainian nationalist underground, the UPA, was distinctly anti-Semitic. Ukrainian nationalist organizations had been ideologically influenced by fascist and Nazi ideology in the prewar years. During the first year of the German occupation, anti-Semitic propaganda and hostile behavior toward Jews were the order of the day within the Ukrainian underground. Some change for the better, especially in the formal decisions and announcements of the Bandera faction, occurred in 1942.[18] Whether these changes influenced the everyday behavior of Ukrainian partisans is questionable. Some Jewish professionals, such as physicians, nurses, and artisans, were encouraged to join the Ukrainian underground, but this was mostly the result of practical necessity.[19]

An exceptional case in the eastern Galician Ukrainian milieu was that of Metropolitan Andrei Sheptyts'kyi, head of the Uniate Church, who saved dozens of Jewish adults and children and appealed to his fellow Ukrainians not to participate in the annihilation of the Jews.[20] The complexity of the Ukrainian situation at the time was underscored by the fact that the very same Sheptyts'kyi who saved Jews supported, out of nationalistic considerations, the establishment of a Ukrainian SS Division. The Ukrainians who collaborated most with the German occupation authorities were the auxiliary militias, which were used as guards during the roundups of Jews and which, at times, even aided in the executions. The local Ukrainian administration assisted the Germans in transferring Jews from small towns and villages into the ghettos.

Starting in February and March of 1944, Soviet partisan and military units gradually advanced into eastern Galicia. Some areas changed hands several times. It was a period of uncertainty, accompanied by growing tension, violence, and chaos. Some Ukrainians and Poles joined the Germans in their westward retreat. The decisive Soviet military thrust in the region occurred in July 1944. The whole of eastern Galicia was under Soviet rule by August.[21]

* * *

The days following the German invasion revealed a mood of growing restlessness among the Soviet administrative personnel in Brzezany. They started evacuating their families. The first German bombardment of Brzezany took place on Saturday, June 28, 1941. It continued on Sunday and

Monday. The bombs caused huge fires. Some public buildings, such as the Sokol and Przyjazn, were hit. A considerable part of the town near the Rynek, Jewish houses along Zbozowa Street in particular, lay in ruins. Rumor had it that Lev Bemko, who was serving in the German Luftwaffe, directed the bombing of the Jewish quarter in town. He was the son of Brzezany's most respected Ukrainian lawyer. During the first two days of July, endless Red Army convoys, including cavalry and horse-drawn artillery, passed through Brzezany as they moved eastward. Small-scale battles and skirmishes were being waged at that time between the Germans and the Russians in the close vicinity of the town and on its outskirts. Armed OUN groups attacked retreating Soviet soldiers. A powerful explosion was heard all over town on Tuesday, July 1. Windows shattered and some roofs collapsed. An ammunition depot, located near the Christian and Jewish cemeteries on the way to Raj, was blown up. This was apparently part of the hasty Soviet retreat. The first Wehrmacht units entered Brzezany on Friday, July 4.[22]

The NKVD started to plan the evacuation of its prisoners as early as June 23. The twelve railway cars that were reserved for Brzezany were part of a detailed plan for Western Ukraine. It seems clear that not all Brzezany prisoners scheduled for evacuation were actually moved to the interior. Sufficient evidence indicates that a considerable number of them were executed. The Brzezany prison was attacked several times by bands of Ukrainian nationalists, but they did not succeed in freeing the inmates. A group of Brzezany prisoners was transferred to the Tarnopol prison on June 26, and some of them were executed there. Daily executions were conducted inside the Brzezany prison between June 27 and 30. Two tractors, their engines constantly running, were stationed nearby to muffle the shots. About 150 people were murdered, but there was not sufficient time for their burial.[23] A gruesome NKVD report stated: "Forty-eight of the inmates in the Brzezany prison weren't buried. Twenty corpses, which couldn't be removed, remained in the prison cellar. Forty corpses were thrown into the river from the bridge." There followed a detailed description of disorder and panic among Soviet prison and army personnel, which was caused by the heavy bombardments.[24] Several dozen prisoners succeeded in escaping during the heavy night-time bombardment between June 30 and July 1.[25]

While the last Soviet officials and military men were leaving Brzezany, the Ukrainian Regional Revolutionary Committee, headed by a Ukrainian lawyer and supported by the OUN, was formed. It appointed local Ukrainians to various city posts. A Ukrainian militia was also organized. Advancing German army units were warmly greeted by the Ukrainian population of Brzezany and the surrounding villages. Triumphal arches were hastily constructed. Bread and salt were offered to the German officers and soldiers. They were perceived by many as liberators from the hated Soviet rule. A Ukrainian newspaper, *Berezhans'ki Visti*, started publishing at the end of July.

It became a mouthpiece for Nazi propaganda and provided a forum for various announcements by the German administration. Anti-Semitic articles were printed there from time to time.

A Ukrainian mass celebration took place in the Brzezany Rynek on Sunday, July 6. The Bandera faction of the OUN had proclaimed the establishment of a Ukrainian state just a few days earlier. The Bolsheviks had disappeared and, in spite of the tragedy of the slain prisoners, the mood was jubilant. Thousands of Ukrainian peasants, including armed OUN units, poured into Brzezany from the surrounding countryside. Leaders of the Ukrainian community and officers of the local German army command mounted a festive platform, which was adorned with German and Ukrainian banners. Father Baczynski delivered a sermon, followed by several speeches. Resolutions were read out and endorsed enthusiastically by the crowd. Among them was a telegram to Hitler proclaiming that "the population of Brzezany and the whole region, liberated from the Bolshevik horror in the course of the invincible march of the German army, extends its greetings and gratitude to the Fuehrer of the mighty German state and the Supreme Commander of the most glorious army in the world." A parade that lasted more than an hour marched through the Rynek to the accompaniment of a Ukrainian brass band from the village of Lapshyn.[26]

Ukrainians broke into the Brzezany prison on July 4, upon the arrival of the Wehrmacht. They discovered mutilated bodies. Floating corpses were seen in the Zlota Lipa River. Corpses were also spotted downriver, near the village of Saranczuki. Some of the dead found in Brzezany were buried in a common grave in the local Christian cemetery. Others were identified by peasant families and taken for burial in their native villages. Dozens of Jews were forced to dig graves and bury the dead in the Brzezany Christian cemetery. Afterward, these Jews were slaughtered right then and there by an enraged Ukrainian mob. Some were killed with their own spades. The effect of the NKVD killing of Ukrainian prisoners, together with powerful emotions evoked by the Sunday rally and the permissive attitude of the local German military, resulted in a town-wide anti-Jewish pogrom. A Ukrainian crowd ran wild through the Jewish quarter and spread out all over town, searching for Jews. People were killed and wounded. Property was seized and looted. Some Ukrainians, especially the local intelligentsia, promised to calm the crowds.[27] Within a few weeks, three mass graves, which contained mostly Ukrainian prisoners murdered by the NKVD, were unearthed in the park surrounding the Sieniawski Castle.[28]

A highly emotional event attended by 20,000 Ukrainians took place on August 31 at the Lysonia Hill, a few kilometers southeast of Brzezany. Lysonia was a commemorative site for battles fought by Ukrainians against Russians and Poles during the First World War. A number of Ukrainian Uniate clergy, headed by Father Baczynski, addressed the crowd. The fallen heroes were mourned. Nationalistic poems were recited. Bands and choirs performed. Dr. Volodymyr Bemko, a longtime member of the OUN and a prominent Ukrainian personality in Brzezany, told the audience that "the last time we could honor our heroes here was in 1929. Poland used to scatter their remains. This is where the infamous Polish pacification was initiated. This is also the site which inspired the souls of thousands of new fighters."[29] Ukrainian public celebrations like that of July 6 in Brzezany and in late August at Lysonia were received with great elation and enthusiasm by the local Ukrainian population, who had been denied public expressions of national identity by the prewar Polish regime.

German administrative personnel began arriving in Brzezany in the fall of 1941. The highest-ranking German official in town, and in the whole Brzezany region, was Kreishauptmann Asbach, a heavyset man in his late 30s. The Asbachs appropriated the best villa in town. It was located near the Rynek, very close to the Farny Church. Asbach also had a summer residence in the Kurzany estate, near Brzezany. The Kreishaupmannschaft, the German administration of the Brzezany region, took over the largest and most impressive building in town, that of the prewar Polish Gimnazjum. It employed a number of Reichsdeutsche, some Volksdeutsche, and quite a large number of low-ranking Polish and Ukrainian personnel. Besides running the administration, requisitioning grain, and arranging for the transfer of locals for labor inside Germany, Asbach had his own private dream. He wanted to transform Brzezany into a modern German-looking town. To this end hundreds of local Jews were forced to raze buildings and prepare open spaces for future construction. Asbach employed a Jewish architect, a refugee from central Poland. He even hid him during one of the roundups. Asbach's architectural fantasies wreaked additional damage upon the already devastated town.[30]

As the occupation continued, a small German community emerged in Brzezany. It consisted mostly of those appointed to various local positions and their families. Fraeulein Schmitz, or Gretel, as some of her friends called her, was Asbach's personal secretary. She was a youngish and exceptionally heavyset single woman from Hamburg. Wives and daughters of other German officials in town worked in the Kreishauptmannschaft. There were also a few German commercial enterprises in Brzezany. The largest was Unduetsch, a branch of a department-store chain with headquarters in Bremen. Herr Mund was in charge of the Brzezany branch. He met Fraeulein Maria in Brzezany. She worked for Asbach. They got married after the war. The head of the Brzezany post office was Herr Plotz-Emden from Frankfurt am Main.

Representatives from VoMi were also in town. They were in charge of appropriating Jewish property for the Volksdeutsche.[31] VoMi was headed by Hubert Kohnen. Kohnen, born in Aachen, had lived in Canada for ten years prior to the war and spoke good English. He was tall and good-looking and could be quite charming when he wanted to be. He assimilated rather well into local society. Krzysia, the daughter of Szymlet, the man who had served as a gunsmith with the 51st Regiment of the Polish Army stationed in Brzezany before the war, became Kohnen's mistress. Krzysia's father and his German "son-in-law" used to rob local Jews of their property. Kohnen and Szymlet accompanied Jews when they were marched to the Okopisko for execution. After the killings, Kohnen and Szymlet sorted out the victims' clothes and deposited them in the VoMi warehouse. Michal Kaminski referred to Szymlet as "Hubert's father-in-law," and maintained that Szymlet made quite a fortune from the Jewish tragedy. "Hubert used to take him to all these 'actions.' Following the executions he would sort out the clothing, looking for gold rings and valuables, and he did quite well, that piece of scum. The Poles in Brzezany didn't like him. The son-of-a-bitch ate Polish bread, served in the Polish army and raised his daughter to be the mistress of a Gestapo man." Kohnen, though his official job was to collect Jewish property, apparently participated in some of the killings. He also shot several Jews who had typhoid. "Hubert," as people called him, was the terror of Brzezany Jews. One of the survivors referred to him as "the Mephisto of the ghetto" and another as "the angel of death."[32]

A number of German officials brought their families to Brzezany. Their children studied in a local German school. The head of the Sonderdienst, Erich Elze, a man in his mid-40s, was a father of five. Schueller, of the Kripo, the local criminal police, had four or five children. Relatives from Germany used to arrive for visits.

The highest-ranking Nazi officer who visited Brzezany was General Jurgen Stroop, the man who mercilessly suppressed the Warsaw Ghetto Uprising.[33] That was in March 1943. As a young officer in the German army during the First World War, Stroop had been stationed in Brzezany for a few weeks. He fell in love with a local Polish beauty during that time and even contemplated marrying her.

In a certain sense, Brzezany became a German town. Street names were changed in November 1941. In some cases these were just translations into German, such as Farnstrasse instead of Farna. In others, distinct Polish names that were affiliated with Polish history and culture were altered altogether. Iwaszkiewicza Street turned into Feldherrnstrasse, Slowackiego became Poststrasse, Mickiewicza-Siegestrasse and Pilsudski Square disappeared altogether. Some streets had been given Ukrainian names, such as Sieniawskich, which became Bogdan Lepkij Street.[34]

Several police units were stationed in town. The German Gendarmerie consisted of nine policemen and was headed by several officers in turn. One of them was Tannenberg, who was from Austria. A particularly vicious Gendarme was Zipprich, a man in his mid-30s. He owned a bulldog, which he would set on smaller dogs and have it tear them to pieces. He was known for his cruelty toward people as well, Jews in particular. Zipprich participated in some of the killings at the Jewish cemetery. There was the Sonderdienst, the Special Police, under the Kreishauptmann. The members were mostly Volksdeutsche. They wore blue uniforms. The Sonderdienst consisted of some thirty men, and its headquarters was near Asbach's mansion. There was also a branch of Kripo, the Criminal Police, some of whose members were Polish. The Ukrainian auxiliary militia was supervised by the Gendarmerie and was headed by a Ukrainian officer. It consisted of a few dozen policemen. They wore blue trousers, dark-gray jackets, and high boots. There was also the Ortskommandantur, the headquarters of the local military command.[35]

Both the Polish and the Ukrainian populations of Brzezany suffered from the harsh wartime conditions. Some had to leave their prewar houses. Food became scarce, and infectious diseases threatened the health of the population. Ukrainian peasants were forced to deliver quotas of grain. Some were taken forcibly to work in Germany. Still, the Ukrainians were better off than the Poles. They enjoyed a preferential status in a public, cultural, and national sense. The local administration of the town was now headed by a Ukrainian, Volodymyr Pryshliak. A Ukrainian was appointed head of the city court; the regional physician was also a Ukrainian, Dr. Lavrovskii. Most of the leading local offices, which had been occupied by Poles in the interwar years, were now held by Ukrainians. A Ukrainian theater was founded. One of the most impressive Ukrainian achievements in wartime Brzezany was the establishment of a Ukrainian educational system. The prewar Brzezany Gimnazjum now became a distinctly Ukrainian institution, the Ukrainian State Gimnazjum. It was located in the Ratusz.[36]

Some conflicts between the Germans and the Ukrainians emerged quite soon after the occupation. Almost all of the local OUN commanders were arrested in mid-September of 1941. Dr. Bemko, who had his office in Lwow at that time, intervened on their behalf, and most of them were eventually released. Bemko also defended several Ukrainians who were accused of hiding and assisting Jews. Increasing numbers of young Ukrainians from Brzezany and the surrounding area joined the UPA underground. The UPA in the Brzezany region appealed to Jewish doctors to join its ranks. Most of them refused. Chmyr, a local UPA leader, supposedly assisted some Brzezany Jews during the German occupation.[37]

Numerous Ukrainians from Brzezany and the region volunteered to serve in the German army. As early as December 1941, about 150 Ukrainians reported for mobilization into the Wehrmacht, but only three were accepted. Another opportunity presented itself in the spring of 1943, when the Ukrainian SS Halychyna Division was being formed. It was wholeheartedly supported by the local Ukrainian intelligentsia and Ukrainian community leaders. Babiak, head of the Brzezany Ukrainian community, and Father

Baczynski, head of the local Ukrainian church, were very active in the mobilization campaign. Almost 3,000 Ukrainians applied from the Brzezany region. Brzezany celebrated the official announcement of the Halychyna Division on April 29. The town was decorated with German and Ukrainian flags, and a parade marched in front of Ukrainian and German officials. Another celebration took place a few weeks later. One of the thirty young men from Brzezany who were accepted to serve in the Halychyna wrote in his memoirs that "the town of Brzezany accompanied its volunteers with music, flowers and girls' kisses."[38]

Official Polish institutions and activities in wartime Brzezany were very modest. The Poles were allowed to maintain a Polish Welfare Committee. The German administration also allowed for a six-grade Polish school. A few classes in the Polish language were also maintained at the local Ukrainian vocational school. Illegal Polish activities centered on the local AK underground and the Polish Scouts. The Polish underground had already appeared in and around Brzezany during the Soviet occupation of 1939–1941. Its members were mostly recent graduates and upperclassmen from the local Gimnazjum as well as members of the local Polish intelligentsia. A separate underground unit was formed by former reserve officers and noncoms of the 51st Regiment. The underground collected intelligence, distributed anti-German leaflets and illegal press reports, and attempted some sabotage, particularly along the railroad tracks. A number of German officers and Gendarmes were killed and wounded. Chief physician of the AK in the Brzezany region was the director of the Brzezany hospital, Dr. Stefan Bilinski. An underground unit consisting of young Polish women was also active. They served mostly as signalers and nurses. Some of them, such as Zofja Sniadecka, helped smuggle people across the Hungarian border.[39]

The prewar Polish Scout organization in Brzezany continued illegal activities under both the Soviets and the Germans. Known during the German occupation as Szare Szeregi, the Gray Ranks, they organized athletic and educational activities for Polish youth. They also assisted the AK in distributing illegal materials and performed "small-type sabotage," such as breaking windows of German offices and stealing weapons from German soldiers. One group attempted to smuggle food into the Brzezany ghetto; some Polish Scouts had close friends among the few assimilated Jewish youngsters in the ghetto. One of them was David Pomeranz, the son of Dr. Pomeranz, whose family converted during the war.[40]

The murder of Dr. Stefan Bilinski, the most prominent Polish personality in Brzezany, was one of the most significant and tragic events for the entire Polish community. Dr. Bilinski had arrived in Brzezany a few years before the war and within a relatively short period became an important community figure. He headed the local hospital and was connected with the AK underground and the Scouts during the war. He was also a member of the local

Welfare Committee. Bilinski was killed by a UPA man in February 1944. His funeral, which was endorsed by the local German authorities, turned into a public demonstration of Polish identity. The first months of 1944 marked an intensification of the Ukrainian-Polish conflict in the Brzezany area. Polish households in mixed Polish-Ukrainian villages as well as in predominantly Polish villages were attacked by the UPA. Houses were burned and their inhabitants murdered and wounded. Particularly brutal murders took place in the village of Buszcze in January 1944. Twenty-two people were murdered in Kuropatniki in early April. Close to 1,000 Poles were apparently murdered by the UPA in the Brzezany region. The Ukrainian underground forcibly requisitioned food and equipment from Ukrainian and Polish peasants. UPA attacks against Poles increased with the steadily approaching front line.

Poles attempted to organize self-defense groups with the assistance of the AK. Some Polish families moved to the Bernardine Cloister and the Farny Church, which turned into Polish defense outposts. The German attitude toward the self-defense of the Poles during the last months of the occupation was fairly permissive. At the same time, Polish underground units in the Brzezany region participated in Operation Storm, "Burza," initiated in January 1944. It was supposed to aid the advancing Red Army and harass the retreating Germans. The relations between the UPA and the Germans were ambivalent. While attacking some Wehrmacht units and Gendarmerie posts in order to get arms and goods, the Ukrainian underground cooperated with other German units in attacking and killing Soviet soldiers and partisans.[41]

The winter and spring of 1944 was a time of uncertainty, fear, and anticipation. Brzezany was bombed several times. Trenches were dug on the outskirts of town. Numerous Poles and Ukrainians, especially among the intelligentsia, started fleeing westward, fearing the return of the Soviets. The first Red Army detachments entered Brzezany on July 22.[42]

Whereas German rule in Brzezany meant inconvenience and suffering for its Polish and Ukrainian inhabitants, it resulted in near-total annihilation for the Jews. The Ukrainian pogroms in the first weeks of the German occupation were an ominous prelude to what would happen in the coming months. A short while after his arrival in Brzezany, Asbach nominated a Jewish Council, the Judenrat. The chairman was Dr. Klarer, and among its members were Dr. Falk, Dr. Pomeranz, and Dr. Wagszal. The Judenrat, here as elsewhere, was supposed to assist the Germans in their anti-Jewish policies. It attempted, as much as it could, to ease the life of the Jews. There was also a local Jewish police force, which aided the Germans and the Ukrainian militia in finding and rounding up Jews.[43]

The first *aktion*, the so-called "intelligentsia roundup," occurred on the eve of Yom Kippur in early October 1941. All Jewish males were required to report to the marketplace. About 600 people, mostly professionals and merchants, were selected and locked up in the Brzezany prison. Asbach promised to help free some of them in return for three kilograms of gold, which he got from the Judenrat. Nobody was released. They were loaded on trucks the next day and driven in the direction of Raj, where all were killed by a contingent of Sipo men from Tarnopol. The bodies were buried in a nearby quarry. Years later the remains would be transferred and reburied at the far edge of the Christian cemetery, behind a monument commemorating Soviet soldiers who fell during the liberation of Brzezany in the summer of 1944. Most of the killings in and around Brzezany were conducted by the Tarnopol Sipo, the German Security Police outpost, headed by SS Sturmbannfuehrer Herman Mueller and his "specialist" on Jewish affairs, Willi Herrmann. The next mass murder took place in mid-December. On Asbach's orders, about 1,000 Jews, mostly the elderly, women, and children, were rounded up by the Jewish and Ukrainian police and Asbach's Sonderdienst on the second day of Hanukkah. They were taken on foot and in horse-drawn carts in the direction of Podhajce. A Sipo detachment, headed by Mueller, was waiting for them in the Litiatyn Forest, halfway between Brzezany and Podhajce. All were shot and buried right there. Brzezany Jews were periodically deported to nearby labor camps. The labor camp roundups were usually carried out by the Ukrainian and Jewish police. Very few returned.[44]

Until mid-January 1942, Jews could move quite freely in and around town. On January 15, an announcement was published in *Berezhans'ki Visti:* "Jews who leave their designated quarter without permission, as well as those who provide them with shelter, are subject to execution."[45] The final establishment of the Brzezany ghetto occurred in the fall. The first massive roundup and deportation to the Belzec death camp was carried out in Brzezany in September 1942. It was directed by the Tarnopol Security Police with the assistance of the local Ukrainian militia. A crowd of Poles, Ukrainians, and Volksdeutsche watched the eerie and tragic scene. Close to 2,000 Jews were loaded onto some fifty freight cars at the Brzezany railway station and transported westward. Only a few, who managed to jump off the train and avoid being killed by the German and Ukrainian escort, made it back to Brzezany.

The next two deportations to Belzec were in October and December.[46] The commander of the Brzezany criminal police reported to his superiors in Lwow that "one hundred bullets were used in the course of the Jewish roundup."[47] During the December deportation, which took place on the first day of Hanukkah, close to 1,000 people were taken to Belzec. The size of the ghetto population shrank considerably. During each one of these deportation roundups, Jews were also shot on the way to the railway station and at the Okopisko. The first roundup of 1943 took place in late March and early April. It lasted three days. Some people were deported to nearby labor camps. Others were executed at the Okopisko. Less than 2,000 Jews remained in the ghetto. The last roundup and the liquidation of the Brzezany ghetto occurred on Saturday, June 12, two days after the Jewish holiday of Shavuot, during the Christian Whitsun, referred to by the locals as the Green Holidays. Both Brzezany Jews and Gentiles would associate this last roundup with summer holidays. Even the "W" group of some 300 Jewish men, who were supposedly needed by the Wehrmacht and were thought to be destined to outlive the rest, were marched to the Okopisko cemetery on that Saturday. Fourteen hundred Jews were shot for several hours, one by one. The corpses were thrown into several pits prepared in advance by the Baudienst. The last roundup and the Okopisko mass killing were directed and supervised by SS Scharfuehrer Willi Herrmann from the Tarnopol SD. According to an eyewitness, "There he was, standing, in front of the Jews, besmeared with blood from top to bottom, looking like a butcher." The Jews were shot by Sipo, the Security Police from Tarnopol, and by local German policemen. Brzezany was now cleansed of Jews—Judenrein.[48]

It is impossible to establish the precise number of Jews who survived the Judenrein roundup. Some went into hiding with Gentile families; others escaped into the forests. Most didn't live to see the end of the German occupation. Brzezany Jews were hidden mostly by Poles, but some were hidden by mixed Polish-Ukrainian families, and a few were hidden by Ukrainians. It seems that the most common motivation for rescuing Jews was remuneration. In some cases, it was pure humanitarianism. Still others, Poles and Ukrainians alike, turned in Jews in hiding. A few dozen survivors, including children, showed up in Brzezany after its liberation by the Red Army in July 1944. Close to 10,000 Jews, including Jewish refugees, had apparently been living in Brzezany at the onset of the German occupation. Massive roundups, killings, and deportations reduced that number to less than 100.[49]

Brzezany went through an enormous demographic upheaval during the three years of German occupation. Some Germans and many more Volksdeutsche arrived in town. They left Brzezany with the retreating German army. The Jewish population ceased to exist. Some Polish and Ukrainian families, fearing the advancing Soviet army, fled westward. In the summer of 1941, more than 20,000 people lived in that town; by the summer of 1944, less than 10,000 people lived there. They were almost exclusively Poles and Ukrainians.[50]

* * *

The German bombing of Brzezany inscribed itself deeply in the memories of its inhabitants. Ludka was in the Rynek when the first German bomber flew over the town. "It suddenly lost altitude and the pilot started shooting. That was my first encounter with the Germans. Many people fled to our house on the outskirts of town. Then we ourselves escaped into the countryside."[51]

Karol clearly remembered that first massive bombing on a summer evening. "People had just left the first showing at the Przyjazn movie theater when a bomb hit the building. The whining of the incendiary bombs was horrifying. Four such bombs fell near our house but, luckily, didn't explode."[52]

Dr. Lipa Wagszal, who was a young Jewish physician at the time, vividly described in his memoirs the first bombardment of Brzezany. He even recalled the exact time. "It was Saturday, four thirty P.M." Lipa and his wife were at their friend's house, sipping tea. "Soon explosions were heard all over. People were running in the streets." The house where his parents lived suffered a direct hit. Lipa's father, an orthodox Jew, was praying nearby with a group of neighbors and survived. His mother was buried under the rubble.[53]

Ruth Wanderer, who turned 6 in April 1941, and her slightly older sister, Rena, remembered running down from their apartment, opposite the Ratusz, and standing at the entrance to the basement. Ruth recalled a blast of air that threw her into the yard. "I remember flying out. I said to myself 'Well, now I'm dead.' I remember being sucked out and wondering whether that's what it looks like after you are dead. Then I realized that I'm still alive. They were bombing the whole night and most of the bombs were firebombs." Rena and Ruth remember after all those years the repulsive lingering smell of the bombings.[54]

Manek Thaler was 6 when Brzezany was bombed. "The German pilots had maps showing the Jewish neighborhoods. They dropped their bombs there because they knew that the majority of the population in those areas was Jewish, not for any military purpose." He must have overheard these remarks from the adults. Manek and his parents stayed on the outskirts of town until the Germans arrived.[55]

Dr. Wagszal recalled the arrival of the first German troops. "It was early in the morning. They were coming downhill on Adamowka Street. First the motorcycles, in pairs, then trucks and buses filled with soldiers, followed by cannons and a few more motorcycles in the rear."[56] Manek returned with his parents from the suburbs to their apartment in the center of Brzezany. "We were walking down this smashed road with dead horses and dead soldiers. At every intersection there were Germans with their square helmets and machine guns."[57]

The arrival of the Germans was perceived by most of the Ukrainians in Brzezany and in the surrounding villages as liberation from the Bolsheviks. Out of curiosity, Karol Codogni, although he himself was Polish, mixed with the predominantly Ukrainian crowd in the center of the town. "The Ukrainians were ecstatic. Throngs of Ukrainian peasants, mostly young people, carrying yellow-and-blue flags adorned with the Ukrainian trident, filled the Rynek and the adjoining streets. They came from the villages, dressed in Ukrainian national costumes, singing their Ukrainian songs. All this was extremely depressing for the Polish population."[58]

Irena Wesolowska, a teenager at the time, recalled that following the arrival of the Germans, "there was celebrating and shooting in the center of town for twenty-four hours straight. Poles and Jews locked themselves in their houses. Windows in Polish and Jewish houses were shattered, and people feared for their lives. Ukrainians celebrated and caroused the whole night, imagining that they would finally have their *samostiina Ukraina—* independent Ukraine. From that moment on, they felt superior."[59]

Dmytro Bartkiw, from Kotow, remembered that during the first weeks of German rule, Ukrainians had high hopes for an independent Ukraine. He and his friends went to the Lysonia Hill, where a Ukrainian national monument was erected. Impressive celebrations attended by huge Ukrainian crowds were held there.[60]

Vasyl Fanga, from Szybalin, recalled the appearance of the Germans in his village but, retrospectively, was quite critical of Ukrainian hopes and expectations. "Once again the peasants made fools of themselves, greeting their 'new liberators' with bread and salt. Yellow-and-blue flags and German swastikas were displayed everywhere. How could the whole Ukrainian leadership be so naive, so stupid, to hope that Hitler would grant them an independent Ukraine?! Instead they brought death, blood, and ruin. The behavior of the entire Ukrainian leadership was utterly disgraceful. People now deny collaborating with the Germans. It's all lies."[61]

Ukrainian celebrations of "liberation" and "independence" in Brzezany and the vicinity were marred by the gruesome sights of the Ukrainian inmates of the Brzezany prison who had been murdered by the Soviets. Vasyl Oleskiw walked from Byszki to Brzezany on the second or third day after the Germans had occupied the town. He and other peasants from his village were worried about the fate of some twenty people from Byszki who had been arrested by the NKVD. Luckily, all of them were alive. However, numerous prisoners from other villages around Brzezany were found dead. "The sights were indescribable, the stench from the corpses. They were spread out on the prison cellar floor. Other corpses were floating in the river, the Zlota Lipa. People blamed the NKVD and the Jews."[62]

Ivan Fanga, from Szybalin, recalled: "I myself, with a group of young boys, went along the river, as far as Saranczuki, where I saw corpses being pulled out of the water. All had been murdered. Women's breasts were cut off, bottles stuffed into their vaginas. It was horrible. I remember it to this day and I shiver when I imagine the dreadful suffering and death of these young men and women."[63] Galina Skaskiv recalled that "after the Soviets retreated, corpses were floating down the river from the Sieniawski Castle. We children pulled them out with pitchforks. Then they were buried in the villages. I saw all that myself. They used to cut off people's noses and tongues. They used to throw people into quicklime."[64]

The prevailing images of Jewish collaboration with the Soviets, which were popular among the Ukrainians in 1939–1941, and the wrath caused by the recent murder of Ukrainian prisoners by the NKVD were, apparently, the principal causes of the Ukrainian anti-Jewish pogrom in Brzezany. Pinhas Fenner was working in a barber shop facing the Brzezany prison. "Thousands of Ukrainians from the surrounding villages arrived in town and gathered in front of the prison. At a certain moment I saw two Ukrainian policemen, wearing blue-and-yellow armbands, escorting a little Jew with a broom in his hand into the building. A few minutes later the Jew, beaten up and bleeding, appeared in a second-floor window. A Ukrainian who stood at his side yelled, 'We just caught a Jew who murdered our brothers.' Suddenly a pistol shot was fired from the crowd and the Jew fell out of the window. Loud cries of 'Death to the Jews' were heard all over. Most of the Jews who perished in Brzezany on that day were murdered with broomsticks with nails attached to them. Crowds of Ukrainians, dressed in their national costumes, marched down the streets shouting 'Death to Jews, Poles, and Communists.'"[65]

Poldek, the young Jewish doctor, witnessed some terrifying scenes during the Ukrainian pogrom. "There were two rows of Ukrainian bandits, holding big sticks. They forced those people, the Jews, in between the two rows and murdered them in cold blood with those sticks. I saw it from the window of our apartment."[66] Rozka Majblum recalled that "Ukrainian terrorists forced Jews to dig pits in the Old Garden. Then some of them were shot or buried alive. Among them was our friend Dziunek Wandmaier. My uncle was there too, and a Ukrainian acquaintance told him to run away."[67] Rena Wanderer's grandfather was beaten up by Ukrainians. "I remember my grandfather being attacked by two Ukrainians and being beaten into a bloody state. They tried to rip off his beard. They hit him in the ear. He was bleeding from one side of his ear."[68]

Manek Thaler, a 6-year-old boy at the time, related what he must have heard from his parents. "The Ukrainian peasants were led into the town and opened up the prisons where Ukrainians had been incarcerated. They released those people from prison, and then they caught as many Jews as they could and massacred them. Then they caught other Jews and forced them to bury the dead, apparently with their bare hands. It was so typically Ukrainian. The Ukrainians don't just kill, they want to have a good time."[69]

There were a few instances when German soldiers interfered with the Ukrainians who were robbing and beating Jews. Although Rena Wanderer refused to tell me how a German saved her grandfather from two Ukrainian thugs, her younger sister Ruth repeated what she had heard from her parents. "There was one soldier there, in a uniform, and my mother said in German 'Save this man,' and he chased them away."[70] When the Thalers returned to their house from the outskirts of Brzezany, they saw Ukrainians removing their furniture. "My mother started screaming at them to stop. A

German officer showed up and she switched into German 'This is our home, please stop it.' The man blew his whistle, drew his pistol, and told them to leave."[71]

Although the Polish population of Brzezany suffered from wartime conditions, life under the Germans seemed better than life under the Soviets. The Germans, according to Tolek Rapf, "made quite a convincing effort vis-à-vis the Poles to appear as their 'saviors' from Bolshevik rule. Local German bureaucrats maintained quite good relations with some of the elite Polish families in town." Tolek himself started working for the German firm Unduetsch, which opened a branch in Brzezany. "Unduetsch was a 'Polish oasis' in Brzezany. The boss, Herr Mund, immediately realized that Poles were different from Ukrainians, most of whom were rabble. Mund's deputy, Herr Tischbein, was definitely pro-Polish and we called him Uncle Tiben."[72]

Ukrainian memories of the German occupation vary. One definite bright spot was the Brzezany Gimnazjum. Although it was moved from its impressive interwar location back to the Ratusz and conditions were quite crowded, it did become a distinctly Ukrainian school. Vasyl Oleskiw attended the Gimnazjum from the fall of 1941 until late winter 1944, when it was closed down because of the approaching front line. "Only Ukrainians went to the Gimnazjum. It was now a Ukrainian State Gimnazjum. Its Ukrainian principal, Stasiuk, was a Gimnazjum professor before the war. There were also other prewar teachers, all Ukrainian. Many students were members of the Ukrainian underground. Some of them feared arrest by the Germans."[73]

Galina Skaskiv, too, was a student of the Gimnazjum. "There were absolutely no Poles there at the time," she remembered. She seemed neither to know nor to care about Polish youth in Brzezany. She did remember, however, walking into the nearby ghetto and being tutored by a Jew. "My landlady recommended her. She spoke five European languages. I used to bring her bread, sugar, and butter." Galina stopped visiting her Jewish teacher when a Ukrainian policeman warned her that she might be caught and executed with the Jews.[74]

Dmytro Bartkiw from Kotow, another Ukrainian Gimnazjum student, recalled "We were extremely happy at school during the German occupation. All the subjects were taught in Ukrainian, and the teachers could discuss Ukrainian history with us. The Germans didn't interfere, except for having a portrait of Hitler hung on the classroom wall." For most of the time, Dmytro lived and studied in close proximity to the ghetto, but he couldn't recall whether he observed what was going on there. "To tell the truth, it didn't interest me. So what if there were Jews in the ghetto? But it did become interesting when the ghetto was being liquidated and the Jews were taken to be shot at the Okopisko, on the way to Raj."[75]

But some Ukrainians recalled their and others' hardships and suffering. Lev Rega started crying when he recalled his arrest by the Germans in

Brzezany in mid-September 1941. "It was like going to the gallows, like visiting Dante's inferno." He recalled the Lacki Street prison in Lwow, where he was interned for some time. One day he saw dead Jews, most of them naked, being loaded into a truck. "Like wood," he commented.

Lev recalled another horrifying scene. "We saw a group of Jews. A German arrived with a huge dog who just skinned them alive, pulling off pieces of flesh." He watched a close friend, a Ukrainian, being taken away and executed. He had been mistaken for a Jew.[76]

Ivan Hrabar, who served for a while in the Ukrainian militia in Brzezany, was arrested and accused of smuggling arms to the Ukrainian underground. He was repeatedly beaten and tortured. "They had a special table with one end lower than the other. I was stretched out on that table and they beat me with rubber truncheons. I screamed. I shouted." Hrabar recalled sharing a cell in the Brzezany prison with a Jewish boy. "I used to get a jar of soup and coffee in a bottle sent from home. I shared it with the boy. I couldn't bear to see him go hungry." After a few weeks, Hrabar was transferred from Brzezany to the Tarnopol prison and finally taken for forced labor in Germany. "I was so weak that I couldn't stand up. It took me a whole year to return to normal."[77]

At the epicenter of human suffering and tragedy in German-occupied Brzezany were, of course, the roundups, deportations, and killings of the Jews. Manek Thaler was 8 at the time. His "darkest hour," as he described it decades later, was during one of the roundups, when he was carried by a friend of his parents inside a garbage can down to the dark basement of the old stone court building in Brzezany. "You lose all concept of time. After a while I began to panic because of all those rats. As I peeked through a grated vent I could see the courtyard where the Gestapo was beating Jews and selecting those who would be deported. They were separating women and old men from the younger men. I was watching for my mother. I was looking for a woman wearing a red kerchief. I thought that every woman with a red kerchief was my mother. I was sure that my mother and father were there and that they would probably be taken away."

In fact, Manek's mother survived that roundup, and his father was taken to a labor camp. Then Manek and his mother went into hiding with a Polish couple on the outskirts of town, near the Okopisko cemetery, which was located on a hill and surrounded by a wall. Manek recalled the sights and scenes which occurred there on the day of the Judenrein action. "The hill was covered with bodies because some of the younger people, when they realized what was happening, jumped over the wall and tried to run down the hill. The Germans shot them with machine guns. I was praying that none of the Jews would make it, because if they did, the Germans would come looking for them and they would find us. As far as I knew, everybody who tried to get away was killed. Years later we found out that one young man actually escaped into the fields and survived."[78] That man was Munio Haber.

Munio was one of those "W" Jews who worked for the German army in Brzezany and were believed to be the most privileged part of the Jewish population. The letter "W" and the Wehrmacht seal supposedly provided the best chance for survival. Munio and his stepfather were among the lucky ones. However, all "W" Jews were executed on the day of the last Judenrein roundup.

Munio distinctly recalled that Saturday, June 12, 1943. The few hundred "W" Jews were held outside the ghetto in a complex of buildings surrounding a courtyard. The gate was locked on Friday evening. "Around eight in the morning an open military truck with four Gestapo men in green uniforms approached on Tarnopolska Street. It was followed by a number of vehicles loaded with soldiers. All of them went in the direction of the local Gestapo office on Sadowa Street. We knew that a roundup was about to begin." Shortly afterward, single shots were heard from the direction of the ghetto. The "W" compound was soon surrounded by soldiers with machine guns. "Around eleven o'clock a distant burst of machine-gun shots was heard, followed by others. We knew very well that these shots marked the final massacre taking place in the cemetery." Munio's stepfather hugged the youngster, whispering, "Mother and the children are no more, apparently, and I too am about to go." He stepped into an adjacent room and closed the door. When, after a few minutes, Munio was called into that room, he saw his stepfather's body lying on one of the bunk beds. The man committed suicide rather than let the Germans kill him.

"The distant machine-gun bursts were heard again and again. After an hour or so everybody was ordered to go down into the courtyard. They formed a column and were marched out of the gate." They were escorted by German and Ukrainian policemen. Munio seemed to recall that "last journey," as he would refer to it years later, almost minute by minute. "The column moved slowly. A group of Gestapo officers was standing at the corner of Tarnopolska and blocked the approach to that street. The column moved on into Ormianska. All intersections were guarded by uniformed Germans with machine guns. Not too far away behind the armed Germans gathered small groups of local people, Poles and Ukrainians, who wouldn't miss our 'procession.' Our last hope was that we might turn left at the town center and then proceed to the railway station. Instead, we were led uphill, in the direction of the cemetery. A subdued but growing murmur arose from the marching column, and for a moment there was a sense of movement, as if the lines were about to break up. It seemed that there, in the large open space in front of the Farny Church, people would start running in all directions. But the noises stopped and nothing happened. It seemed again that the crowd was going to break up and run into the surrounding fields when we approached the cemetery. However, only a few men tried their luck. They were shot and killed on the run."[79]

Tolek Rapf was watching the last roundup in Brzezany from his Unduetsch office window. "They were walking in a column, with Ukrainian policemen and a few Gestapo men on either side. Shots were fired from time to time, and a wheelbarrow moved along collecting the corpses. They marched up the street. It was an unforgettable sight. I probably knew many of them, but it was particularly Dr. Pomeranz, our family doctor, who remains imprinted in my memory. And Sylka Finkelstein, my classmate, a beautiful girl with long braids who used to sit very close to my bench. I can see Pomeranz as if it were today, walking proudly, his shirt collar wide open, his jacket over his shoulders. I'll never forget that sight. They marched right under our windows, turning left toward the church, in the direction of the Jewish cemetery, the Okopisko. All this was terribly shocking, especially in such a small town, where almost everyone knew everyone else."[80]

Halszka, Tolek's younger sister, also recalled that roundup. "I had just left the Farny Church and was walking down Iwaszkiewicza Street. A large flat cart was moving in the opposite direction and it was filled to the brim with bodies of people killed on the street. They were killed on their way to Okopisko. I remember that horrible pile. A hand was sticking out of one corner and a leg out of another. A head was hanging over the side. I ran down the street, screaming."[81]

Stanislawa Sabi lived opposite the Okopisko cemetery. "I saw what was happening. I became hysterical and ran down into the cellar. I saw how they dug a huge pit. I saw how the Germans led along the Seifert family, the women. They were beautiful, with beautiful children. These Jews were stripped naked. They were holding their children in their arms. It was a horrible sight. The Germans shot them from behind. They fell into the pit. Some of them were still stirring. I ran away, crying hysterically." Stanislawa never went near the ghetto. "I was terrified by the Germans. Once I was returning to town from the countryside during a roundup. 'Oh my God,' I thought, 'I'm going to die. They are killing my friends.' I thought I'm going to drop dead from fear. Once I saw a Jewish girl who used to sit next to me at school. She sat leaning on a stone. I'm not sure whether she was alive." Asked about Polish attitudes toward Jews under the German occupation, she maintained that "everybody felt for them. Of course, everybody was worried about himself, too. Everybody wanted to live. Germans killed Poles as well as Jews."[82]

Vasyl Oleskiw, a student at the Ukrainian Gimnazjum in Brzezany at the time, was living in a rented room near the Okopisko cemetery. One afternoon Vasyl and a friend were watching the killings. "I saw how they brought a group of Jews. They undressed, and then were led, one by one, to that pit, where they were shot." On another occasion he witnessed one of the roundups. "A column of Jews was marched to the Okopisko. Old Jews, men, women, and children. They were escorted by Jewish militia and by drunken Gestapo men. One of the Germans had a gold tooth and looked like a murderer. He shot Jews from time to time, as they were walking. We saw them falling. A few minutes after that dreadful procession marched by, my mother came running. She looked as though she had gone crazy." Oleskiw's mother had just arrived from the village with some food for her son when the roundup took place. Asked about assistance to Jews in the Ukrainian countryside near Brzezany, Vasyl was sure that "the Ukrainians sympathized with them. I know of no case where the Ukrainians in the villages betrayed Jews. The underground had a favorable attitude toward them."[83]

Ivan Fanga, from Szybalin, recalled an execution of Jews at the Okopisko. "A pit was dug and a narrow footbridge erected. This German, Zipprich, placed five or six Jews in a straight line and shot them with a single bullet. Little children were thrown into the pit on top of these corpses, and everything was covered up. After such an operation Zipprich would take off his gloves and throw them into the pit." Fanga, himself a member of the Ukrainian underground at that time, was sure that many Jews served in the ranks of the UPA. "They served as doctors, dentists, and nurses. There were even some Jews from Brzezany." Asked about Ukrainian assistance to Jews, he maintained that "Ukrainian people used to hide Jews. Many Jews were hiding in our village."[84]

Galina Skaskiv, a student at the Gimnazjum in German-occupied Brzezany, stated that "the Ukrainians commiserated very much with the Jews. Even our high school youth, who were pretty rough and tough, sympathized with the Jews, especially when we watched them being led to the Okopisko. The way they went, mothers with children. You would have to be an animal to be glad about it. The ground moved and blood flew all over. It was a terrible sight." Galina was amazed that "some Jews collaborated with the Germans, like the Jewish militia in Brzezany. I saw it from my balcony, near the Gimnazjum. Jewish militiamen ran along the roofs, chasing people. They dragged others from cellars. I was amazed how people could do it to their own. Our Ukrainian militia was somehow neutral. I never saw Ukrainian militiamen arresting Jews."[85]

Aleksandr Pankiv was 9 when he was taken for a Jewish boy by the Germans and almost shot at the Okopisko. "It was a beautiful day during the summer vacation. We went to watch the Germans. I was dark with curly black hair and looked like a Jew. They caught me and made me join a group of Jews. I marched with them for about forty minutes. Everybody was crying. They knew that they were going to die. When we reached the Okopisko we were told to undress and we were led to the edge of the pit. At the last minute a Ukrainian policeman recognized me. He kicked me in my behind and told me to get lost. I was completely naked. I ran like mad and jumped over the cemetery wall. I was terrified, and I'll remember it to my dying day." A few weeks later, during another roundup, Aleksandr, with other boys, Poles and Ukrainians, ran to the Storozysko hill to watch the executions. When I asked him how he could watch it such a short time after he was almost shot himself, Pankiv casually remarked "It was interesting."[86]

The executioners' testimonies were mostly matter-of-fact accounts of the killings. When asked during an interrogation more than thirty years later about the killings, SS Sturmbahnfuerer Mueller described those "routine" executions. "The victims remained at a distance of about fifty meters from the pit. They had to sit or stand with their backs facing the pit. They were dispatched to the pit according to the number of riflemen available. If eight men were shooting, eight Jews were sent. Those who waited their turn could hear the shots. I never made the victims dig their own pits or undress, since that went against my beliefs. In other places, executions were carried out with machine guns or submachine guns. This method could inflict unnecessary pain, since imprecise shots didn't always kill instantaneously. Therefore I refused to use rifles, machine guns or submachine guns. I tried to shorten the victims' ordeal. My men knew that I used a 7.65 caliber pistol exclusively."

Mueller recalled his first roundup of Jews in Brzezany. "It must have been in the summer of 1942 and was ordered by SiPo, the Security Police. On that day we left Tarnopol for Brzezany early in the morning. We were supposed to return before sunset. The site of the execution was on the outskirts of Brzezany. I was in town with my men, searching the Jewish quarter for Jews. Then I escorted the first group of Jews, by foot, to the execution site. The victims were shot with pistols, in the neck." As for his knowledge of Nazi policies concerning the Final Solution, Mueller stated "I learned about the intention to kill all Jews only after leaving Galicia. No reasons for the execution of Jews were given. They were justified, however, by the necessity to secure the rear against sabotage and espionage. These measures weren't criticized by anyone, although everyone knew about them. Nobody expressed any opinion. Nobody said it was murder."[87]

Willi Herrmann, who served under Mueller in the Tarnopol SD, recalled the December 1941 roundup in Brzezany. "This was the first time I saw Jews being killed. In the morning we drove from Tarnopol to a forest near Brzezany and met a group of German policemen. Then, several horse-drawn vehicles, crammed with Jews, arrived. These were only men, as I recall. The vehicles, driven by farmers, left and we secured the area immediately. The Jews were killed by the German police. After the execution was completed, we left."

Herrmann participated in the last Judenrein roundup in Brzezany. "We traveled by truck to Brzezany and met there the Ukrainian militia and the German Gendarmerie. Then, all the remaining Jews were taken from the ghetto to the cemetery. They weren't allowed to take any luggage. Everything was already set up at the cemetery. The pits had been dug by the Baudienst. They were about two meters deep, four meters wide, and three meters long. The Jews had to undress, but some remained with their underwear on. I don't know how the execution was carried out. We left after the roundup. The clothes of the dead were collected by the Volksdeutsche Mittelstelle."[88]

Hubert Kohnen was the representative of the Volksdeutsche Mittelstelle, or VoMi, in Brzezany. Although his official duty was to collect Jewish property, he also used to volunteer to chase and even kill Jews. Numerous interviewees, especially Poles and Jews, remembered this tall, blue-eyed, and English-speaking German who was a sort of a "man about town" in German-occupied Brzezany. Ruth Wanderer recalled Hubert's "visits" to their apartment. Their grandmother, Fruma, knew German well and had often traveled to Vienna before the war to purchase various items of merchandise for their Brzezany store. "Hubert used to taunt my Grandmother Fruma. He would sit down with her and pick up something, like a copper pot or hand-painted pastels, and she would tell him the story of the item. When she finished talking, he would say, 'I'm taking it with me.' He always made sure that he knew the 'history' of the item, and she was helpless to do anything about it. This was his shtick."[89]

Once, when Krystyna Gryczynska, a Polish woman who was in her early 20s at that time, was traveling in a crowded train from Lwow to Brzezany, a man in a uniform invited her to join him in the "Germans only" section of the train. It was Kohnen. He later arranged a job for her in one of the German offices in town. "This Hubert Kohnen used to visit my mother. She spoke excellent German. He and my mother used to sit in easy chairs and chat. I would go in from time to time and listen to their conversation. Mother would tell him 'Jews are people too. They are unfortunate.' Hubert would laugh and remark 'Really now! Have you ever heard such a thing?!'"[90]

Hans-Adolf Asbach, Kreishauptmann of the Brzezany region, presented a quite peaceful and almost idyllic image of Brzezany when he was interrogated in the mid-fifties. "In 1941, the Jews of Brzezany were not living in a separate area. They mixed with the non-Jewish population, Poles, Ukrainians, and Germans. There were no executions by the SS in Brzezany in 1941. Only roundups were conducted, during which those fit for labor were taken away. A large number of Jews were deported from Brzezany in the fall of 1942. The SS had had those Jews deported, by freight train, in the direction of Tarnopol. These roundups were conducted suddenly and the Kreishauptmannschaft was never notified in advance."[91]

Asbach was interrogated again in the mid-sixties, at which time he was accused of collaborating in the killing of Brzezany Jews. He continued to distance himself from the German security and terror apparatus and stressed the conflict of interests between the local German administration and the SS. "I was aware of the fact that Jews from the countryside were assembled in towns and cities. However, I wasn't sure for what purpose. I do recall that the Jews of Brzezany were forced to wear a yellow star. I have no recollection of why this was done. Only a very small circle of SS members were informed about the so-called *'aktionen.'* The German population in Brzezany generally had no knowledge about the anti-Jewish measures." When asked about specific killings in and around Brzezany, Asbach's answer was "I neither witnessed nor heard about Jews being killed in the Brzezany region."

Asbach continued to present an almost serene image of everyday life in town. "Jews, Poles and Ukrainians mingled with each other. They even shared the same houses. Only on very special occasions were people asked to leave their houses. Those who were dislocated, Jews, Poles and Ukrainians, could select their new dwellings." As for his relations with the SS, Asbach recalled that "the SS men called me a sissy and frequently complained about my rather mild attitude toward the Jewish population. Eventually, in early 1943, I asked to be transferred from my post because of the increasing deportations of Brzezany Jews. I didn't want to remain Kreishauptmann, when my conscience couldn't be appeased anymore."[92]

Somehow, Hans-Hermann Mund, another German who lived at that very time in Brzezany and headed a commercial enterprise, a branch of the Unduetsch firm, recalled rather precisely what happened to the Jews. "I do know that above half a dozen extermination roundups occurred in Brzezany. Every time Willi Herrmann appeared in town everybody knew that something bad was going to happen to the Jews." Mund witnessed one of the deportations at the local railroad station. "I saw the ill-fated procession of the Jews reach the station: men, women and children. It was a dreadful scene, particularly because of the little children. I knew then that all these Jews were being taken to an extermination camp, that they were doomed."

Mund also spoke, in his modest manner, of assisting some of his Jewish employees on some occasions. "They often hid in the storage rooms and stayed there during the roundups. However, this didn't save them. This was only a short-term delay. All were eventually killed." Mund, unlike most of the interrogated Germans who had lived in Brzezany, vividly recalled the last Judenrein roundup in mid-June 1943. "I saw how Jews were being shot at the Jewish cemetery. The distance to the cemetery was about 2,500 meters and I couldn't identify those who were firing. I heard that Willi Herrmann participated in that roundup. For days afterwards, the wind carried a strong poisonous smell all over. There were no more Jews left in Brzezany after this roundup."[93]

Johann, a Luftwaffe officer, arrived in Brzezany in the spring of 1943 and served in an air-force intelligence unit that was stationed on the bank of the Staw. He remembered quite well the Judenrein roundup on a Saturday in mid-June of that year. "From our observation site we were able to observe the Jewish cemetery. Our powerful binoculars made it easy to observe, at close range, what was going on. I saw that the Jews were brought in groups, men, women and children. They were ordered to undress by German and Ukrainian policemen and were placed close to the pit. A row of victims started out from the undressing site and ended at the pit. They were pushed and dragged to the edge of the pit and then shot by a uniformed man. The man pointed his gun at each victim's neck, shot, and then pushed him with his foot into the pit."

Johann and another German officer by the name of Kane, who owned a camera, decided to get closer to the scene of the execution. "When we got close to the cemetery we saw individual Jews trying to run away. We saw a naked Jew at the foot of a tree. He was shot on the run. Kane took a picture of him. He was in the Brzezany district long before me and was very interested in these Jewish roundups. As a devout Catholic, he was a firm opponent of the Nazis."[94]

Menachem Dul, an out-of-town Jew who survived the Holocaust in Brzezany by pretending to be a Karaite, described in his memoirs an unusual encounter with a German soldier in the summer of 1943.[95] "It was a hot day in June. I was walking alongside the lake and saw a Wehrmacht man. He looked sad, stopped near me and initiated a conversation. He told me that he was a Bavarian and a Catholic. He felt for the local population, which was suffering as a result of the war. His brother had been killed at the front and some of his relatives were in prison. He himself was about to leave for the front. The man bitterly complained about what he was supposed to fight and die for."[96]

Frau D., who worked at the Brzezany Kreishauptmannschaft, saw a column of Jews being led to the Okopisko during that last Saturday roundup. "I saw how a few hundred Jews, men, women and children, were taken from the Jewish quarter to the Jewish cemetery. I saw that dreadful column from a short distance. They passed right by me. After that roundup, there were no more Jews in Brzezany. Following that last roundup, signs were posted at the entrance to the town: 'This Place is Judenfrei.'"[97]

Assistance to and rescue of Jews were never clear-cut and simple matters. It is necessary, therefore, to consider all sides involved; in our case, the Jews, Poles, and Ukrainians in Brzezany and in its surroundings.

Dr. Lipa Wagszal-Shaklai related the story of his family's survival in his memoirs. The Wagszals—father, mother Pepka, and a little boy, Matus— were assisted in various ways by the doctor's Polish acquaintances and friends. Among them were a nurse, Anna, and a colleague, Dr. Danek. Both worked with Dr. Wagszal in the Brzezany hospital. Dr. Danek helped the Wagszals to escape to the countryside and kept some of their valuables, which he later passed on to the peasants who hid them. Lipa sensed that Anna, who did not particularly like Jews, had a soft spot for him. On one occasion she suggested hiding him alone at her parents' farm, which was in a distant village. He politely refused. The Wagszals hid together at various locations in and around the villages of Potutory and Demnia, south of Brzezany. Some of the peasants who helped them were the doctor's former patients. Most of the time, though, they stayed with the extremely poor family of Franio and Doska Szczepanski. Franio was an illegitimate son of a Polish father and a Ukrainian mother. His motivation for helping the Jewish doctor's family was a strange mixture of greed and compassion.[98]

The Wanderers, father, mother, and two girls, Rena and Ruth, left the Brzezany ghetto a few weeks before the last roundup. First they stayed with a Polish woman, Karolina Nowak, in a village several kilometers out of town. Isaac Wanderer knew Karolina's son, Juzek, who casually asked him one day "How would you like to have a place to hide for you and your family?" When they climbed down into the hiding place dug under Karolina's barn they found there two Brzezany Jews, Itschie Nadler and his nephew Sanek Goldberg. Ruth recalled "We were shocked. Juzek never told us that there were other Jews in there. Juzek was a gambler, and that was our good fortune. Only those who gambled took Jews in. Our father paid a fortune in dollars. Living with two strangers in extremely crowded conditions was nerve-racking. To kill time we played cards with paper money that we made, promising to pay up later, if we survived."

The Wanderers had to leave Karolina's house sometime in March or April 1944, when Ukrainians started burning down Polish houses in the vicinity. They stayed for a short while with another Polish family and ended up in a hiding place in the house of Zofia and Jozef Regula, where they stayed until the liberation. Rena recalled that "the Regulas were first paid in dollars and when these ran out, with jewelry. Finally, no jewelry was left and my mother gave them her wedding ring." Ruth remembered that one midsummer Sunday Jozef suggested something very unusual, that they come up from their "bunker" and have a meal in the living room. "So, there we were, sitting with them, frightened of our own shadow. And finally one of them said 'You are free, you can go home. You've been free since yesterday.'" Ruth remembered distinctly that before they left the Regulas, "they made us swear that we would never tell anybody who saved us. They were afraid of people knowing about the money they got from us and of being accused of being Jew-lovers. And so we never ever had anything to do with them afterwards."[99]

Anna Herzog was saved by a Polish priest. The priest, who came from a poor Brzezany family, had studied in a theological seminary before the war, and Grandpa Herzog had helped subsidize him. When the situation of the Jews in the ghetto became desperate, Anna traveled under an assumed Polish name to the village where this priest lived and preached. He was ready to help, and Anna began to play the organ in his church. That's were she met Lech, with whom she fell in love. Before marrying him, Anna was converted to Catholicism by the priest. "I revealed my identity to Lech and he was moved to tears. Lech came from a rather poor mixed Polish-Ukrainian family. His mother told me to consider myself her daughter." Anna, her mother, and her father, not knowing the whereabouts of each other, survived the German occupation and were later reunited. Her mother, too, became a Catholic, and although the father never converted officially, they lived as a devout Catholic family in postwar Poland.[100]

Poldek survived the Holocaust in a very unusual way, serving as a doctor with the Ukrainian nationalist underground, the UPA. "My father went to Lavrovskii, a local Ukrainian physician who worked for the Germans, and he sent me to the village of Koniuchy, north of Brzezany. I spoke Ukrainian fluently and very soon established a good reputation. I used to treat sick peasants not only in Koniuchy but also in Baranowka and Kuropatniki. My patients knew that I was Jewish. I used to do immunization and minor surgery; I pulled teeth and delivered babies."

Poldek became friendly with a man by the name of Chmyr, head of the Ukrainian police in Koniuchy, who was also a member of the UPA. He treated him for typhoid. "This Chmyr became very fond of me and suggested that I work as a doctor for the UPA and made the necessary contacts. I was asked to translate books of basic medicine from Polish and German into Ukrainian and to teach young Ukrainian women to be nurses for the underground. Everybody knew that I was Jewish." Poldek recalled an incident involving one of the Ukrainian women partisans. "This woman, who didn't know how to use a pistol, shot herself in the belly, and they told me to operate. 'I'm not a surgeon,' I told them. 'How can I operate without anesthesia?' But they said 'You operate!' So, I operated. I didn't find the bullet. I couldn't have. It was like finding a needle in a haystack. She died, but they didn't blame me for it. They had so much confidence in me that I not only treated them as patients, I would also sing Ukrainian songs with them, in their choir." When I asked the 82-year-old doctor to sing one of those Ukrainian songs for me, he carried the tune fairly well in his somewhat trembling voice. "'*Oy ne khody Rysiu, tay na vechernytsiu. Luchshe bylo ne khodyty, luchshe bylo ne tuzhyty*' (Don't go, Rysiv, to the party. Better not to go there. Better not to yearn for a sweetheart). I was a good baritone and they made me sing all their nationalist songs." Nevertheless, Poldek was always fearful of being murdered.

In the early spring of 1944, Soviet partisans and paratroopers started showing up in the forests. Some were apprehended by the UPA. One day a man was brought to Poldek and he was told "to cut him open and experiment on him, in order to get some more practice. Without any anesthesia, of course. The UPA officer said 'You do it, or if you don't do it, we'll do it to you.' That was the worst moment in my life. I refused, and I expected the worst. After a day or two the UPA officer said, 'OK, forget about it.' Another time, a wounded SS man who had been captured by the Ukrainians was brought to me and I was asked to treat him. The German was pleading with me and telling me that he had a family and children and didn't want to die. I didn't do it, I didn't lift a finger."

Poldek didn't know for sure where the front line was, but he had been hearing artillery poundings for some time, which then became quiet. He decided that this was the time to defect. "I had to get away from them. I didn't care if I died. I just had to run away." He somehow was able to return to Brzezany, where he met Dr. Wagszal. "Dr. Wagszal and his wife, Pepka, were concerned about me and told me that some Ukrainian peasants had inquired about my whereabouts. I suspected that the UPA was after me and, with Wagszal's assistance, I succeeded in leaving Brzezany."[101]

Zbigniew Rusinski claimed that there was an organized effort by the illegal Polish Scouts underground in Brzezany to supply food to the ghetto. He himself was wounded by a Ukrainian policeman during such an attempt and was treated by Dr. Pomeranz. After a few days of convalescing inside the ghetto, Rusinski was wrapped in sheets and loaded onto a cart with corpses. "My bare feet, whitened by chalk, were sticking out from underneath the bodies. When the cart reached Okopisko some people were waiting for me there. They took me to my family, and within hours I was on a bus to Lwow."[102]

The Drobnicki sisters, Maria, Zofia, and Rozalia, hid Jews at one time or another. Nusia, Maria's daughter, was a teenager during the war. Her mother, a widow, was living with her three children near the village of Posuchow, south of Brzezany. Nusia recounted those times in her belated memoirs. "Our farm was on the edge of the forest, quite distant from other houses. We built a hiding place for six persons underneath one of the rooms. My mother contacted a relative, Karol Codogni, who was friendly with Jews in Brzezany, and offered the hiding place to a Jewish pharmacist, the richest Jew in town. However, nothing came of it. Instead, we ended up hiding Mrs. Roza Goldman and her daughter Bela. Mrs. Goldman's husband and son had gone to Palestine before the war." At a certain point in time, Maria and Nusia told the Goldman women that they could not keep them anymore. "They fell to their knees and wept. Bela despaired that she would never live to see her father and brother again. Mrs. Goldman begged and promised that after the war she would give my mother half of their family house in Brzezany. This pledge was written down on a piece of paper which my mother kept till the end of her life." Nusia told Karol Codogni years later that the Goldman women also threatened that they would turn her mother in to the Germans if she forced them to leave.

Besides Roza and Bela Goldman, Maria and Nusia Drobnicki hid two Jewish men during the last few months of the German occupation. One of them was young and attractive. His name was Sanek Goldberg. Nusia recalled that "there was a lot of bickering among the Jews. My mother and the two Jewish women were against the idea of keeping these men. I liked that young Sanek Goldberg very much. He would certainly have been killed wandering in the woods." All four survived, hidden by the Drobnickis. Years later, Nusia remarked in her memoirs that "Sanek could have arranged for me the Medal for the Righteous. This would have been proof that my wartime stories were true."

Nusia's Aunt Zofia and her husband, Jozef Regula, hid the Wanderer family. "There was a father, a mother, and two daughters. The name of one of them was Ruth. I heard that they had settled in the U.S. I assume that they would agree to apply for the Righteous Gentile Medal for us. Perhaps this could be arranged by the two girls, who should be middle-aged women by now." Nusia's Aunt Rozalia, and her husband, Wladyslaw Regula, hid a number of Jews at different times. Among them was Rozka Majblum. Nusia presented a "saviors statistics" in her memoirs and calculated that every tenth Jewish survivor in Brzezany was saved by the Drobnickis.[103]

Zofia Sniadecka was an exceptional young Polish woman. She was 28 when the Germans occupied Brzezany. A teacher by profession, she was active in a number of Polish organizations in prewar Brzezany. She was recruited by the Polish underground following the Soviet occupation in the fall of 1939. During the German occupation Zofia worked for a German firm and became increasingly involved in assisting Jews. She was particularly active in smuggling out Jewish children from the Brzezany ghetto and finding them foster homes with Polish families.

The persecution of the Jews in Brzezany had a deep effect on Zofia. In her deposition to Yad Vashem, she described a nightmarish scene which she witnessed at the Brzezany lake, the Staw. "The Germans were chasing a group of Jews of all ages, shooting at them. They made them run into the water. People were drowning. Those who managed to climb back to the bank were mercilessly beaten. I'll never forget it. From that time on, my apartment turned into a shelter. At first, I was extremely scared, and that fear almost paralyzed me, but gradually I started to gain confidence and strength. I felt compassion for these people, especially for the children. I decided that I had to be strong. People needed me."

Among those who were assisted by Zofia was Emil Orenstein, a young Jewish dentist from Brzezany, whose wife had died before the war. Zofia found a Polish foster family for his 5-year-old son and a shelter for Orenstein's sister and husband. After liberation, Zofia married Orenstein, who converted to Catholicism. All in all, Zofia Sniadecka aided in the survival of eleven Jews and helped on various occasions additional Jews who didn't survive. She received her Righteous Gentile award in 1986.

During the last years of her life, Zofia was a broken person. Her Polish family never understood her deeds. Jewish survivors, including her own husband, didn't appreciate what she'd done for them. In a letter to Yad Vashem, she wrote "My family disowned me. Not even a single Jew remembers me now. I died time and again with your martyred people and will never forget those terrible times. I'm writing this letter and crying. I've ceased to believe in both people and God." Zofia died, a bitter and lonely woman, at the age of 83.[104]

Although Ukrainian assistance to Brzezany Jews was quite rare, there were a few such cases. Rozka Majblum and her mother hid in Dr. Bemko's house during one of the roundups. They were friendly with his sister, Mrs. Parasie-wiczowa. They were hiding there again, for a short while, during the last roundup in June 1943.[105] Ivan Hrabar recalled how he helped his father deliver food from their farm in Posuchow to a Jewish woman in Brzezany. Her father had been friendly with Ivan's father before the war.[106] Vasyl Oleskiw recalled how he and some of the Ukrainian Gimnazjum students gave bread to Jews who worked near the Ukrainian dormitory.[107] Then, of course, there was Tanka Kontsevych from the village of Raj.

There is a significant discrepancy between what actually happened and the prevailing opinions among Ukrainians from Brzezany and the nearby villages concerning Ukrainians' assistance to Jews. Vasyl Fanga, from Szy-balin, maintained that "Ukrainians cursed the Germans for murdering in-nocent people. Most of them were decent people. Of course, there may be monsters in any family. People used to bring food to the ghetto to help out the suffering Jews."[108] Ivan Fanga, also from Szybalin, was convinced that "numerous Jews served in the UPA as doctors, nurses and dentists. Many Jews were hiding even in our own village."[109] Lev Rega stated unequivocally that "we had clear instructions in the UPA not to fight against the Jews. There was no outright hatred of Jews. Many Ukrainians sympathized with them."[110] Dmytro Bartkiw, from Kotow, had a slightly different view of Ukrai-nian-Jewish relations. "I was thinking why local people didn't save more Jews. They didn't fraternize with the locals before the war, so that when bad times arrived, there was nobody to turn to. It was terrible."[111]

Poles and Ukrainians from Brzezany and the countryside recalled Polish-Ukrainian tensions and acts of violence. Tolek Rapf recalled that the Polish underground around Brzezany was concerned mainly with self-defense against the UPA. "They used to attack a Polish village and murder everybody. But it's not only that. They tortured and massacred. They thrived on it." Some of Tolek's closest friends were killed by Ukrainians.[112] Irena remem-bered Ukrainian acts of terror in the villages around Brzezany. She used to help out at that time in the local hospital, headed by Dr. Bilinski, and saw the victims at close range. "Those Poles who succeeded in escaping the Ukraini-ans would arrive in town from the nearby villages early in the morning. Some of them had lost a hand, some had their breasts or noses cut off. We young girls cut old linen into strips and used them to bandage the wounds."[113]

Dr. Bilinski, the most outstanding Polish personality in wartime Brzezany, was assassinated by a UPA man in early 1944. Tolek recalled his funeral. "Everybody knew that Bilinski was the most important Pole in Brzezany. All Polish Brzezany attended his funeral. This was a rare event during the Ger-man occupation. The casket was draped in Polish national colors. It was followed by a red-and-white wreath representing the Polish community of

the town and by a wreath with a swastika, sent by the Kreishauptmann."
Tolek, a tall young man at that time, was among the first four pallbearers.
"The casket was not mounted on the hearse, as originally planned. It was
passed along and carried all the way to the cemetery."[114] Halszka, Tolek's
younger sister, recalled that "1944 was the worst time. We were afraid when
the Germans started leaving. That's when many Polish families, mainly from
the nearby villages, moved to the Bernardine Cloister. One could see flames
rising around the town almost every night. These were Polish houses set on
fire by the Ukrainians."[115]

Galina Skaskiv spoke of both Polish and Ukrainian atrocities. "My brother
was in the Kholm region. He came back and told us about these horrible
murders, how Poles murdered Ukrainians. They grabbed children by their
feet and threw them against a wall. People told us about a Ukrainian priest
whose throat was cut with a saw. And then came the moment of revenge. I
remember how one day, at noon, some men from our street grabbed scythes,
pitchforks, and axes, and ran out to Polish villages."[116]

There were also somewhat different memories of Polish-Ukrainian relations during the German occupation. Ludka Michorowska continued to be
friendly with some young Brzezany Ukrainians, former Gimnazjum students. "These were mostly older classmates. I even had a Ukrainian boyfriend for a while. One of my Ukrainian acquaintances who was serving in
the local Ukrainian militia helped me when I stood in line for bread."[117]
Oksana Baczynska, the daughter of the Ukrainian priest in Brzezany who
had been friendly with the Rapf girls before the war, maintained friendly
relations in spite of becoming an extreme Ukrainian nationalist. It was
rumored in town that Oksana had warned Dr. Bilinski of a possible UPA
attempt on his life.[118] Lev Rega recalled that after he had been arrested by
the Germans he was approached on one occasion by a Polish prisoner who
wanted to exchange his gold watch for a piece of bread. Lev told him, "Even
though I'm Ukrainian I won't take it. We are both political prisoners. I'll
share it with you."[119]

* * *

The three years of the German occupation of Brzezany affected the lives
and attitudes of the three ethnic communities in different ways. For many
Poles, the arrival of the Germans meant liberation from the hated Bolshevik
regime. The German occupation, in spite of the inconveniences of everyday
life, was considered much less traumatic than the preceding Soviet rule.[120]
German anti-Polish terror in eastern Galicia was indeed milder than in
central Poland. Polish attitudes toward the Germans were, therefore, considerably more positive there than in other parts of the country. The affiliation of some local Poles with the German language and culture, which went
back to the Hapsburg times, also had a positive effect. Since the Ukrainians

were seen by the Poles as an immediate threat, and since the Soviets were always perceived as a potential danger, the German threat, by contrast, seemed relatively moderate.

The Poles were quite depressed as they witnessed the elation and triumph of their Ukrainian neighbors during the first weeks of the German occupation. The Polish population in eastern Galicia, Polish peasants in particular, were severely traumatized by increasing Ukrainian acts of terror. Polish narrators laid particular emphasis on Ukrainian cruelty. Some Polish narrators also spoke of immoral Ukrainian attitudes and behavior toward Jews. However, there were also other, more positive, Polish memories.

Polish attitudes toward the Jewish tragedy were not uniform. Poles were often criticized for traditional anti-Semitism, indifference, lack of moral sensitivity, and even outright enmity toward their Jewish neighbors. The separation between the Polish and Jewish communities in prewar Poland is considered by some to have been a major cause of Polish wartime conduct.[121] A recent study revealed that Poles brutally murdered the whole Jewish population of a town a few days after its occupation by the Germans.[122]

German atrocities against Brzezany Jews became imprinted in the memory of their Polish neighbors. Time and again Polish narrators recalled groups of Jews being marched to the Okopisko and the subsequent execution scenes. Some Poles were particularly affected when they recognized familiar faces. Others, however, remembered these sights as spectacles. There was also some ugly and vicious voyeurism and gossip about naked Jewish women identified on their way to the death pit. The close-up view of the plight and killing of the Jewish neighbors created a kind of small-town intimacy in both a moral and an immoral sense.

A number of Brzezany Poles argued that the prevailing Polish attitudes were those of sensitivity, compassion, and assistance. The recollections of surviving Brzezany Jews tell a rather different story. In most cases, the primary motive for assisting Jews was material gain. However, more than once, there was a mixture of greed and compassion. At times romance, love, and sex were intertwined with material expectations. It seems that the most humanitarian motive for rescuing Jews in Brzezany was that of Zofia Sniadecka.

The Ukrainian population, which had been increasingly repressed in prewar Poland and had suffered from Soviet terror in the years 1939 to 1941, greeted the Germans as liberators. Ukrainians pinned high hopes on Hitler for establishing *samostiina Ukraina,* an independent Ukraine. Many Ukrainians considered the Germans to be natural allies. There was also the memory of the First World War and of the preceding Hapsburg times, which associated all things German with civility and culture. Although Ukrainian hopes for independence were not fully realized and everyday life wasn't easy, the Ukrainians were still the most preferred of the three ethnic groups. Frustration and rage followed the discovery of the Ukrainian prisoners who were murdered in Brzezany by the NKVD. Ukrainian narrators vividly remembered those frightful sights in and around Brzezany. The murder of Jews by Ukrainians in Brzezany and elsewhere in eastern Galicia was, perhaps, an act of transferred aggression and punishment by proxy. The hated Bolsheviks disappeared from the scene. The Jews, who were perceived by the Ukrainians to be Soviet collaborators, were there, helpless, fair game for the enraged Ukrainian mob. None of the Ukrainian narrators mentioned the Ukrainian pogrom against Jews in Brzezany.

Like Poles, local Ukrainians witnessed the steadily deteriorating situation of the Jews in Brzezany, the ghettoization, the deportations, and the killings. They seem to have distanced themselves more than the Poles from the suffering Jews. Some of them had personal contacts with Jews at that time. When Ukrainians described Brzezany Jews marching to the Okopisko, they didn't mention their Ukrainian escort. What was usually pointed out was the fact that the Jews didn't resist. A Ukrainian woman spoke of the cunning and cruelty of the Jewish militia toward their fellow Jews.

Almost all Ukrainian narrators claimed that the Ukrainian population was friendly and compassionate toward the Jews.[123] Some narrators maintained that the Ukrainian underground, the UPA, assisted and saved large numbers of Jews. Jewish medical personnel were usually mentioned in this context. Some Ukrainians, such as Lev Rega and Ivan Hrabar, both of whom were arrested and traumatized by the Germans, showed genuine compassion for the Jews. The most perplexing case was that of young Aleksandr Pankiv, who was mistakenly marched to the Okopisko Jewish cemetery and almost killed there as a Jew. In spite of this traumatic experience, he ran to watch the murder of another group of Jews a few weeks later. For him, too, as for other Poles and Ukrainians in Brzezany, the Okopisko executions were a spectacle and a show.

Ukrainian attitudes toward Poles and Jews were shaped to a great extent by the radicalization of Ukrainian nationalism.[124] Prewar frustrations and new wartime realities of terror and violence had a significant impact upon Ukrainian nationalists, particularly the young. Naively, they hoped against hope that Ukrainian independence might come after the war ended. This, in turn, justified ethnic cleansing; that is, getting rid of the local Polish population, which would be achieved through intimidation and terror.

The Jews of Brzezany, both natives and refugees, were almost completely annihilated. Only a few could testify to what had happened there during the Holocaust. Trauma, helplessness, and distrust emerged in the narrations of Brzezany survivors. They usually viewed their Polish and Ukrainian neighbors as indifferent bystanders, at the least. At the same time, Brzezany Jews used their sense of ingenuity and persistence to try to save their own lives and those closest to them.

An overwhelming sense of loss in a personal and community sense usually excluded any compassion for the plight of their neighbors, the Poles and the Ukrainians. Still, there were a few positive comments. Ruth Wanderer was willing and able to tell how a German soldier saved her grandfather from Ukrainian thugs. The overall message of Poldek, the young Jewish doctor, was undoubtedly about Ukrainian cruelty and anti-Semitism. But his memory also registered some moments of togetherness and intimacy. Dr. Lipa Wagszal disclosed a sentimental memory of Anna, the Polish nurse. There was also the exceptional and unusual story of Anna Herzog, the convert. She would carry a parallel, and at times conflicting, Jewish and Polish identity throughout her life.

German memories, unlike the interviews with Poles, Jews, and Ukrainians, were culled from legal and judicial documentation and were, apparently, manipulated and distorted. Still, some genuine attitudes and responses as well as a certain measure of authenticity could be discerned. The Germans lived in Brzezany within their own microcommunity, making their lives as comfortable as possible, often at the expense of the locals. Kreishauptmann Asbach, not unlike a provincial governor of a mighty empire, appropriated the best villa in town for himself as well as an estate in the country. He drove cars and rode horses and attempted to realize his grand architectural dreams in Brzezany. He, as well as other German bureaucrats and members of their families, could speak German with quite a number of the local middle class and intelligentsia, whether they were Poles, Jews, or Ukrainians. Mund, head of the Unduetsch firm, lived in Dr. Bilinski's house and was very friendly with the doctor. The Brzezany branch of Unduetsch was an "enclave" of unusually friendly German-Polish relations. Mund cared for both his Polish and Jewish employees.

Most of the Germans who lived and worked in Brzezany denied and repressed recollections concerning Jews. Asbach consistently denied any direct linkage to anti-Jewish measures. He distinctly separated his administrative functions from the German Security Police's actions against Jews. He attempted to draw an almost idyllic picture of a normal town, where for most of the time the three local ethnic communities lived peacefully together. Mund clearly recalled the plight of the Jews. But even Mund, like some Polish and Ukrainian narrators, couldn't understand why "Jews didn't resist." Like Poles and Ukrainians, he couldn't identify with Jewish solitude and helplessness. There was also the VoMi man Hubert Kohnen, who was vividly remembered by both Poles and Jews. He could be friendly and charming at one time, greedy and deadly dangerous at another.

Then there were the professional killers from Tarnopol, such as Mueller and Herrmann. Both submitted detailed and matter-of-fact descriptions of the executions. Mueller perceived himself as a "humane" killer. He never forced his victims to dig their own graves and made sure that they were shot instantly. Willi Herrmann, who was always immaculately dressed, a white scarf tucked in the front of his SS uniform, argued that the killing scenes touched him deeply and made him feel miserable.[125]

The German occupation of Brzezany resulted in a total transformation of the town and in a radicalization of people's attitudes. The Jewish community ceased to exist. The few Jewish survivors and those Brzezany Jews who emigrated before the war whose families were murdered remained permanently scarred by the trauma of the Holocaust. Many would harbor accusatory feelings not only toward the German perpetrators but also toward their neighbors, the Ukrainians and the Poles. Tensions which existed in the prewar years between Poles and Ukrainians would create an unbridgeable chasm in the wake of wartime terror and murder. Poles would tend to remember the atrocities perpetrated by the UPA. Ukrainians, those who remained in and around Brzezany as well as those who left for the West, would harbor a feeling of disappointment and victimization, which was augmented by Ukrainian suffering under the Soviet regime after the war.

FIGURE 26.   Identification of exhumed remains of prisoners executed by the NKVD in Brzezany in June 1941. October 1941. Courtesy of Zbigniew Rusinski.

FIGURE 27.   Slowackiego Street, renamed Poststrasse during the German occupation of Brzezany. On the far left: the prewar Brzezany county office building. On the right: the prewar savings bank building, which served as Wehrmacht headquarters during the German occupation. On the left, more distant: the post office building.

FIGURE 28.
(above, left) SS Scharfuehrer Willi
Herrmann, 1941. Courtesy of Yad
Vashem Archives, Jerusalem.

FIGURE 29.
(above, right) Hubert Kohnen, VoMi
representative in Brzezany.
Courtesy of Bundesarchiv, Berlin.

FIGURE 30.
(left) Herr Mund, director of
Unduetsch. Courtesy of Yad
Vashem Archives, Jerusalem.

FIGURE 31.   The funeral of Dr. Stefan Bilinski, February 1944. First on the left: Tolek Rapf. Courtesy of Tolek Rapf.

FIGURE 32.   Okopisko, 1991.

FIGURE 33. Monument to fallen Red Army soldiers on the edge
of the Christian cemetery, on the way to Raj.

FIGURE 34.   Monument to fallen UPA partisans, facing the Red Army monument.

6

THE AFTERMATH, 1944–1945

We returned to Brzezany from Raj in the summer of 1944 and left the town a year later. Although I whispered and limped for weeks as a result of our living in small and crowded hideouts, I have quite cheerful memories of that last year in Brzezany. I do not recall any sadness. Most of my family, including my father, were no more, but their absence didn't seem to bother me too much. I just didn't think about them. And if the memory of my father did occur from time to time, during that first year after the liberation as well as in the subsequent years of my adolescence, I hoped that he would somehow reappear.

Those few Brzezany Jews who survived lived in the center of town. There was a group of children of various ages. My closest friends were Matus, the son of Dr. Wagszal, and his older cousin Marek. There were also Manek Thaler and Rena, Munio's younger sister. We played and spoke with each other for hours on end in the courtyards. The Wagszals gave Matus a small dog and named him Herut, Hebrew for freedom. We ran around for hours with that dog. In the afternoons we used to sit on a bench in between the Ratusz and the Ukrainian Church. A whole upper-floor wall of the Ratusz building was covered with a huge painting, which I recall in detail even now. Three soldiers wearing their distinctive helmets and uniforms stood side by side: the Russian, the British, and the American. Three flags fluttered in the background.

We boys were fascinated by the Red Army soldiers. Marek recently reminded me of how we used to walk to the army encampments that were scattered around town. The soldiers must have taught us those popular Soviet wartime tunes, which were incessantly repeated on the loudspeakers. Ever since then I have had a sentimental weak spot for such songs as "Katiusha," "Tiomnaya noch'," and "Ogoniok." There were also impressive daily announcements about the advancement of the Soviet Army and its occupation of various cities along the route to Berlin.

I vaguely recall the school. I was accepted into the third grade, though I had never attended the first two. My first tutor was Grandpa Fishl, who taught me to read and write Polish during those long months of hiding. After a few months at school, my Russian exceeded that of our Polish teacher. The closest friend I had at school was a Polish boy, Bolek Teperowicz. I visited him quite often and we used to play in the garden outside his house. The most dramatic event I recall from my visits there was the premeditated "execution" of a frog, which was pushed into a glass jar. We bombarded the jar with stones until the poor animal froze. When I was again in Brzezany decades later, I tried to find Teperowicz. And there was indeed a Bolek Teperowicz, who lived in a small, dilapidated house with some grass around it. The man had recently had brain surgery and was hardly coherent. The house and the man depressed me. Could that have been my friend when we were boys of 9 and 10? Could that have been the garden where we "massacred" that frog?

I must have been a voracious reader of books. I recall pleasant walks to a lending library on the outskirts of Brzezany. I also used to visit very often a small Russian bookstore on the way to the Farny Church. It offered all kinds of pamphlets about Russian generals and marshals. Marek Glazer recalled that on one occasion while we waited for our shoes to be mended in a shoemakers' workshop, I read aloud from a book to the shoemakers. In a letter written years later by Mrs. Freundlich, who had worked as a librarian in the Brzezany library, to Pepka, Dr. Wagszal's wife, she mentioned "little Szymek Redlich, five years old, who used to borrow books written in four languages, Polish, Ukrainian, Russian, and Yiddish. He not only read those books, but actually devoured them. He used to come daily to our library. We suspected that he wasn't really reading those books and demanded that he report on their contents, which he did, in great detail." I was 9 at the time, but I might have looked like 5 or 6. I also doubt whether I could read books in Yiddish or Ukrainian. Mrs. Freundlich must have exaggerated.

The most dramatic event in Brzezany during that single year after liberation was the hanging of a man. It was winter. I stood near a window facing the Rynek. With me in that room were several people. One of them was Bela, Natan's sister, who sat at the piano. Out there, in the far end of the Rynek was a small crowd. It was snowing. A truck appeared and stopped in the middle of the crowd. On its platform were a few people. One of them seemed to read something from a piece of paper. After a few minutes the truck moved with those standing on the platform. Except one. That man remained, hanging, his body dangling from side to side. Bela was playing Chopin's mourning march. I was told that the man who was hanged was a banderovits, a Ukrainian nationalist. People were talking about atrocities committed by the banderovtsi against the Soviets.

I remembered for years the military funerals in liberated Brzezany. I must have watched with fascination the marching soldiers, their uniforms, the band, and most of all, the open Soviet-style caskets with the upper part of the body and face of the deceased in full view. There were also wreaths and

*flowers. After a short ceremony, they were interred in graves dug beforehand, in
a small square just outside the Ratusz. The slim, cone-shaped tombstones
erected later on top of these graves had a red star on their top. Beautiful,
aromatic flowers, mostly violets, were grown at their feet. I can still smell their
scent. When I returned to Brzezany, I was eager to find the site, but it had just
disappeared. I was told later that this "minute cemetery" of the fallen Soviet
soldiers was moved to another place.*

*We spent the last few weeks before leaving Brzezany camping in the open air
along the railroad station in Potutory. It was very hot. People gathered in
groups and talked. Kids played and had a good time. It was like vacation.
Finally, we were loaded, with our meager belongings, on an open freight train.
It would be forty-six years before I saw Brzezany again.*

As a result of the Teheran, Yalta, and Potsdam agreements concerning the
borders of postwar Poland, eastern Galicia became part of the Soviet Ukrainian Republic. This had fateful and far-reaching effects on the local population, which, after the mass murder of the Jews, consisted mainly of Ukrainians
and Poles. The Ukrainians, beginning in the summer of 1944, went through
a process of forced re-Sovietization. The majority of the Poles left eastern
Galicia within two to three years and resettled in the so-called "recovered
territories" in southwest Poland. The few Jewish survivors joined the Poles in
their westward trek.

The Soviets, who resumed ruling Western Ukraine in the course of the
spring and summer of 1944, sought to bring the local population into confor-
mity with the Soviet system. The arrival of the Red Army reminded many
Ukrainians of the traumatic encounter of 1939–1941. They were mostly antagonistic, and the Soviets now faced a substantial and well-armed Ukrainian
underground that was popular with the masses. The peasants were terrified by
the prospect of collectivization. Most of the Ukrainian youth and the local
Ukrainian intelligentsia who did not escape westward were committed to
Ukrainian nationalism and considered the Soviet Union to be its greatest
enemy. The three years of German rule, in spite of hardship and suffering,
were a time of relative ideological and cultural flexibility for the Ukrainians.
The change, as far as they were concerned, was definitely for the worse.[1]

Ukrainian cultural organizations and associations, which had been allowed to function under German rule, were disbanded. Ukrainians, who
held various administrative positions during the German occupation, were
considered disloyal. Ukrainians from the Soviet part of Ukraine as well as
ethnic Russians were appointed to most of the administrative and Party
posts. Assignment to Western Ukraine was regarded as highly desirable,
since in terms of consumer goods it compared favorably with the rest of the
war-ravished Soviet Union.

A most significant stronghold of Ukrainian national identity, the Greek Catholic Uniate Church, was, in fact, liquidated. The Soviet authorities displayed a rather tolerant attitude toward the Church during the first months of the reoccupation of Western Ukraine. However, after the Yalta Conference recognized the Soviet annexation of the region in early 1945 and with the imminent Soviet victory over Germany, a full-fledged campaign against the Uniate Church was launched in March of that year. Metropolitan Sheptyts'kyi, the revered head of the Church, had died a few months earlier. The authorities began instituting Soviet laws regarding religion. Uniate priests were cajoled and forced to convert to Russian Orthodoxy, the only official and collaborative Christian church in the Soviet Union. Greek Catholic priests were arrested, and St. George's complex, the seat of the Uniate metropoly, was raided in April 1945. The Ukrainian Uniate Church, at least officially, ceased to exist.[2]

The Soviets, who were at war with Germany until the spring of 1945 and were drained of material and human resources, faced a most complex and at times frustrating situation. Their effort to pacify and administer the newly conquered West Ukrainian territories faced serious obstacles. Ukrainian teenagers and young adults took to the forests by the thousands. Evading mobilization into the Red Army, they either joined the UPA underground or formed marauding bandit groups. Numerous peasant households had dugouts, which were stockpiled with food, weapons, and ammunition. The cities and towns were in Soviet hands, but the villages and the forests were mostly UPA territory or no-man's land. The UPA staged attacks designed to interfere with the ongoing Sovietization. They specially targeted the Soviet security apparatus and those who collaborated with the Soviets. Soviet security and military forces staged blockades of UPA enclaves and attempted to infiltrate the Ukrainian underground. For a number of years it was nearly impossible to wipe out the Ukrainian resistance.[3]

The Soviets conducted numerous punitive campaigns against the UPA throughout Western Ukraine in the early months of 1945. In less than two months, in January and February of that year, 11,000 UPA men were killed. One way to scare off the local Ukrainian population and discourage it from joining and supporting the underground was to publicly execute *banderovtsi*. A report of the Drohobych Regional Communist Party Committee spoke of a public hanging. "On January 9, 1945 two members of the UPA were hanged in the market square following a sentence by the Military Tribunal. Close to 8,000 people were present at the execution. The hanging was greeted by loud applause. It is assumed that up to 20 active members of nationalist bands will be sentenced and executed by hanging in various towns of the region." The hanging of the UPA man in the Brzezany Rynek must have been part of this campaign.[4]

144

The number of victims on both sides, even during the initial stage of the confrontation in the years 1944–1945, was vast. According to one estimate, the Ukrainian underground had killed more than 30,000 Soviet soldiers, security personnel, and local collaborators by the end of 1945. The scale of the Soviet repression was even more staggering. More than 90,000 Ukrainians were killed by the Soviet security forces through the summer of 1945. More than 10,000 Ukrainian families were deported. Increasing wide-scale deportations adversely affected the base of support enjoyed by the Ukrainian underground. Close to half a million West Ukrainians would be deported to the Soviet interior before the end of the decade.[5]

The ongoing struggle between the Soviets and the Ukrainian underground abounded in mutual atrocities. Particularly ruthless and atrocious acts of violence were performed by the Ukrainian underground. UPA instructions spoke of explicit procedures for executions. The violation of corpses was a common occurrence. Corpses were stripped of shoes and clothing, heads were severed, faces were cut to pieces. The most severe violence and violations were reserved for the "outsiders," Soviet military and security personnel, as well as for local "traitors." Harsh terrorist methods were used against their families.[6]

One of the means used by the Soviets to suppress the Ukrainian underground, mostly in the early phase of the reoccupation of Western Ukraine, when Soviet manpower was still needed for the war effort, was the *istrebitelnye batalliony*, the "destruction battalions." They consisted, usually, of local young and middle-aged people who were not fit for regular army service and were headed by Soviet security officers. More than 200 such "battalions" were active in early 1945. They consisted mainly of Poles, who considered their somewhat strange new status as Soviet "policemen" to be useful for the protection of the local Polish population as well as for taking revenge on the UPA. The Soviets, though fully aware of anti-Soviet attitudes common among the Poles, considered them to be a convenient and necessary, if only temporary, "ally" in their war against a mutual enemy, the Ukrainian nationalist underground.[7] The "destruction battalions" in the Tarnopol region in early 1945 consisted of more than 4,000 people—Poles, Ukrainians, and Russians. The Poles formed close to 60 percent.[8]

Polish-Ukrainian relations didn't improve after the Soviet reoccupation of Western Ukraine. Poles and Ukrainians had mutually exclusive claims on the region and nourished conflicting hopes for its future. The former would have liked to believe that prewar eastern Galicia would be part of postwar Poland; the latter were toying with the idea that international politics would bring about Ukrainian independence. Tensions, enmity, and mutual killings continued. The fall of 1944 and the spring of 1945 witnessed large-scale anti-Polish assaults by the Ukrainian underground. The number of Polish victims in the Tarnopol region was particularly high.[9] Estimates of the number of Poles killed by the UPA in the course of both the German and the Soviet occupation range from tens to hundreds of thousands.[10]

Relations between the Soviet regime and the Polish population in the former Polish eastern borderlands, which turned now into Soviet Western Ukraine, were ambivalent. The traumatic events of 1939–1941—the arrests, deportations, and executions—were still fresh in the minds and hearts of the Poles. At the same time, however, local nationalist Ukrainians were their common enemy and the Soviet Union supported the establishment of a postwar Polish state, whose future political nature was still vague. Polish attitudes toward the "liberating" Red Army were a mixture of relief and apprehension. There was a prevailing sense of uncertainty. There were rumors of deportation, either to Poland proper or to Siberia.

Although the Poles hoped that eastern Galicia and its principal city, Lwow, would remain Polish, Stalin's plans were entirely different. Mass arrests of Polish intellectuals and activists of the Polish underground were conducted by the Soviet security forces in Lwow in early 1945. The trial of a group of leading officers of the Polish underground, the AK, was staged in Moscow in the summer of 1945. Life, especially in the Ukrainian-dominated countryside, where the UPA was still going strong, was far from secure. It also became increasingly evident in the course of 1945 that there would be ample space for resettlement in the "recovered territories" that were detached from Germany. Many Poles realized that the only way out was to pack their belongings and board the trains.[11]

It is believed that thousands of Poles left eastern Galicia during the German occupation. At least 100,000 Poles left Western Ukraine even before official Soviet-approved repatriation to Poland commenced. The precondition for official large-scale population movements was an agreement between the Soviets and the Polski Komitet Wolnosci Narodowej (PKWN), the temporary Polish pro-Communist government, which was signed in the fall of 1944. Additional agreements were signed in 1945. In the course of 1945, more than half a million Poles, including Polish Jews, were repatriated from Western Ukraine to Poland. The summer of 1945 was the most intensive period of repatriation. Around 160,000 repatriates left the Tarnopol district, where Brzezany was located, between October 1944 and October 1945. The total number of those who left that district to settle in Poland was more than 200,000. Among them were 5,500 Jews. Ten thousand repatriates had already left the Brzezany region by April 1946. By the end of 1946, close to 800,000 Polish repatriates had left Western Ukraine for Poland. About 30,000 of them were Jews, both Holocaust survivors and those who survived the war inside the Soviet Union. Eastern Galicia, now part of Soviet Western Ukraine, lost significant proportions of its prewar population.[12]

The Jewish population of eastern Galicia was close to 600,000 on the eve of the war. It has been estimated that only 2 percent survived the German occupation. A few thousand east Galician Jews who lived during the war inside Russia, some of whom had been mobilized by the Red Army, started returning to their prewar homes in 1944. Their homes, however, were no more, and their families had perished in the Holocaust. The general mood of the Jewish survivors was one of gloom. Hardly any of them considered staying. While they lived there for a few months after liberation, they didn't feel welcome or wanted. The local population, and especially the nationalist-minded Ukrainians, the Ukrainian underground in particular, was quite hostile. The UPA renewed its claims of Judeo-Bolshevism, accusing the Jews of collaborating with the Soviet administration. The Poles weren't too friendly, either. Even among the Soviet "liberators" there were indications of anti-Semitism. The very fact that some Jews survived was viewed by the Soviets with suspicion. It's no wonder, therefore, that those indigenous Jews who still lived in Western Ukraine in the years 1944–1945, including the few Brzezany survivors, left for Poland. Most of them would eventually emigrate to Israel and North America.[13]

Eastern Galicia, now part of Soviet Western Ukraine, which prior to the Second World War was populated by Poles, Ukrainians, and Jews, was drastically changing its demographic profile. It would soon be populated almost entirely by Ukrainians and Russians, among them numerous newcomers from the Soviet interior. Native east Galicians would barely reach 5 percent of the local population in the 1990s.[14]

* * *

The first Red Army units entered Brzezany in the early hours of July 22, 1944. The town was completely different from what it used to be before the war and during the first Soviet occupation of 1939–1941. Its population had shrunk to a few thousand. Part of it lay in ruins.

The Polish AK underground, which was active in the vicinity of Brzezany, established immediate contact with the Soviet army, security police, and administration. AK units, wearing red-and-white armbands, marched into town and reported at the local Soviet command on July 23. Following negotiations between AK commanders and the Soviet authorities, some 150 AK men joined the local "destruction battalion." Besides the Poles, there were also a number of Russians and Ukrainians in the Brzezany battalion. The principal motivation of the Poles for joining the battalion was the defense of the local Polish population from the Ukrainian underground. The Brzezany "destruction battalion" participated in close to 100 skirmishes with the UPA in the years 1944–1945. During one such event, in September 1944, the Soviet public prosecutor of the Brzezany region was killed by Ukrainian partisans in the vicinity of Narajow. Some of his Russian and Polish guards were killed as well. Their mutilated corpses, some with fingers and genitals cut off, were brought to town the next day. The Red Army soldiers and officers were buried in the town square, near the Ratusz; the Poles were buried in the Christian cemetery on the way to Raj.[15]

The Soviet-Ukrainian armed conflict that raged throughout Western Ukraine also affected the Brzezany region. Hardly a week passed without people being killed and wounded on all sides. The UPA attacked a Soviet unit in the village of Troscianiec, south of Brzezany, on August 11, 1944. A retaliatory action was conducted in Troscianiec by Soviet security forces, including the "destruction battalion" from Brzezany, two weeks later. Some of the local Ukrainian peasants were beaten and wounded, mostly by Polish *strebki*.[16] The Ukrainian underground attacked Polish households in the village of Kurzany, southwest of Brzezany, on August 12, 1944. Twenty Polish peasants were killed, including children. Seventy Polish households went up in flames. A number of Poles who were working in the Soviet administration were apprehended and murdered. Soviet security conducted an extensive punitive campaign in the Brzezany region in September 1944. Numerous Ukrainian village households were burned and destroyed. Another Soviet effort to wipe out the UPA, known as the Khrushchev campaign, was conducted in the spring of 1945. One of the fiercest battles took place in the Troscianiec Forest.[17]

The Polish population of Brzezany, which enjoyed a certain amount of security in view of the mostly Polish local "destruction battalion," wasn't sure of its future. Like Poles throughout Soviet-occupied Western Ukraine, they hoped that their region would eventually become part of postwar Poland. However, most of them soon realized that the uprooting from their native places, as difficult and traumatic as it was, and their westward repatriation to the "recovered territories" in Poland was preferable to life in Soviet Ukraine.

The few remaining Brzezany Jews lived in the shadow of their immense loss. The Okopisko cemetery, with its mass graves, reminded them day by day of the fact that Jewish Brzezany was no more. A "Special State Commission" founded by the Soviet government to investigate Nazi crimes cooperated with numerous local committees that had been established in the territories liberated by the Red Army. The Brzezany Committee, established in October 1944, compiled its report in the early summer of 1945. A major part of the report dealt with the Okopisko executions. One of its fifteen signatories, the only Jew among them, was Dr. Lipa Gershovich Wagszal. The report, drafted in official Soviet phraseology of the period, spoke of the 16,000 Jews who were killed and buried on the grounds of the Okopisko cemetery. Another 600 Jews were killed and buried near the village of Litiatyn. Among the German executioners mentioned in the report were Hubert and Herrmann. At one point all committee members, including some local witnesses to the executions, visited the Okopisko site. The report concluded that "there were 6 larger and 15 smaller pits. One of them was 20 meters long, 3 meters wide and more than 3 meters deep. The length of the remaining pits ranged from 20 to 12 meters."

Stanislaw Sawczak, the Polish man who had been in charge of the Christian cemetery in Brzezany before the war, during the war, and after the Soviet reoccupation, told the committee that about 12,000 Jews were buried in the Okopisko cemetery and that none of the local population participated in the killings. The executions, according to Sawczak, were conducted solely by the German Criminal Police, the Kripo. "Among them were Herrmann—the man in charge, his deputy—Mueller—Zipprich, and Hubert, who [was] used to finish off the Jews."[18]

Most of the local Poles, as well as the few Jewish survivors, left Brzezany in the course of 1945. Since the railroad tracks leading to Brzezany had been destroyed by the Germans before the arrival of the Soviets, they boarded the freight trains in Potutory with all their belongings, including cows and goats. An eyewitness recalled that "near the Potutory railway station, in an open field, we built huts out of boards and tree branches. That's where we settled and waited for the train. We didn't know where we were going, we weren't sure at all of the future. We camped for almost a month, with the smoke of the campfires getting constantly into our eyes and the hungry cattle bellowing all the time."[19]

* * *

Dr. Lipa Wagszal started writing his wartime memoirs on the train to Poland. He recalled that day a year earlier, in July 1944, when, with his wife and little Matus, who was wearing dirty rags, they had returned to Brzezany. "We settled as far from the ghetto area as we could. We didn't even look in that direction. Our only wish was to distance ourselves from that frightful place." Lipa was fearful of the local population as well as of the returning Soviets. His gut feeling was that both disliked Jews. He himself had been ordered several times to the local NKVD and Narodnyi Komissariat Gosudarstrennoi Bezopasnosti (NKGB, People's Commissariat of State Security) offices. Their most persistent questioning concerned his survival during the German occupation. They suspected him of collaboration. "We hoped for the moment when we could get away from our hometown and from our anti-Semitic neighbors. Life in Brzezany was sad. People were depressed. Most of the town was ruined and dirty. The stores were closed and the streets were completely dark in the evenings. Unpleasant memories and fears were in the air." Lipa recalled that the small Jewish community of survivors used to pray in one of the apartments. None of the numerous prewar Jewish prayer houses existed anymore. The only place left intact, the Large Synagogue, was turned into a grain depot. Nevertheless, there were some joyful moments. "Some of the young people who survived the war in Russia, including those who served in the Red Army, started returning. Some of them decided to get married, and we prepared the weddings."[20]

When I met a few years ago with some Brzezany survivors, most of whom were women in their 70s and 80s, their reminiscing about postwar Brzezany centered on these strange weddings. Mania's wedding was the first Jewish wedding in Brzezany after the liberation. She married Itschie Nadler in March 1945. She was 21. Most of her family, including her parents, had been killed. Itschie was 35, and he had been married before the war. His wife and 4-year-old son had apparently perished in Belzec. Mania recalled, "When I left the hideout I weighed 35 kilograms. I was very sick and almost died. They called for a Soviet army doctor who happened to be Jewish. I'll never forget him. He was very good-looking, like Robert Taylor. He spoke Yiddish and took good care of me. He even gave me 500 rubles, which was a lot of money at that time, and he wanted to marry me." Mania married Itschie Nadler in Wanderer's apartment. "Wanderer was like a father to me. Unbelievable. He sat with me during those hours before the wedding when I had to fast and talked with me about those terrible times, about our lost families. Then they brought in food and drinks."

Rachel was the only bride whose parents survived. She married in May. "The wedding was in our apartment, on Kolejowa. I wore a pink dress. The dress was kept, with some other of our family's belongings, by my father's prewar customer, Zuczkowski, who used to work as a warden in the Brzezany prison. The Jewish women prepared the food, mostly fish. It was impossible to get kosher meat. Everything was *kedat ukdin*. The *huppa* and everything else. It was a real *simhe*. We were like one big family."[21]

Every interviewee who was in Brzezany at that time remembered the hanging in the Rynek. Zbigniew Zuczkowski was 15 and attended the Brzezany Soviet high school. "The whole school was ordered to go and watch the execution. We stood down there, in the Rynek. I was standing right there, about fifty meters from that place. The man had a board attached to his chest, with his name on it, Ivan Lev. There was a rumor that when he was caught he had a trophy on him, fifty-three human ears, cut off the heads of those whom he killed, apparently Russians and Poles. A huge Studebaker truck stopped in the middle of the Rynek. On its open deck, close to the edge, stood a man who was surrounded by a number of elegantly dressed NKVD officers wearing white fur jackets. The Russian judge read out the verdict and commanded the truck to move on. The car moved and the man remained hanging. His body swayed back and forth. It remained there for two days."[22]

Karol Codogni was also in that crowd, watching the execution. He recalled that the man was hanged directly opposite our prewar cloth store. "He remained there, hanging, a couple of days. As he was hanged, he must have urinated, and there was this icicle hanging down his pants." Karol also remembered corpses of Ukrainian UPA men displayed on Slowacki Street. "They used to bring them in the morning and set them against the wall. Then some peasant women would arrive from nearby villages and identify the bodies. There was a lot of yelling. The Soviets wanted both to frighten the Ukrainians and get the families and relatives of the killed. Many were then deported to Siberia."[23]

Ivan Fanga, from Szybalin, recalled the Red Army "liberation" as a nightmare. He was at that time a member of the UPA. "There they were, the NKVD, the Polish *strebki*, our own traitors who collaborated with the Bolsheviks. That immense force fought against us. We had many dead and wounded. Weapons and munitions became scarce. We moved from one encirclement to another and there was no end to the battles." Ivan became sick with typhoid and was eventually arrested by the Soviets. "They tried and sentenced me in Brzezany and I faced execution. I spent about two weeks in the 'death cell.' One Sunday they took the three of us, tied us with ropes, and led us out of the prison. People had just left the church, and a whole bunch of them started following us. Suddenly I saw my mother in that crowd. She tried to hand me some milk, but one of the soldiers hit her over the head and she fell down. The milk spilled on the pavement. People helped her to get up. She had blood all over her face."

Ivan and the other two Ukrainian prisoners were marched in the direction of the cemetery. "As we stood close to this huge pit, prepared in advance, I saw a number of horse carts filled with corpses. On each cart there was an NKVD man. Some of them rode horses. Polish *strebki* started to unload the corpses and lay them down along the pit." Ivan was sure that he would be executed right there. "I was hit over the head and lost consciousness. Then I heard somebody yelling 'Stop it, stop it, take them back.' The three of us were taken back to the prison cellar. Our death sentence was commuted to twenty years of labor camps in the remote regions of the Soviet Union." Ivan Fanga was imprisoned for the next twelve years in Vorkuta.[24]

* * *

The immediate "post-liberation" years were a time of instability and upheaval in Western Ukraine. The Ukrainians suffered the most. For many of them, the war still continued. It was waged now by a formidable enemy, Stalin's victorious Russia. The Ukrainian nationalist underground fought ferociously, taking terrible revenge. Violence, atrocities, and the violation of corpses were quite common. The Soviets consistently terrorized their real and potential Ukrainian opponents. Those postwar years of suffering would turn into a traumatic memory for many West Ukrainians. At the same time, however, the memory of a sustained armed resistance against all odds and acts of hopeless sacrifice and valor would become a major component of their national identity. The mourning and admiration for the fallen UPA fighters would only become public and official in the nineties, following Ukraine's independence.

The Poles would remember the disappointment and frustration of losing their eastern borderlands, the Kresy, and becoming part of the Soviet empire. Brzezany Poles, like their compatriots from all over Western Ukraine, would bear in their minds and hearts the tragedy of uprooting from native land and landscape. The Ukrainian-Polish conflict, which continued throughout the "post-liberation" period, would leave deep scars of animosity and mistrust on both sides of the new borderline for a long time.

The few surviving Jews, overwhelmed by their tragedy and loss, considered 1944–1945 to be a time of transition. Still, there was occasionally a feeling of revival and continuity. There were some happy moments, such as those Jewish weddings. The small communities of survivors in various towns, including Brzezany, sensed a strong bond, a kind of togetherness. Child survivors were considered to be walking miracles. They were everybody's children. People wanted to leave the ghost towns, the cemeteries, and the sites of execution as soon as they could. They had a strong urge to move to places where there was a chance to live within some sort of a Jewish community. Some would stay for a number of years in postwar Poland. Others would move on to points of departure, mostly in West Germany, on their way to Israel and North America.

7

THEIR RETURN

My return to Brzezany was part of a wider trend, the return of people to their birthplaces throughout Eastern Europe. Although some visits by Poles, Jews, Ukrainians, and others to their hometowns had occurred in the years since the end of the Second World War, these pilgrimages to the past became frequent only after the collapse of communism. The forty-odd years of closed borders and inaccessible sites turned people's birthplaces into something remote, an imaginary world of magic, dreams, and nightmares. Feelings and attitudes toward these places were diverse. For decades, Poles and Ukrainians saw their native lands ruled by hated Communist governments. Jewish survivors and Jews originating from these areas were deeply affected by the trauma of the Holocaust. Their feelings about it were directed not only toward the Germans but also toward the Jews' former Polish and Ukrainian neighbors. Since Eastern Europe was for many both a birthplace where normal and happy lives were once lived and the site of suffering and tragedy, common human nostalgia assumed a very unique and conflicting quality. People felt simultaneously attracted and repelled. In spite of their tragedies and losses, Poles, Jews, and Ukrainians who left their birthplaces maintained and nurtured idealized and mythologized images of a "native homeland" that was associated mostly with the prewar years. These images were usually linked to their childhood and adolescence.

Although each of the three Brzezany diasporas acted in a similar manner to preserve memories, their acts were always inner-oriented. The Brzezany Ukrainian memorial book that was published in the U.S. and the Brzezany Jewish memorial book that was published in Israel are a case in point.[1] Postwar reunions of former Brzezanyites were exclusively mono-ethnic. No group was even aware that the other groups had founded their particular organizations and met from time to time. It seemed as if the war and the conflicts among Poles, Ukrainians, and Jews and their different tragic fates prevented any kind of common memory. People who once lived close to each other and had relations with their neighbors became completely separated. The act of returning to Brzezany was also separate. Each group tended to return to its specific sites from its own particular past, not to the common past of Brzezany. But there were some exceptions.

* * *

One of the first Poles to return was Ryszard Brzezinski. His parents were married in Brzezany after the Soviet reoccupation of the town in 1944, and shortly thereafter they resettled in Poland. Ryszard was born in Gliwice, in Polish Silesia, in early September 1945. In the summer of 1953, a few months after Stalin's death, his grandmother was allowed to visit a brother, one of the few Poles who had stayed in Brzezany. The 8-year-old boy went with her. Following that first journey to Brzezany, Ryszard continued to return for family visits almost every summer. He used to wander around the town looking for interesting things. He became particularly fascinated by the old, half-ruined Sieniawski Castle, where he often searched for "treasures." As he grew older, Ryszard became increasingly interested in the history and memorabilia of Brzezany. He started collecting various Brzezany souvenirs. On one occasion, he found a Jewish Sabbath chandelier in his uncle's house. When I questioned Ryszard about the motivation behind his "Brzezany craze," Ryszard quoted from a poem he had recently written: "My heart is always near you, land of Brzezany."

The two old Brzezany cemeteries, the Christian and the Jewish one, which are both on the way to the village of Raj, held a special attraction for Ryszard. He used to visit the graves of his family and was always saddened by the growing neglect that was typical of the Soviet era. What enraged him most was the gradual destruction of the Jewish cemetery on the Okopisko hill, overlooking the town. According to Ryszard, the cemetery had remained quite intact throughout the fifties. Then buildings were constructed on part of the site. Tombstones were dislodged and were used to build sidewalks. Their inscribed surfaces were usually laid face up, "to prevent slipping on rainy days." The wall surrounding the cemetery also disappeared in time. The place turned into a neglected and dirty stretch of pasture for cows, chicken, and geese.

Ryszard also witnessed the gradual decline of the impressive Brzezany synagogue. For a while it was used for grain storage, but once it lost its usefulness, for whatever reason, it started falling apart. The beautiful Polish Catholic Farny Church near the Rynek was remade into a sports hall. Ryszard had a special feeling for the age-old Sieniawski Castle and chapel. Both were now almost completely ruined. Among the souvenirs which Ryszard brought with him from Brzezany were some bricks from the castle entrance. Ryszard made numerous appeals to various Polish ministries, imploring them to renovate some historical Brzezany sites, first and foremost the Sieniawski chapel. Ryszard's dream was to establish a Brzezany museum in his country house.[2]

Zbigniew Rusinski was 15 when he and his family left Brzezany in the fall of 1945. During the war he had been active in the Polish Scout underground, and after the Soviet reoccupation he joined a local auxiliary police force that assisted the NKVD, forerunner of the KGB, in its fight against the Ukrainian underground. Rusinski inherited part of his impressive Brzezany collection from his father. His initial interests were the Polish Scout organization and the AK Polish underground in Brzezany and the vicinity. In time, he started collecting nearly everything connected with his hometown, from old archival documents to a Jewish shofar, which he once found in a Brzezany dunghill. In his Rybnik home, where I visited him, Rusinski has a long, narrow room full of all kinds of Brzezany memorabilia. Collecting such items has become Rusinski's hobby and his obsession.[3]

Rusinski visited Brzezany for the first time after forty years. "I couldn't recognize the place. I was appalled by what I saw there. The Jewish cemetery was all in ruins, the tombstones were broken, some having been used for the construction of houses for high-ranking local Soviet dignitaries. Some tombstones were still erect and looked like sentinels, guarding whatever remained." The place had changed so much that he wasn't sure that this was actually the prewar Jewish Okopisko cemetery. A woman tending a flock of geese that was grazing near the broken tombstones remarked matter-of-factly, "Yes, you are standing on top of those mass graves." Rusinski, recalling his Jewish friend David Pomerantz, who was murdered with his parents at the Okopisko, placed a bunch of flowers and left.[4]

Halszka Rapf traveled from Warsaw to Brzezany after fifty-four years. Her first reaction was shock. "Whatever I remembered was entirely different from what I saw there. Our house was still there, but for half a century nobody had taken care of it. It's old and neglected. Our beautiful garden, once overflowing with flowers, narrowed now by a widened road, is overgrown with weeds." Another ghastly sight was that of the nearby Farny Church. Equally terrible was the present state of the Bernardine Cloister on the hill overlooking Brzezany. The Cloister had been turned by the Soviets into a prison and correctional institute for young criminals and was surrounded by ugly walls and barbed wire. Still another disappointment was the Christian cemetery. "This was one of the most beautiful cemeteries in the whole region. There were those age-old trees. Children used to run along the pathways on holidays. Now almost all the trees have been chopped down, and only sad tombstones remain."

Halszka was pleasantly surprised by the appearance of the town center and the prewar Ratusz, which had been turned into a museum. Her encounters with people were also encouraging. She even found Olga, her family's prewar Ukrainian chambermaid. Their reunion was quite emotional. "And so I thought to myself that friendship with Ukrainians shouldn't be so difficult. I loved Olga once and even held her baby daughter at the christening.

I'm aware, however, that other Ukrainians caused us great harm." When I asked Halszka about her thoughts when she was leaving Brzezany, her short comment was, "I thought that I was lucky to see Brzezany before I die."[5]

Halszka's older brother, Tolek, never returned. Following my last visit to Brzezany, I sent him a letter with a picture of what used to be the Rapf villa. In his reply Tolek remarked, "I would very much like to visit my home town but I'm afraid of the shock I would get comparing contemporary Brzezany with the place where I spent a marvelous childhood."[6]

* * *

Israel Ne'eman returned to Narajow, a small town northwest of Brzezany, in the summer of 1997. Sixty-two years had passed since he had left it and emigrated to Palestine. He was then a young Zionist pioneer of 21. Although he had been active in the Brzezany-Narajow *landsmannschaft* in Israel for years, the idea of actually visiting the sites of his youth occurred to him only after retirement. What really motivated Israel was his hope and belief that "something could be found," perhaps some books from his grandfather's extensive Judaica library or some Jewish tombstones. Anything which might bear witness to prewar Jewish life. "An enormous disappointment. Nothing. I went to look for the Beit Hamidrash and the Synagogue. No remnants at all." What he did find, however, was the family house, rebuilt beyond recognition, painted blue and turned into a mini-market. "It was a gray, rainy day in mid-June, and after seeing the house I didn't feel well. I started to vomit, right there, my guts spilled out. Is this the shtetl that it once was? It had been full of life, youth movements, Chasidim, people dancing with torahs on Simhat Torah."

When the group returned to the hotel in Tarnopol, Israel was really sick. What soothed him, though, were the green hilly landscapes around Brzezany and Narajow, which he remembered so well. When I asked him whether he would like to go there once more, the answer was surprisingly positive. In spite of his disappointment, if there were another opportunity, he would still try to find "something."[7]

Natan Goldman left Brzezany for Palestine a few weeks before the war. He was then 18, having just graduated from the Gimnazjum. He returned in the summer of 1997. I had interviewed him a few months earlier and told him about the reunion planned by Brzezany Poles in Ustron. Natan decided not only to travel to the reunion but also to organize a group of Israeli Brzezanyites and take them to Brzezany. In Ustron, Natan seemed to be in his element. He spent most of the time with his Polish classmates from the Gimnazjum, arguing, reminiscing, and exchanging old photos. The most intimate meeting was with his old school-friend Tolek Rapf. Tolek was sick and couldn't come to Ustron. Natan traveled for hours by train to Tolek's home in the northern port city of Gdansk. They spent the whole night talking. Natan summed up his visit to Poland: "I'm glad I went to the reunion. It was good to be in Poland and to meet the closest Polish friend I ever had in Brzezany."

The first familiar site Natan saw on arriving in Brzezany was the lake, the Brzezany Staw. "This was the most exciting moment for me. I spent a great part of my life right there. I was an excellent swimmer. There was only one youngster who swam better, Bolko, a Ukrainian." Natan went to see his family's prewar house, the half-ruined synagogue, and the Gimnazjum building. Another site he made sure he saw was the Sieniawski Castle and the "Old Garden" around it. Natan complained that he could not find time alone during his trip, since other members of the group demanded his attention and guidance. When I asked him to sum up his visit to Poland and Brzezany, Natan concluded, "I'm glad I went. This was an experience. I'm glad I saw my friends."[8]

Bela Feld was apparently the oldest person who returned to Brzezany. In spite of her age and some health problems, she decided to join Natan on his journey to Poland and Brzezany. Bela had emigrated to Palestine in 1935 and visited her family in Brzezany in 1937. That was the last time she saw them. All of Bela's immediate family were killed, either in Brzezany or in the Belzec death camp. "From the first moment I heard that I was the only one left from my whole family and that all the others were murdered, I sensed a feeling of guilt. It was difficult to accept the fact that nobody survived. I had to return to Brzezany. If I didn't, I would be betraying my family. I had to bow down in front of their graves, to see those places once more. I had to go."[9]

At the Brzezany reunion in Ustron, Bela asked to speak to a small group of people who gathered around her. We were sitting around a table, sipping tea and coffee. Bela shared some of her apprehensions concerning her imminent visit to Brzezany. "I've been carrying a certain image of the town in my memory and I don't want to ruin it when I face reality. I don't have the slightest idea in which direction I should bow to pay tribute to those who were dear to me. There is no tombstone, there were no funerals. There was nothing."[10]

Bela, Natan, and a few other Brzezany Jews arrived in town on a midsummer Sunday, on the day commemorating the constitution of new, independent Ukraine. As their conspicuous red minibus arrived in the Rynek, they saw a crowd. Bela recalled that moment. "As we stopped, we faced a procession. They were all Ukrainians, many dressed in their colorful peasant folk costumes. For a split second it seemed to me like a crusaders' column marching towards us and about to attack. My immediate impulse was to run away, to disappear. There were hundreds of people, marching. At the same time, I looked up and saw some of the old buildings around the Rynek, where Jews had lived and had their stores. It was terrible. I suddenly recalled all of them. I could tell you which store belonged to whom. And now there were no more Jews." The combination of a Ukrainian crowd celebrating a holiday and bygone images of prewar Jewish Brzezany had an extremely powerful effect on Bela.[11]

Soon some people gathered around the unusual "tourists," and Bela tried to inquire about old-time friends and acquaintances. A name which she kept repeating was that of Halyna Dydyk, a Ukrainian with whom she attended the Brzezany Women Teachers' Seminary more than sixty years earlier. Halyna was one of Bela's closest friends in those days. Bela never imagined that Halyna would turn into one of Brzezany's contemporary Ukrainian heroes.

Halyna's life, spanning the Polish, German, and Soviet times, epitomizes, in a way, the history of the Ukrainians in eastern Galicia during most of the twentieth century.[12] She was born in 1912, in the village of Szybalin. When Bela met her at the teachers' seminary, Halyna was already a staunch Ukrainian nationalist. She was a member of the illegal Ukrainian Plast youth movement. Bela belonged to the Brzezany branch of the Hanoar Hatzioni Zionist youth organization. As for her unusual friendship with Halyna, Bela confided in me: "I really loved her. She was tall and she sang beautifully. We really had a lot in common. We wanted to sing in a quartet, but since there were only the two of us, we used to stand and sing in front of the mirror." Both were young, educated girls, optimistic and enthusiastic about the future, each in her own way. Halyna believed in a free and independent Ukraine. Bela planned to emigrate to Palestine. Bela recently sent me an old gray envelope which once contained a letter sent to her by Halyna, back in 1931. The letter was lost, but the seemingly insignificant envelope was indicative of Halyna's convictions. The stamps were Polish, but the addresses were in Ukrainian.

Bela, who emigrated to Palestine in the mid-thirties, never heard from her Ukrainian friend again. She often wondered how Halyna behaved toward Jews during the German occupation. There is no information about that. What is known is that Halyna was active in the OUN, the Organization of Ukrainian Nationalists, and joined the UPA underground during the war. She was arrested by the NKVD sometime in 1940 and was held in the Brzezany prison until the Soviet retreat in the summer of 1941.

While in the UPA, Halyna headed the underground Ukrainian Red Cross in the region. She was also very close to UPA leader Roman Shukhevych. Halyna was arrested in the early spring of 1950, when Shukhevych's hideout, near Lwow, was discovered by the Soviets. Shukhevych committed suicide. Halyna tried to poison herself. "They saved me, half conscious, in order to torture me. They beat me mercilessly, day after day. They prevented me from sleeping at night. This continued for two years."[13] Halyna was sentenced to twenty-five years in labor camps. All that while she remained loyal to Ukrainian nationalism and to her deceased commander, "Chuprynka" Shukhevych.

In spite of her own hopeless situation she was always helping and encouraging her fellow prisoners. Halyna was finally released in 1971. She was then close to 60, a sick and broken woman. She died in 1979, twelve years before her lifelong dream of an independent Ukraine was realized. She was buried in the Brzezany cemetery.

The crowd of curious onlookers surrounded Bela and urged her to visit Halyna's burial site and say a few words about her erstwhile friend. Bela became frightened. "I felt like running away. I didn't want to go there. I was emotionally exhausted." She wasn't sure how to behave in that situation. She remembered that my Aunt Malcia and Rozka Majblum, as well as other Jewish survivors from Brzezany who arrived in Israel after the war, told her that the Bandera people, the members of the Ukrainian underground, were the worst. "I remembered Halyna the way she was before the war, before all that. And suddenly she turned into a hero and a martyr, associated with that name, Bandera. I knew that something was wrong, *'s'iz nisht git.'*" Bela politely refused the invitation.

Like the others in her group, Bela wanted to see the sites of her childhood and youth. She looked for her family's house on Tarnopolska Street, but what she found were straight rows of trees. "I walked between the trees and sat down on a bench. I wanted to feel something. For a moment I thought I was losing my mind. And then I pulled myself together." Like the others, Bela went to the Okopisko cemetery. "I wanted to remember. I wanted to feel the soil, to smell. Perhaps I could sense something. There was a multitude of emotions." Bela also went to see the remains of the Brzezany synagogue. "I remembered it in my subconscious. As if from a page of an old album. I visualized the synagogue as it was once. And now it was all in ruins. It looked like a huge, wounded animal." Summing up her journey to Brzezany, Bela sadly remarked, "I really traveled to see 'nothing.'"

Mike (Manek) Thaler spent three hours in Brzezany in the spring of 1998 during the Jewish Passover week. He e-mailed me some of his impressions and reactions to his visit in the Ukraine. "I visited two Ukraines, a Jewish one and a non-Jewish one. Brzezany stood between them like a bone stuck in my throat, reminding me of the immense distance between the two worlds. As for my feelings about Ukrainians, I feel strangely distant from them, so I hardly feel anything. I automatically distrust and dislike the older ones." As for the younger ones, Mike dryly commented, "I never discussed Jewish issues with them, except once, in Brzezany, when a 21-year-old reporter asked me why I was there. I simply told her, 'So I would never have to come back again.' Then I just walked away, because I felt that to discuss the Shoah with them would be useless and degrading to the people who were killed." Mike found and identified the house where he had lived inside the ghetto, as well as the house near the Okopisko cemetery where they had stayed with a Polish family. He also recognized the old courthouse building where he lay hidden in the cellar while many Brzezany Jews were taken away. He was both amazed and angered by his visit to the town museum in the Ratusz building. "There, on the second floor, a 1,000-year-old history of Brzezany is on display, without even a hint that Jews had lived there."[14]

Judge Doron Majblum didn't have any personal memories of the town, since he was born in Palestine. Nevertheless, he knew a lot about the town, its Jews, and his own family. His father and mother, both of whom had emigrated from Brzezany to Palestine before the war, often spoke about the families they left behind. The only one who survived was his father's younger sister, Rozka. A few years before Doron's visit to Brzezany, during one of the holidays when the family, including Doron's children, got together, Rozka told her Holocaust story in detail. Doron told what happened: "Everybody was sitting around her. I'll never forget it. It's one of my most distressing memories. Rozia was telling a heartbreaking story late into the night, about her survival, about her parents, about Grandpa's murder. When I was planning my journey to Brzezany I recalled Rozia's memories." His parents and his aunt had described scenes of Brzezany from which Doron constructed an image of the town. "I saw this town in my imagination and I knew that a day would come and I'd get there."

When he finally got to Brzezany via Lwow, although he had never been there before, he became extremely agitated as he approached the town. "I was all emotion. I felt that a dream was coming true, that I was about to touch it." Doron walked frantically around Brzezany, trying to identify familiar sites, those he remembered from his family's stories. "The feeling was like being in a dream, a dream which would soon evaporate, disappear. I ran around and took pictures of nearly everything." Doron remembered that when his Ukrainian-speaking driver helped him by asking one of the locals to direct him to the synagogue, the man remarked that one needed a strong heart to see the sight. Doron was overwhelmed and depressed upon seeing the synagogue. He decided, on the spot, to take a small part of it back with him to Israel. With the aid of the driver, they pulled out a single brick from one of the crumbling walls. "I took the brick with me. It traveled with me back to Israel. It's in my house now. I look at it sometimes. Perhaps, many years ago, it heard my grandfather's prayer or a Torah reading of one of my relatives." When Doron returned to Lwow, he realized it was Yom Kippur, the Day of Atonement. On that very day, back in 1941, his grandfather was murdered by the Germans near the village of Raj. In his closing remarks, Doron returned to the synagogue brick. "Perhaps, one day, when I die, they should throw it into my grave."[15] Doron Majblum died of a sudden heart attack in the summer of 1999. I called his widow and told her about his thoughts concerning the synagogue brick. She thanked me and said that she would make sure it was used in the construction of the tombstone.

Dmytro Bartkiw settled in England after the war and lost contact with his parents, who had remained in the village of Kotow, near Brzezany. In the mid-sixties, after hearing from a cousin in America who had succeeded in corresponding with their family, Bartkiw sent them a letter. His mother had already died by that time, and his father died two years later. After the war, Dmytro never saw his parents again. In 1981, when he traveled to Moscow and Kiev as part of an exchange group, he wasn't allowed to travel to Western Ukraine. Instead, his two sisters, one living in Kotow and the other in Tarnopol, came to see him. Bartkiw visited Kotow only after the establishment of independent Ukraine in 1992. "Most of the men of my age had perished. Some had been killed while serving in the UPA underground, and others had been drafted into the Red Army and killed in action." His visit to Brzezany was a disappointment. He saw the Rynek, the Ratusz, and the Gimnazjum, but the town as a whole looked much worse than the way he remembered it.[16]

Vasyl Oleskiw, from Byszki, settled in London after the war and had no news of his family until 1956. For twelve long years, he knew nothing about his parents and his sister. "I took it very hard. I used to have nightmares, very realistic ones. I saw my mother, my father, our neighbors. When I returned to the Ukraine for the first time, I didn't believe I was really there. I thought it was a dream. I was barely conscious." He returned for the first time in 1992 and stayed in Kiev and Lwow. His parents had died by then. Oleskiw had seen them for the last time in 1944. When he traveled to the Ukraine again, he visited Byszki and Brzezany. He, too, was disappointed. "There are no beautiful villas, the lake is not the same, and everything looks so poor, so neglected. Even the people look different."[17]

In 1993, Ivan Hrabar traveled from London to his native village of Posuchow after half a century. By then he had already retired and had suffered a heart attack. The last time he saw his parents and his younger brother was in 1942, when he was arrested by the Germans. His father died in 1986, his mother in 1990. He missed her by three years. But he did meet his brother. "I went to my village. My brother met me there when I got off the train. We cried. It was very emotional." When I asked Hrabar about his feelings toward his old country, his response both surprised and moved me. "I want to go and die in my country, in Ukraine. My mother and father are there in Posuchow, buried in one grave, side by side. I told my brother that I would like to be buried near my parents in Posuchow, four kilometers from Berezhany."[18]

* * *

The urge to return to the sites of one's childhood is universal. What makes the return to Eastern Europe and to places such as Brzezany unique is the historical and political reality which has unfolded since the Second World War. This part of Europe was barely accessible until the momentous changes of the late eighties and the final collapse of communism. Decades of physical, political, and cultural distance intensified nostalgia, imagination, and dreams. This was apparently the reason for the powerful emotional reaction to the confrontation with objects, places, and scenes from the past. The first moments were usually overwhelming. Then there followed a search for places connected to one's physical presence in the past. Not all visitors were able to identify the specific places which had had significance for them, since physical and architectural structures had changed over the years. Thus, some visitors were frustrated in their search for meaningful sites. However, most of the public places and structures were easy to recognize and remember. They seemed to bridge the past and the present. The Brzezany sites most often mentioned were the Staw, the Rynek, the Ratusz, and the Gimnazjum.

Each ethnic/religious group returned to its places of worship and burial: Jews, to the dilapidated synagogue building; Poles, to the Farny Church; and Ukrainians, to the Uniate Church opposite the Ratusz. Poles returned to the Christian cemetery on the way to Raj, and Jews returned to the Jewish Okopisko cemetery. Whereas Poles, in spite of long years of neglect, could still identify graves and tombstones, Jews could mourn for their dead only in a symbolic way, since their cemetery had been almost completely destroyed. Most of the tombstones had been removed, and the few that remained were overturned and broken. It was impossible to identify the mass graves, the pits into which the Jewish victims were thrown.

Returnees usually wanted to take back something which would remind them of their return and renew their links with the past. This was done mainly by taking pictures or looking for memorabilia. A most unique way was that of Ryszard Brzezinski and Doron Majblum, both "second-generation" Brzezanyites. The former brought back some bricks from the Sieniawski Castle; the latter, a single brick from the crumbling Brzezany synagogue.

Poles, Jews, and Ukrainians each returned to "their" Brzezany, to places and structures identified with their particular past. There were, however, a few exceptions. Zbigniew Rusinski and Ryszard Brzezinski visited the Jewish Okopisko cemetery and showed strong personal and emotional involvement. There was no case, as far as I know, except for myself, of a Jewish visitor who went to the Christian cemetery. Would I have done it if I were not a historian? The exclusive focus of Brzezany Jews on specific Jewish objects of the past was a result of their enormous tragedy. Loss and mourning were also common among Poles and Ukrainians. However, in the case of Brzezany Jews, they were overwhelming. Brzezany Poles and Ukrainians were indeed affected by the war. Some were killed, some were deported, many were resettled. But almost all Brzezany Jews perished. Their deaths were linked in the memory of their relatives not only with the German perpetrators but also with their Ukrainian and Polish neighbors. This made an emotional crossing of boundaries so difficult, if not impossible.

CONCLUDING REMARKS

For me Brzezany is both history and autobiography. The two are almost inseparable. A return to one's roots is usually a mono-ethnic experience. My intent was to present the multi-ethnic community of Brzezany, where Poles, Jews, and Ukrainians lived side by side. I was also interested in the way each group remembered its past. Collectives tend, quite naturally, to view the past from an inner-oriented perspective. The more traumatic that past, the more particular and exclusive the perspective. The war and the Holocaust are a striking example. Poles, Ukrainians, and, most of all, Jews were at the epicenter of suffering. It has been very difficult, nearly impossible, for them to view with empathy and understanding the plight of the others. Decades of communism, with its ideological and manipulative restrictions, made a genuine and honest facing of their common past highly unlikely.

Although it was primarily Hitler's Germany and Stalin's Russia which caused wartime violence and brutality, Poles and Ukrainians also fought bitterly with each other and preserved their selective, mutually hostile memories. The Jews, the ultimate victims of Nazi Germany, were treated mostly with indifference and sometimes with outright hostility by their prewar neighbors. Jewish memories of Poles and Ukrainians are usually negative. The complex and tragic past of the Jews, Poles, and Ukrainians and their conviction of exclusive victimhood resulted, mostly, in separate self-centered memories. Only empathy and a breakthrough in mental and emotional patterns can bring about mutual understanding of that past. This is not easy for anyone, including a historian. There is also another obstacle. People tend to interpret certain periods in the past in view of subsequent events. Each period should be viewed separately. This is particularly necessary when a collective trauma casts its long shadow both backward and forward. It is, therefore, of paramount importance not to view prewar Brzezany through the prism of the war and the Holocaust. We should try to face it as it actually was during its "normal" times as well as during the time of turmoil, hate, suffering, and loss.

At least some of the Hapsburg legacy of multiculturalism and moderation seemed to prevail in interwar Brzezany. Although "Polishness" was a dominating feature, Jews and Ukrainians weren't completely alienated. Each group tended to keep to itself, but there were also varying degrees of interethnic relations. Some anti-Semitic events did occur, but there was never a pogrom-like atmosphere in town. Anti-Ukrainian pacification campaigns and the suppression of Ukrainian culture and nationalism affected Polish-Ukrainian relations. Still, this was a far cry from subsequent confrontations. The Soviet occupation of Brzezany brought about a weakening of interethnic cohesion. For the Jews, the Soviet rule was a lesser evil. It was tragedy and trauma for most Poles and Ukrainians. The disintegration of prewar frameworks and the chaos of transition resulted in outbursts of violence. The Polish-Jewish-Ukrainian community had already begun to disintegrate before the Germans arrived.

Interethnic indifference and outright hostility increased during the German occupation. A Ukrainian pogrom, during which dozens of Jews were killed and wounded, occurred in Brzezany. Jews were isolated from their prewar Polish and Ukrainian neighbors and, subsequently, deported and killed. The Jews would remember those terrible years as the end of their community. The killings in the Okopisko cemetery were viewed by some Poles and Ukrainians with empathy. For others, it was just a spectacle. Nobody could understand Jewish helplessness. The motives of those who helped and rescued Jews were largely a mixture of greed and compassion. The Ukrainian-Polish conflict intensified and took its painful toll. The Poles would carry bitter memories of Ukrainian terror. The Ukrainians would remember Polish-Soviet cooperation in the suppression of the Ukrainian underground. The Jews would nurture an overpowering sensation of loss, accompanied by strong accusatory feelings, not only toward the German perpetrators but also toward their Polish and Ukrainian neighbors.

When the Soviets reoccupied Brzezany, there were almost no Jews left. Most of the Poles were subsequently repatriated to Poland. Some Ukrainians left with the Germans; others were deported by the Soviets. Those Ukrainians who stayed in Brzezany went through a painful process of Sovietization, which brought more terror and suffering. Only a small part of its prewar population, mostly Ukrainians, stayed on. Prewar multi-ethnic Brzezany no longer existed.

Poles, Jews, and Ukrainians lived side by side in Brzezany for many years. They lived together and apart at the same time. Their "togetherness" could hold only during periods of relative stability. When destabilization came, the Polish-Ukrainian-Jewish "triangle" started to disintegrate. The unprecedented wartime circumstances and the brutality of life under both Soviets and Germans brought out the worst in human nature. Ordinary morality was tested by extraordinary circumstances. Poles, Jews, and Ukrainians lived through difficult and cruel times. But there was a difference: whereas Poles and Ukrainians reversed roles as oppressors and oppressed, the Jews were always powerless victims. Most of the Poles and Ukrainians survived the war. The Jews didn't.

* * *

The research and the writing of this book were both a professional and a personal experience for me. As a historian I wanted to place my past within a wider historical context. But most of all, I had an irresistible urge to return both mentally and physically to the sites of my childhood. But maybe there is something more to it. Going back to Brzezany made me happy. Was I chasing after my good childhood years, before life was shattered? Did I look for proof that once I too had a normal life?

There was more than curiosity in my search. There was also excitement. The reading of the Brzezany newspaper made me feel as if I was right there at the town square, watching the marching soldiers, hearing the military band play. There was the geographical proximity of the Lwow and Tarnopol archives to Brzezany. The most meaningful and moving part of my research, though, was the interviews. Somehow, an immediate bond emerged—not only with Jews but also with Poles, and even with Ukrainians. Was this related to Karol and Tanka? Was it part of my general optimistic and perhaps naive worldview? I was, indeed, looking for the humane and the good in man. I even found my good German. I identified with Bela Feld, with Halszka Rapf, with Ivan Hrabar, and with Anna Herzog. I tried to verify my memories and to relive my past through theirs. I became a memory collector.

I could not, of course, present a complete and detailed image of Brzezany in my book. I hope that what I did accomplish will be of some value for the understanding of one specific community and, perhaps, of humanity.

POLES

Brzezinski, Ryszard. Ustron, June 1997.
Cwynar-Baranek, Wladyslawa. Ustron, June 1997.
Czajkowska-Sabi, Stanislawa. Ustron, June 1997.
Codogni, Karol. Omer, May 1986.
Herzog, Anna (pseudonym). Bytom, July 1998.
Kaminski, Michal. Ustron, June 1997.
Lubelska-Michorowska, Ludmila. Warsaw, June 1997.
Partynska-Wesolowska, Irena. Ustron, June 1997.
Rapf, Witold (Tolek). Gdansk, July 1998.
Rapf-Wierzbicka, Halszka. Warsaw, June 1997; Gdansk, July 1998.
Rusinski, Zbigniew. Ustron, June 1997.
Skrzypek, Stanislaw. Arlington, Virginia, September 1998.
Slotwinski, Jozef. Obory, July 1998.
Stronska-Gryczynska, Krystyna. Ustron, June 1997.
Zuczkowski, Zbigniew. Warsaw, June 1997.

JEWS

Feld-Danieli, Bela. Tel-Aviv, March 1997; April 1998.
Goldman, Natan. Haifa, February 1997; March 1998.
Goldschlag, Samuel A. Telephone interview. September 1998.
Grossfeld, Seweryn. Jerusalem, July 1997.
Katz, Menachem (Munio Haber). Haifa, February 1997.
Majblum, Doron. Tel-Aviv, June 1997.
Majblum, Mordechai. Yokneam, October 1997.
Majblum-Sandel, Rozka. Haifa, February 1997.
Meser-Meler, Rachel. Tel-Aviv, April 1997.
Nadler, Miriam. Tel-Aviv, April 1997.
Ne'eman-Neumann, Israel. Tel-Aviv, April 1997.
Nir, Reuven. Haifa, March 1998.

Poldek, L. Queens, New York, September 1998.
Prizand-Bone, Batya. Haifa, February 1997.
Schmidt, Efraim. Haifa, February 1997.
Shaklai, Matityahu. Tel-Aviv, August 1999.
Szotenberg, Zeev. Alfei-Menashe, Summer 1996.
Thaler, Michael. Holocaust Oral History Project, San Francisco, California, September 1989.
Wanderer-Biheller, Rena. Lakeview, New Jersey, September 1998.
Wanderer-Stolarsky, Ruth. Lakeview, New Jersey, September 1998.

UKRAINIANS

Bartkiw, Dmytro. London, October 1997.
Dudar, Stepan. Berezhany, February 1997.
Fanga, Ivan. Berezhany, August 1997.
Fanga, Vasyl. Berezhany, August 1997.
Hajwa, Marian-Dmytro. London, October 1997.
Hrabar, Ivan. London, October 1997.
Kontsevych, Ania. Berezhany, January 1997.
Kontsevych, Tatiana. Berezhany, August 1991.
Labunka, Myroslav. (Interview by Jan T. Gross.) Philadelphia, Pennsylvania, Spring 1981.
Milsztok-Lysak, Anna. Berezhany, July 1998.
Oleskiw, Vasyl. London, October 1997.
Pankiv, Aleksandr. Berezhany, July 1998.
Pavliv, Iulian. Lviv, March 1997.
Rega, Lev. Berezhany, August 1997.
Skaskiv, Galina. Lviv, August 1997.

NOTES

1. MY RETURN

1. *Berezhans'ka zemlia: Istorichno-memuarnii zbirnik,* Vol. 2 (Toronto: Berezhany Regional Committee, 1998), 624.

2. Plan-skhema mista Berezhany, Berezhany Ethnographic Museum. For an interwar map of Brzezany, see Menachem Katz, ed., *Brzezany Memorial Book* (Hebrew) (Haifa: Irgun yots'e Bz'ez'ani Narayuv veha-sevivah be-Yisra'el uve-Artsot ha-Berit, 1978), 219. Ryszard Brzezinski exhibited a detailed map of interwar Brzezany at the Brzezany reunion of 1998. That map is now in the author's possession. For a list of street names during the German occupation of Brzezany, see *Berezhans'ki Visti,* November 27, 1941.

3. Demographic data on interwar Brzezany and the Brzezany district (*powiat*) were culled from *Pinkas Hakehillot: Encyclopedia of Jewish Communities. Poland,* Vol. 2, *Eastern Galicia* (Hebrew) (Jerusalem: Yad va-shem, rashut ha-zikaron la-Sho'ah vela-gevurah, 1980), 107 (hereafter *Pinkas Hakehillot*); *Glos Brzezanski* 1 (1932), 12–13; *Glos Brzezanski* 18 (1938), 5; Keren Hayesod Collection, KH4B-1774, Central Zionist Archives, Jerusalem; *Kresy Wschodnie II Rzeczypospolitcy: Brezany* (brochure) (Krakow: n.p., 1993); Krzysztof Maziakowski, *Zycie codzienne w Brzezanach w latach 1932–1939 w swietle "Glosu Brzezanskiego." Praca magisterska* (Wroclaw: Uniwersytet Wroclawski, 1993), 4–5; *Berezhans'ka zemlia: Istorychno-memuarnyi zbirnyk,* Vol. 1 (New York: Berezhany Regional Committee, 1970), 52–56 (hereafter *Berezhans'ka zemlia* 1).

4. *Glos Brzezanski* 14 (1939), 5.

5. See comments to Brzezinski's map of interwar Brzezany.

6. See Stanislaw Wiszniewski, ed., *Przewodnik po Brzezanach i okolicy* (N.p., n.d.), 5–10; Katz, ed., *Brzezany Memorial Book,* 14–18.

7. For a detailed description of the Brzezany Synagogue, see Katz, ed., *Brzezany Memorial Book,* 221–230. For information on churches in Brzezany, see Zbigniew Rusinski, "Brzezany." Vol. I. Rybnik, 1993. Unpublished manuscript.

2. CLOSE AND DISTANT NEIGHBORS

1. Interview with Batya Prizand-Bone, Haifa, February 1997.

2. Interview with Bela Feld-Danieli, Tel-Aviv, March 1997.

3. Interview with Israel Ne'eman-Neumann, Tel-Aviv, April 1997.

4. The Memorial Book of the Jewish community in Brzezany, meant to commemorate Jews and Jewish life in that town.

5. Interview with Menachem Katz, Haifa, February 1997; Menachem Ben Shimon Katz, *Path of Hope* (Hebrew) (Tel-Aviv: 'Eked, 1992).

6. Interview with Natan Goldman, Haifa, February 1997.

7. Interview with Rena Wanderer-Stolarsky and Ruth Wanderer-Biheller, Lakeview, New Jersey, September 1998.

8. Interview with L. Poldek, Queens, N.Y., September 1998.

9. The Harcerstwo was the Polish counterpart of the Boy Scouts that became a paramilitary youth organization in the context of World War II. Chapter 3 describes the activities of the Harcerzy before and during the war in great detail.

10. Interview with Dr. Stanislaw Skrzypek, Arlington, Va., September 1998.

11. Personal communication from Prof. Michael Thaler.

12. Interview with Prof. Matityahu Shaklai, Tel-Aviv, August 1999.

13. Interview with Zbigniew Rusinski, Ustron, June 1997; Correspondence with Zbigniew Rusinski; Zbigniew Rusinski, *Tryptyk Brzezanski* (Wroclaw: W kolorach teczy, Oficyna Artystyczno-Wydawnicza, 1998), 130.

14. Interview with Halszka Rapf-Wierzbicka, Warsaw, June 1997; Interview with Tolek Rapf, Gdansk, July 1998.

15. Interview with Ludka Lubelska-Michorowska, Warsaw, June 1997.

16. Interview with Ryszard Brzezinski, Ustron, June 1997.

17. Interview with Jozef Slotwinski, Obory near Warsaw, July 1998.

18. Interview with Anna Herzog, Bytom, July 1998.

19. Telephone interview with S. A. Goldschlag, September 1998.

20. Interview with Iulian Pavliv, Lviv, March 1997.

21. Interview with Lev Rega, Berezhany, August 1997.

22. Interview with Galina Skaskiv, Lviv, August 1997. The interview was published in *Ukraina Moderna* 2–3 (1999): 273–308.

23. Interview with Marian Hajwa, London, October 1997.

24. Interview with Ivan Hrabar, London, October 1997.

25. Interview with Dmytro Bartkiw, London, October 1997.

26. Interview with Vasyl Oleskiw, London, October 1997.

27. Interview with Aleksandr Pankiv, Berezhany, July 1998.

28. TR-10/518, Yad Vashem Archives, Jerusalem (hereafter YVA); Asbach Case, AR-Z 76/61, 202, Ludwigsburg Archives, Zentrale Stelle der Landesjustizverwaltungen zur Verfolgung nationalsozialistischer Verbrechen, Ludwigsburg, Germany (hereafter LA); Dieter Pohl, *Nationalsozialistische Judenverfolgung in Ostgalizien, 1941–1944* (München: Oldenbourg, 1997), 411; Thomas Sandkühler, *"Endloesung" in Galizien: Der Judenmord in Ostpolen und die Rettungsinitiativen von Bertold Beitz, 1941–1944* (Bonn: Dietz, 1996), 453.

29. TR-10/518, LA; Asbach Case, AR-Z 76/61, 208, 308, YVA; Pohl, *Nationalsozialistische Judenverfolgung in Ostgalizien*, 418; Sandkühler, *"Endloesung" in Galizien*, 442.

30. TR-10/518, LA; Asbach Case, AR-Z 76/61, 202, YVA; Pohl, *Nationalsozialistische Judenverfolgung in Ostgalizien*, 415; Sandkühler, *"Endloesung" in Galizien*, 260, 267.

31. Hubert Kohnen, NSDAP Personal File, Bundesarchiv, Berlin; Becker et al. Case, AR 797/66, 208, LA.

32. Asbach Case, AR-Z 76/61, 208, LA.

3. THE GOOD YEARS, 1919–1939

1. Jerzy Tomaszewski, *Ojczyzna nie tylko Polakow: Mniejszosci narodowe w Polsce w latach 1918–1939* (Warsaw: Mlodziezowa Agencja Wydawnicza, 1985), 52, 97, 173; Tomaszewski, *Rzeczpospolita wielu narodow* (Warsaw: Czytelnik, 1985), 35; Tomaszewski, "Czesc II: Niepodlegla Rzeczpospolita," in *Najnowsze dzieje Zydów w Polsce w zarysie, do 1950 roku,* ed. Jerzy Tomaszewski (Warsaw: Wydawn. Nauk. PWN, 1993), 161; Zbigniew Pucek, "Galicyjskie doswiadczenie wielokulturowosci a problem wiezi spolecznej," in *Galicja i jej dziedzictwo,* Vol. 2, *Spoleczenstwo i gospodarka,* ed. Jerzy Chlopecki and Helena Madurowicz-Urbanska (Rzeszow: WSP, 1995), 11; Zhanna Kovba, *Liudianist' u bezodni pekla: povedinka mistsevoho naselennia skhidnoï Halychyny v roky "Ostatochnoho rozv'iazannia ievreis'koho pytannia"* (Kiev: Sfera, 1998), 18–19. According to Kovba, the Ukrainians constituted as much as 73 percent of the population in eastern Galicia.

2. Jozef Buszko, "Galicyjskie dziedzictwo II Rzeczypospolitej," in *Galicja i jej dziedzictwo,* Vol. 1, *Historia i polityka,* ed. Wlodzimierz Bonusiak and Jozef Buszko (Rzeszow: WSP, 1994), 187–197; Jerzy Chlopecki, "Galicja—skrzyzowanie drog," in *Galicja i jej dziedzictwo,* Vol. 2, *Spoleczenstwo i gospodarka,* ed. Jerzy Chlopecki and Helena Madurowicz-Urbanska (Rzeszow: WSP, 1995), 27–47; Kovba, *Liudianist' u bezodni pekla,* 208. For a discussion of the Hapsburg era in Galicia and its multi-cultural background, see also Israel Bartal and Antony Polonsky, "Introduction: The Jews of Galicia under the Habsburgs"; John-Paul Himka, "Dimensions of a Triangle: Polish-Ukrainian-Jewish Relations in Austrian Galicia"; and Jerzy Holzer, "Enlightenment, Assimilation, and Modern Identity: The Jewish Elite in Galicia." All in *Polin: Studies in Polish Jewry,* Vol. 12, *Focusing on Galicia: Jews, Poles and Ukrainians, 1772–1918,* ed. Israel Bartal and Antony Polonsky (London and Portland, Ore.: Littman Library of Jewish Civilization, 1999).

3. Norman Davies, *God's Playground: A History of Poland,* Vol. 2 (Oxford: Clarendon, 1981), 404.

4. For a discussion of Polish nationality policies in the interwar years, see Andrzej Chojnowski, *Koncepcje polityki narodowosciowej rzadów polskich w latach 1921–1939* (Wroclaw: Zaklad Narodowy im. Ossolinskich, 1979).

5. For a discussion of politics in interwar Poland, see Antony Polonsky, *Politics in Independent Poland, 1921–1939: The Crisis of Constitutional Government* (Oxford: Clarendon, 1972); and Davies, *God's Playground.*

6. The Ridna Shkola Society, established in the late nineteenth century, promoted Ukranian-language education.

7. Paul R. Magocsi, *Morality and Reality: The Life and Times of Andrei Sheptyts'kyi* (Edmonton: Canadian Institute of Ukrainian Studies, University of Alberta, 1989).

8. John-Paul Himka, "Western Ukraine in the Interwar Period," *Nationalities Papers* 22, no. 2 (Fall 1994): 347–363; Shimon Redlich, "Jewish-Ukrainian Relations in Inter-war Poland as Reflected in Some Ukrainian Publications," in *Polin: Studies in Polish Jewry,* Vol. 11, *Focusing on Aspects and Experiences of Religion,* ed. Antony Polonsky (Portland, Ore.: Littman Library of Jewish Civilization, 1998), 232–246.

9. Orest Subtelny, *Ukraine: A History* (Toronto: University of Toronto Press, 1988), 444–446.

10. Chojnowski, *Koncepcje polityki narodowosciowej,* 206–239.

11. Ezra Mendelsohn, *The Jews of East-Central Europe between the World Wars* (Bloomington: Indiana University Press, 1983), 18–19, 24–26.

12. Piotr Wrobel, "Czesc I: Przed odzyskaniem niepodleglosci," in *Najnowsze dzieje Zydów w Polsce w zarysie, do 1950 roku,* ed. Jerzy Tomaszewski (Warsaw: Wydawn. Nauk. PWN, 1993), 108–109.

13. General Jozef Haller, heading an army of 60,000 troops, arrived in Poland from France in the early summer of 1919 and had conquered the whole of eastern Galicia by early June.

14. For the most balanced discussion of Polish-Jewish relations in the interwar period, see Mendelsohn, *The Jews of East-Central Europe,* 37–42, 69–74; and Ezra Mendelsohn, "Interwar Poland: Good for the Jews or Bad for the Jews?" in *The Jews in Poland,* ed. Chimen Abramsky, Maciej Jachimczyk, and Antony Polonsky (Oxford: Basil Blackwell, 1986), 130–139. See also Eva Hoffman, *Shtetl: The Life and Death of a Small Town and the World of Polish Jews* (New York: Houghton Mifflin, 1997) 194, 199. For a discussion of conflicting historiographical views on Polish-Jewish relations, see Mendelsohn, "Interwar Poland," 130–136.

15. Mendelsohn, *The Jews of East-Central Europe,* 19, 51–52; Mendelsohn, *Zionism in Poland: The Formative Years, 1915–1926* (New Haven, Conn.: Yale University Press, 1981), 97–101.

16. Redlich, "Jewish-Ukrainian Relations in Inter-war Poland," 232–246.

17. Mendelsohn, *The Jews of East-Central Europe,* 47; Hoffman, *Shtetl,* 175.

18. Mendelsohn, *The Jews of East-Central Europe,* 48, 60; Mendelsohn, *Zionism in Poland,* 81. According to Samuel D. Kassow, the Jewish youth movements performed the function of a counterculture; they provided "a home away from home." See Yisrael Gutman, Ezra Mendelsohn, Yehuda Reinharz, and Chone Shmeruk, eds., *The Jews of Poland between Two World Wars* (Hanover, N.H.: University Press of New England, 1989), 202, 216–219.

19. Wrobel, "Czesc I," 88; Tomaszewski, "Czesc II," 162–167.

20. For information on Brzezany during the First World War and the immediate postwar years, see Stanislaw Wiszniewski, *Brzezanczycy przy odbudowie Panstwa Polskiego od 1831 do 1920 r* (Lwow: Drukarnia Wydawnicza, 1938), 139–159; and Wiszniewski, *Brzezany i kresy polodniowo-wschodnie Rzeczypospolitej Polskiej, 1918–1919* (Lwow: Biblioteka kresowa, 1935), passim.

21. Maziakowski, *Zycie codzienne w Brzezanach,* 44–47; *Glos Brzezanski* 15/16 (1936), 10; *Glos Brzezanski* 6 (1937), 7; *Glos Brzezanski* 24 (1937), 8.

22. Maziakowski, *Zycie codzienne w Brzezanach,* 58; *Brzezany 1530–1930* (Brzezany: J. Landesberg, 1930), 72–76.

23. *Glos Brzezanski* 3 (1932), 6–7.

24. *Glos Brzezanski* 7 (1933), 3–4.

25. *Glos Brzezanski* 11 (1935), 1–2.

26. For information on the Polish Scouts in Brzezany, see Zbigniew Rusinski, Hufiec Brzezany, 1911–1939. 3 volumes. Rybnik, 1996. Unpublished manuscript.

27. *Stulecie Gimnazyum Brzezanskiego, 1806–1906* (Brzezany: Komitet Jubileuszowy, 1907).

28. Ibid., 163–175.

29. *Glos Brzezanski* 15/16 (1936), 9.

30. Ibid.; *Brzezany: Jednodniowka Akademicka 1927* (Lwow: Inauguracyjne wydaw-nictwo Polskiego Akademickiego Kola Brzezanczykow we Lwowie, 1927), 67–74.

31. Based on a picture of the 1934 graduating class that includes teachers and personal communication from Jan Wojciechowski, one of the graduates.

32. Katz, ed., *Brzezany Memorial Book*, 134–135; Interview with Efraim (Froyko) Schmidt, Haifa, February 1997.

33. For information on the history of the 51st Regiment, see Leszek Zachuta, *51 Pulk Piechoty Strzelcow Kresowych im. Giuseppe Garibaldiego* (Pruszkow: Oficyna Wy-dawnicza "Ajaks," 1992).

34. *Glos Brzezanski* 17 (1936), 2.

35. Anna Kolbekowna, "Marszalek Edward Smigly-Rydz, Syn ziemi Brzezanskiej," in *Jednodniowka mlodziezy Gimnazjum Panstwowego im. Marszalka Edwarda Smiglego-Rydza w Brzezanach* (Brzezany: Nakladem Gminy Szkolnej Gimnazjum Panstwowego im. Marszalka Edwarda Smiglego-Rydza, 1937), 6–7; Marek Jablonowski and Piotr Stawecki, *Nastepca Komendanta: Edward Smigly-Rydz. Materialy do biografii* (Pultusk: Wyzsza Szkola Humanistyczna, 1998).

36. *Glos Brzezanski* 7 (1937), 1.

37. Ibid., 2–5; Rusinski, "Hufiec Brzezany."

38. *Brzezany, 1530–1930*, 13–15.

39. For information on Jewish organizations and associations in Brzezany, see Katz, ed., *Brzezany Memorial Book*. Short official reports on the various Jewish associa-tions in interwar Brzezany are located in Derzhavnyi Arkhiv Ternopil'skoi Oblasti, Ternopil' (hereafter DATO).

40. Katz, ed., *Brzezany Memorial Book*, 106–119.

41. Fond 338, op. 1, File 231, 21, 23, Tsentral'nyi Derzhavnyi Istoricheskii Arkhiv, L'viv (hereafter TsDIAL); Fond 7, op. 1, File 164, 1, 2, 4, DATO; File 260, 1–3, DATO.

42. Fond 342, op. 1, File 17, passim, TsDIAL. According to Samuel D. Kassow, Jewish community activities in the shtetl usually depended on a small core of people. See Gutman, *The Jews of Poland between Two World Wars*, 207.

43. Prosvita societies throughout eastern Galicia promoted Ukrainian literacy and culture. They were active in establishing Ukrainian school, libraries, and read-ing rooms.

44. Fond 348, op. 1, File 1025, 21, 23, TsDIAL.

45. Fond 348, op. 1, File 1025, 48, TsDIAL.

46. Fond 348, op. 1, File 1025, 79–81, TsDIAL.

47. Fond 348, op. 1, File 1029, 11–12; File 1030, 93–100, TsDIAL.

48. Fond 348, op. 1, File 1030, 117, TsDIAL.

49. Fond 348, op. 1, File 1029, 19–20, TsDIAL.

50. Fond 348, op. 1, File 1030, 245, TsDIAL.

51. *Berezhans'ka zemlia* 1: 124–134.

52. Fond 206, op. 1, File 435, 64, TsDIAL.

53. Fond 206, op. 1, File 436, 94–95, TsDIAL.

54. Fond 206, op. 1, File 438, 22, TsDIAL.

55. Fond 389, op. 1, File 209, 26–28, TsDIAL; File 210, 3, TsDIAL.

56. *Glos Brzezanski* 2 (1933), 10.

57. *Glos Brzezanski* 11 (1933), 4; *Glos Brzezanski* 5 (1934), 5.

58. *Glos Brzezanski* 4 (1933), 10; *Glos Brzezanski* 11 (1933), 10.

59. *Glos Brzezanski* 11 (1933), 8.

60. *Berezhans'ka zemlia* 1: 241–248.

61. *Glos Brzezanski* 5 (1934), 11; *Glos Brzezanski* 6 (1934), 11.

62. *Glos Brzezanski* 17 (1935), 1, 3.

63. *Glos Brzezanski* 11 (1936), 5.

64. *Glos Brzezanski* 13 (1937), 1.

65. *Hajdamaks* is a pejorative Polish term from the eighteenth century for Ukrainian robbers and highwaymen. *Glos Brzezanski* 1 (1938), 6; *Glos Brzezanski* 3 (1938), 8.

66. *Glos Brzezanski* 1 (1939), 7.

67. *Glos Brzezanski* 6 (1939), 8.

68. *Glos Brzezanski* 12 (1939), 7.

69. *Berezhans'ka zemlia* 1: 276–277.

70. Fond 7, op. 1, File 191, 2–3, DATO.

71. Fond 7, op. 1, File 191, 6, DATO.

72. *Glos Brzezanski* 6 (1932), 13.

73. *Glos Brzezanski* 5 (1933), 6, 12.

74. *Glos Brzezanski* 12 (1937), 1, 12.

75. Personal communication from Mundek Sauberberg-Harpaz.

76. Ibid.

77. Interview with Tolek Rapf, Gdansk, July 1998.

78. Interview with Halszka Rapf-Wierzbicka, Warsaw, June 1997.

79. Interview with Batya Prizand-Bone, Haifa, February 1997.

80. Interview with Vasyl Oleskiw, London, October 1997.

81. Interview with Tolek Rapf.

82. Interview with Stanislaw Skrzypek, Arlington, Virginia, September 1998.

83. Interview with Wladyslawa Cwynar-Baranek, Ustron, June 1997.

84. Interview with Karol Codogni, Omer, May 1986.

85. Interview with Lev Rega, Berezhany, July 1998.

86. Interview with Vasyl Oleskiw.

87. Interview with Dmytro Bartkiw, London, October 1997.

88. Interview with Vasyl Fanga, Berezhany, August 1997.

89. Interview with Israel Ne'eman-Neumann, Tel-Aviv, April 1997.

90. Interview with Tolek Rapf.

91. Interview with Halszka Rapf-Wierzbicka, Warsaw, June 1997.

92. Interview with Stanislaw Skrzypek.

93. Interview with L. Poldek, Queens, New York, September 1998.

94. Interview with Jozef Slotwinski, Obory, July 1998.

95. Interview with Natan Goldman, Haifa, February 1997.

96. Telephone interview with S. A. Goldschlag, September 1998.

97. Interview with Anna Herzog, Bytom, July 1998.

98. Telephone interview with S. A. Goldschlag.

99. Interview with Lev Rega.

100. Interview with Galina Skaskiv, Lviv, August 1997.

101. Interview with Jozef Slotwinski.

102. Interview with Batya Prizand-Bone.

103. Interview with Bela Feld-Danieli, March 1997.

104. Interview with Tolek Rapf.

105. Interview with Batya Prizand-Bone.

106. Interview with Michal Kaminski, Ustron, June 1997. Endek was a member of Endecja, an extremely nationalist and anti-Semitic party in interwar Poland.

107. Interview with Israel Ne'eman-Neumann.

108. Interview with Mordechai Majblum, Yokneam, October 1997.

109. Interview with L. Poldek.

110. Interview with Lev Rega.

111. Interview with Marian-Dmytro Hajwa, London, October 1997.

112. Interview with Vasyl Oleskiw.

113. Interview with Dmytro Bartkiw.

114. Interview with Galina Skaskiv.

115. Interview with Vasyl Fanga.

4. THE SOVIET INTERLUDE, 1939–1941

1. Jan Tomasz Gross, *Revolution from Abroad: The Soviet Conquest of Poland's Western Ukraine and Western Belorussia* (Princeton, N.J.: Princeton University Press, 1988), passim.

2. Ibid., 25–27.

3. Irena Grudzinska-Gross and Jan Tomasz Gross, *War through Children's Eyes: The Soviet Occupation of Poland and the Deportations, 1939–1941* (Stanford, Calif.: Hoover Institution Press, 1981), 6–7.

4. Gross, *Revolution from Abroad*, 29–35.

5. Ben-Cion Pinchuk, *Shtetl Jews under Soviet Rule: Eastern Poland on the Eve of the Holocaust* (Cambridge, Mass.: Basil Blackwell, 1990), 26.

6. Gross, *Revolution from Abroad*, 52, 55.

7. Orest Subtelny, *Ukraine: A History* (Toronto: University of Toronto Press, 1988), 454.

8. Pinchuk, *Shtetl Jews under Soviet Rule*, 89, 97.

9. David R. Marples, "The Ukrainians in Eastern Poland under Soviet Occupation, 1939–1941: A Study in Soviet Rural Policy," in *The Soviet Takeover of the Polish Eastern Provinces*, ed. Keith Sword (Basingstoke: Macmillan, 1991), 236–252.

10. After the outbreak of World War II, the NKVD was in charge of massive arrests and deportations from the annexed Polish territories, in addition to other security tasks.

11. Grudzinska-Gross and Gross, *War through Children's Eyes*, 13–17; Pinchuk, *Shtetl Jews under Soviet Rule*, 93–94.

12. Gross, *Revolution from Abroad*, 126–138.

13. Keith Sword, *Deportation and Exile: Poles in the Soviet Union, 1939–1948* (London: Macmillan, 1994), 5–7.

14. Subtelny, *Ukraine: A History*, 457.

15. Ibid., 13–19, 25–27.

16. The description of Brzezany under Soviet rule in 1939–1941 is based on *Berezhans'ka zemlia* 1: 278–297; Katz, ed., *Brzezany Memorial Book*, 98–103; Zbigniew Rusinski, *Tryptyk Brzezanski* (Wroclaw: "W kolorach teczy," Oficyna Artystyczno-Wydawnicza, 1998), 14–26.

17. Leszek Zachuta, *51 Pulk Piechoty Strzelcow Kresowych im. Giuseppe Garibaldiego* (Pruszkow: Oficyna Wydawnicza "Ajaks," 1992), 23–24.

18. *Chervona berezhanshchina,* June 4, 1941.

19. Katz, ed., *Brzezany Memorial Book,* 101.

20. *Chervona berezhanshchina,* October 9, 1939.

21. Interview with Tolek Rapf, Gdansk, July 1998.

22. Testimony by Sima Kvodi-Ehre, 03–9534, YVA.

23. Interview with Iulian Pavliv, Lviv, March 1997.

24. Interview with Myroslav Labunka by Jan T. Gross, Philadelphia, Spring 1981; Gross, *Revolution from Abroad,* 44; Janina Karnilowska, "Zbrodnia na Proboszczu," *Gosc Niedzielny,* Katowice, July 23, 1989, 2; Vasil' Rabik, *Trostianets: Naris istorii sela* (Berezhani: Published by the author, 1999), 41.

25. Interview with Tolek Rapf.

26. Interview with Halszka Rapf-Wierzbicka, Warsaw, June 1997.

27. Interview with Menachem Katz, Haifa, February 1997.

28. Interview with Efraim Schmidt, Haifa, February 1997.

29. Interview with Rozka Majblum-Sandel, Haifa, February 1997.

30. Interview with Iulian Pavliv.

31. Interview with Vasyl Fanga, Berezhany, August 1997.

32. Interview with Galina Skaskiv, Lviv, August 1997.

33. Interview with Vasyl Oleskiw, London, October 1997.

34. Interview with Ludmila Lubelska-Michorowska, Warsaw, June 1997.

35. Interview with Halszka Rapf-Wierzbicka.

36. Interview with Rozka Majblum-Sandel, Haifa, February 1997.

37. Interview with Wladyslawa Cwynar-Baranek, Ustron, June 1997.

38. Interview with Vasyl Oleskiw.

39. Interview with Vasyl Fanga.

40. Interview with Seweryn Grossfeld, Jerusalem, July 1997.

41. Interview with Tolek Rapf.

42. Interview with Halszka Rapf-Wierzbicka, Warsaw, June 1997.

43. Interview with Iulian Pavliv.

44. Interview with Ludmila Lubelska-Michorowska.

45. Interview with Wladyslawa Cwynar-Baranek.

46. Interview with Menachem Katz.

47. Interview with L. Poldek, Queens, New York, September 1998.

48. Letter from Chana Feld to Bela Feld-Danieli, undated, copy in author's possession; Interview with Bela Feld-Danieli, March 1997.

49. Interview with Menachem Katz.

50. Joseph Soski, "Memories of a Vanished World," unpublished memoirs, 1991, 38–44; and Soski's letter to the author, July 20, 1998.

5. THE GERMAN OCCUPATION, 1941–1944

1. Dieter Pohl, *Nationalsozialistische Judenverfolgung in Ostgalizien, 1941–1944* (München: Oldenbourg, 1997), 301, 399–310.

2. For a discussion of the Poles under German rule in the District of Galicia, see

Wlodzimierz Bonusiak, *Malopolska Wschodnia pod rzadami Trzeciej Rzeszy* (Rzeszow: WSP, 1990); Ryszard Torzecki, *Polacy i Ukraincy: Sprawa ukrainska w czasie II wojny swiatowej na terenie II Rzeczypospolitej* (Warsaw: Wydawn. Nauk. PWN, 1993); and J. Lukaszow (T. A. Olszanski), "Walki polsko-ukrainskie, 1943–1947," *Zeszyty Historyczne* 90 (1989): 159–199.

3. Jan Tomasz Gross, *Revolution from Abroad: The Soviet Conquest of Poland's Western Ukraine and Western Belorussia* (Princeton, N.J.: Princeton University Press, 1988), 179; Ivan Bilas, *Represyvno-karal'na systema v Ukraini, 1917–1953*, Vol. 2 (Kiev: "Lybid'," 1994), 225. For an extensive discussion of the massacres, see Bogdan Musial, *"Konterrevolutionäre Elemente sind zu erschiessen": die Brutalisierung des deutsch-sowjetischen Krieges im Sommer 1941* (Berlin: Propyläen, 2000), 102–142. Musial argues that what looked like evidence of torture resulted mostly from machine-gun and hand-grenade killings. According to Musial, some of the corpses were mutilated posthumously by Ukrainian nationalists in order to support their anti-Bolshevik and anti-Jewish propaganda (262–269). The total number of prisoners deported to the Soviet interior was, according to Musial, 16,340, and the number of those murdered was close to 10,000 (200–210). Among the murdered prisoners were also Poles and Jews. This fact was usually omitted by German and Ukrainian accounts.

4. Gross, *Revolution from Abroad*, 181–186; Andrzej Zbikowski, "Local Anti-Jewish Pogroms in the Occupied Territories of Eastern Poland, June–July 1941," in *The Holocaust in the Soviet Union*, ed. Lucjan Dobroszycki and Jeffrey S. Gurock (Armonk, N.J.: M. E. Sharpe, 1993), 173–179; Jan Tomasz Gross, *Sasiedzi: historia zaglady zydowskiego miasteczka* (Sejny: Pogranicze, 2000). For German anti-Jewish propaganda and the incitement of the local population against Jews, see Zhanna Kovba, *Liudianist' u bezodni pekla: povedinka mistsevoho naselennia skhidnoï Halychyny v roky "Ostatochnoho rozv'iazannia ievreis'koho pytannia"* (Kiev: Sfera, 1998), 70–76, 100–101; and Musial, *"Konterrevolutionäre Elemente sind zu erschiessen,"* 200–210. Musial discusses anti-Jewish pogroms in eastern Galicia on 172–199.

5. Orest Subtelny, *Ukraine: A History* (Toronto: University of Toronto Press, 1988), 463–465.

6. Pohl, *Nationalsozialistische Judenverfolgung in Ostgalizien*, 312.

7. Jan Tomasz Gross, *Polish Society under German Occupation: The Generalgouvernement, 1939–1941* (Princeton, N.J.: Princeton University Press, 1979), 189; Subtelny, *Ukraine: A History*, 468; Torzecki, *Polacy i Ukraincy*, 47.

8. Lukaszow, "Walki polsko-ukrainskie," 163.

9. Ibid., 173.

10. Pohl, *Nationalsozialistische Judenverfolgung in Ostgalizien*, 54–65; Ia. S. Khonigsman, O. Ia. Naiman, and F. Ia. Gorovskii, *Evrei Ukrainy*, Vol. 2 (Kiev: Ukrainsko-finskii in-t menedzhmenta i biznesa, 1995), 129–131. For a discussion of German and Ukrainian attitudes toward and images of Jews in the newly occupied ex-Soviet territories, see Musial, *"Konterrevolutionäre Elemente sind zu erschiessen."*

11. For a discussion of the mass killings of Jews in eastern Galicia, see Pohl, *Nationalsozialistische Judenverfolgung in Ostgalizien*; Eliyahu Jones, *The Jews of Lvov during the Second World War and in the Holocaust* (Russian) (Jerusalem: Rossiiskaia Biblioteka Kholokosta, 1999); and Musial, *"Konterrevolutionäre Elemente sind zu erschiessen."* On the VoMi, see Valdis O. Lumans, *Himmler's Auxiliaries: The Volksdeutsche*

Mittelstelle and the German National Minorities of Europe, 1933–1945 (Chapel Hill: University of North Carolina Press, 1993); and Pohl, *Nationalsozialistische Judenverfolgung in Ostgalizien,* 297–300.

12. For a discussion of the Judenraete, see Isaiah Trunk, *Judenrat: The Jewish Councils in Eastern Europe under Nazi Occupation* (New York: Macmillan, 1972).

13. Pohl, *Nationalsozialistische Judenverfolgung in Ostgalizien,* 13.

14. *Pinkas Hakehillot:* kaf khet; see also Pohl, *Nationalsozialistische Judenverfolgung in Ostgalizien,* 253.

15. Pohl, *Nationalsozialistische Judenverfolgung in Ostgalizien,* 178–179.

16. For a discussion of Gentile rescuers of Jews, see Nechama Tec, *When Light Pierced the Darkness: Righteous Christians and the Polish Jews* (New York: Oxford University Press, 1986); and S. P. Oliner and P. M. Oliner, *The Altruistic Personality: Rescuers of Jews in Nazi Europe* (New York: Free Press, 1988). For Ukrainian rescuers of Jews in eastern Galicia, see Kovba, *Liudianist' u bezodni pekla,* 154–202.

17. Pohl, *Nationalsozialistische Judenverfolgung in Ostgalizien,* 363.

18. A. Wais, "Some Circles of the Ukrainian National Movement and the Problem of Jews during the Second World War." (Russian) *Vestnik evreiskogo universiteta v Moskve* (Moscow-Jerusalem) 2, no. 9 (1995): 104–113.

19. The issue of Jews serving in the UPA is discussed in Philip Friedman, "Ukrainian-Jewish Relations during the Nazi Occupation," in *Roads to Extinction: Essays on the Holocaust,* ed. Ada June Friedman (New York: Jewish Publication Society of America, 1980), 188; Taras Hunczak, "Ukrainian-Jewish Relations during the Soviet and Nazi Occupations," in *Ukraine during World War II: History and Its Aftermath,* edited by Yury Boshyk (Edmonton: Canadian Institute of Ukrainian Studies, University of Alberta, 1986), 42; Edward Prus, *Holocaust po Banderowsku: czy Zydzi byli w UPA?* (Wroclaw: Wydawn. "Nortom," 1995), 153–172; Kovba, *Liudianist' u bezodni pekla,* 108–115, 224–230.

20. For a discussion of Sheptyts'kyi's attitude and behavior toward Jews, see Shimon Redlich, "Sheptyts'kyi and the Jews during World War II," *Magocsi* (1989): 145–162.

21. Pohl, *Nationalsozialistische Judenverfolgung in Ostgalizien,* 381–385.

22. Zbigniew Rusinski, *Tryptyk Brzezanski* (Wroclaw: W kolorach teczy, Oficyna Artystyczno-Wydawnicza, 1998), 27; *Berezhans'ki Visti* 4 (1941).

23. Ivan Bilas, *Represyvno-karal'na systema v Ukraini, 1917–1953,* Vol. 2 (Kiev: "Lybid'," 1994), 222–225, 230–234; Rusinski, *Tryptyk Brzezanski,* 32; *Berezhans'ki Visti* 1, July 24, 1941. The overcrowded prison in Brzezany was inhabited by 351 prisoners. Its prewar capacity was 160. See Musial, *"Konterrevolutionäre Elemente sind zu erschiessen,"* 96.

24. Bilas, *Represyvno-karal'na systema v Ukraini,* 248–249.

25. *Berezhans'ki Visti* 2, July 27, 1941.

26. *Berezhans'ki Visti* 1, July 24, 1941; *Berezhans'ka zemlia* 1: 300.

27. *Berezhans'ki Visti* 1, July 24, 1941; Rusinski, *Tryptyk Brzezanski,* 33; Menachem Ben Shimon Katz, ed., *Brzezany Memorial Book* (Hebrew) (Haifa: Irgun yots'e Bz'ez'ani Narayuv veha-sevivah be-Yisra'el uve-Artsot ha-Berit, 1978), 261.

28. Rusinski, *Tryptyk Brzezanski,* 33–34.

29. *Berezhans'ki Visti* 14, September 4, 1941; *Berezhans'ka zemlia* 1: 301.

30. Rusinski, *Tryptyk Brzezanski,* 36–37; *Berezhans'ka zemlia* 1: 304–305.

31. Miroslaw Kushnir, "Dnevnik. Zoshit siomii," *Volia i bat'kivshchina* 2 (11/27/1998): 85; AK Report, June 10, 1943, 203/XV-7, Archiwum Akt Nowych, Warsaw (hereafter AAN).

32. For information concerning Hubert Kohnen, see Brzezany Collection of witnesses' testimonies, peh ain/01167, YVA and 208 AR 797/66, LA. See also interview with Michal Kaminski, Ustron, June 1997.

33. Kazimierz Moczarski, *Rozmowy z katem* (Warsaw: Wydawnictwo Naukowe PWN, 1977. Hebrew version, Tel-Aviv: ha-Kibuts ha-me'uhad, 1979), 40–41, 136.

34. *Berezhans'ki Visti* 35, November 27, 1941.

35. For information on the various police units in Brzezany, see Asbach Case, AR-Z 76/61, 202, LA; *Berezhans'ka zemlia* 1: 303.

36. *Berezhans'ki Visti* 23, October 5, 1941; *Berezhans'ki Visti* 32, November 13, 1941; *Berezhans'ki Visti* 33, November 16, 1941.

37. *Berezhans'ka zemlia* 1: 311–312; *Ukrainians and Jews: A Symposium* (New York: Ukranian Congress Committee of America, Inc., 1966), 123–126; *Berezhans'ka zemlia* 1: 812.

38. Lev Stetkevych, *Iak z Berezhan do kadry: spogady z divizii,* (Ternopil': "Dzhura," 1998), 16; AK Report, July 1, 1943, 203/XV-41, AAN; Kushnir, "Dnevnik. Zoshit siomii," 73.

39. Rusinski, *Tryptyk Brzezanski,* 71–89.

40. Ibid., 117–135.

41. Ibid., 37–47, 83–87, 128; Gestapo Report, May 22, 1944, 0–32/99, YVA.

42. Rusinski, *Tryptyk Brzezanski,* 87; AK Reports, 203/XV-16 and 203/XV-28, AAN.

43. Katz, ed., *Brzezany Memorial Book,* 264–271.

44. Ibid., 266–268; 271–273.

45. *Berezhans'ki Visti* 3(46), January 15, 1942.

46. Katz, ed., *Brzezany Memorial Book,* 308–313, 321–323, 328–329. For different estimates of the number of Jews taken from Brzezany to Belzec, see Robin O'Neil, "Belzec: A Reassessment of the Number of Victims," *East European Jewish Affairs* 29, no. 1–2 (Summer–Winter 1999): 95, 99, 100, 102. According to O'Neil, the total number of Brzezany Jews who arrived in Belzec was 3,600.

47. Police Reports to Lemberg Kripo, 1942–1944, p. 4, R-36/1/6, DALO.

48. Katz, ed., *Brzezany Memorial Book,* 331–332; 337–339; Testimony by Dr. Elieser Schaklai, Asbach Case, AR-Z 76/61, 208, LA; Kushnir, "Dnevnik. Zoshit siomii," 83–85. For the last roundup of Jews in Brzezany, see also letter by Stanislaw Czerwinski, November 3, 1946, 03/3307, YVA; letter by Dr. Alfred Schuessel, November 25, 1944, M-49, 4225, YVA; Thomas Sandkühler, *"Endloesung" in Galizien: Der Judenmord in Ostpolen und die Rettungsinitiativen von Bertold Beitz, 1941–1944* (Bonn: Dietz, 1996), 267.

49. Katz, ed., *Brzezany Memorial Book,* 342–344. For an account of attempts by Ukrainians in Brzezany and in the surrounding villages to assist Jews, see *Ukrainians and Jews: A Symposium,* 123–126. Assistance to Jews by the Polish parish priest in Brzezany, Rev. Adam Lancucki, and by the Ukrainian priest Stepan Baczynski is discussed in *Ukrainians and Jews: A Symposium,* 124; and in Michal Grynberg, ed., *Ksiega Sprawiedliwych* (Warsaw: Wydawn. Nauk. PWN, 1993), 89, 562.

50. According to a German newspaper published in Lwow in December 1942,

the population of Brzezany was then 13,649 (4,181 Ukrainians, 3,832 Poles, and 5,636 Jews). Quoted in Kovba, *Liudianist' u bezodni pekla*, 150. Baedecker's *Travelguide for the Generalgouvernement*, published in 1943, mentioned 8,400 residents in Brzezany. A publication of the Office of Statistics of the Generalgouvernement, published in 1943, mentioned 10,297 inhabitants in Brzezany. See *Das Generalgouvernement, Reisehandbuch* (Leipzig: Baedeker, 1943), 231; *Amtliches Gemeinde- und Dorfverzeichnis für das General-gouvernement* (Krakau: Burgverlag Krakau g.m.b.h., 1943), 3.

51. Interview with Ludmila Lubelska-Michorowska, Warsaw, June 1997.

52. Interview with Karol Codogni, Omer, May 1986.

53. Eliezer Wagszal-Shaklai, "Memoirs," unpublished manuscript, n.d.; Elyashiv Oren, *Doctor's Come Back* (Hebrew) (Tel-Aviv: Sifriyat po'alim, 1981); Katz, ed., *Brzezany Memorial Book*, 271, 336.

54. Interviews with Rena Wanderer-Stolarsky and Ruth Wanderer-Biheller.

55. Interview with Prof. Michael Thaler, Holocaust Oral History Project, San Francisco, September 1989.

56. Wagszal-Shaklai, "Memoirs."

57. Interview with Michael Thaler.

58. Interview with Karol Codogni.

59. Interview with Irena Partynska-Wesolowska, Ustron, June 1997.

60. Interview with Dmytro Bartkiw, London, October 1997.

61. Interview with Vasyl Fanga, Berezhany, August 1997.

62. Interview with Vasyl Oleskiw, London, October 1997.

63. Interview with Ivan Fanga, Berezhany, August 1997.

64. Interview with Galina Skaskiv, Lviv, August 1997.

65. Testimony by Pinhas Fenner, M-1/E, 263, YVA.

66. Interview with L. Poldek, Queens, New York, September 1998.

67. Interview with Rozka Majblum-Sandel, Haifa, February 1997.

68. Interviews with Rena Wanderer-Stolarsky and Ruth Wanderer-Biheller, Lakeview, New Jersey, September 1998.

69. Interview with Michael Thaler.

70. Interviews with Rena Wanderer-Stolarsky and Ruth Wanderer-Biheller.

71. Interview with Michael Thaler.

72. Interview with Tolek Rapf, Gdansk, July 1998.

73. Interview with Vasyl Oleskiw.

74. Interview with Galina Skaskiv.

75. Interview with Dmytro Bartkiw.

76. Interview with Lev Rega, Berezhany, August 1997.

77. Interview with Ivan Hrabar, London, October 1997.

78. Interview with Michael Thaler.

79. Menachem Ben Shimon Katz, *Path of Hope* (Hebrew) (Tel-Aviv: 'Eked, 1992), 9–26.

80. Interview with Tolek Rapf.

81. Interview with Halszka Rapf-Wierzbicka, Warsaw, June 1997.

82. Interview with Stanislawa Czajkowska-Sabi, Ustron, June 1997.

83. Interview with Vasyl Oleskiw.

84. Interview with Ivan Fanga, Berezhany, August 1997.

85. Interview with Galina Skaskiv.

86. Interview with Aleksandr Pankiv, Berezhany, July 1998.

87. Asbach Case, AR-Z 76/61, 208, LA.

88. Asbach Case, AR-Z 76/61, 202, LA.

89. Interviews with Rena Wanderer-Stolarsky and Ruth Wanderer-Biheller.

90. Interview with Krystyna Stronska-Gryczynska, Ustron, June 1997.

91. Asbach Case, AR-Z 76/61, 202, LA.

92. Ibid.

93. Asbach Case, AR-Z 76/61, 208, LA.

94. Ibid.

95. The Karaites were descendants of a sect that originated in Judaism. They were usually not persecuted by the Nazis.

96. Menachem Dul, *Z otchlani* (Haifa: Published by the author, 1967), 70.

97. Asbach Case, AR-Z 76/61, 208, LA.

98. Wagszal-Shaklai, "Memoirs"; Oren, *Doctor's Come Back.*

99. Interview with Rena Wanderer-Stolarsky and Ruth Wanderer-Biheller.

100. Interview with Anna Herzog, Bytom, July 1998.

101. Interview with L. Poldek.

102. Interview with Zbigniew Rusinski; Rusinski, *Tryptyk Brzezanski,* 126–130.

103. Janina Drobnicka-Oleksyn, unpublished memoirs, Olawa, 1990.

104. Zofia Sniadecka-Ornatowska File, Righteous Gentiles Collection, YVA.

105. Interview with Rozka Majblum-Sandel, Haifa, February 1997.

106. Interview with Ivan Hrabar.

107. Interview with Vasyl Oleskiw.

108. Interview with Vasyl Fanga.

109. Interview with Ivan Fanga.

110. Interview with Lev Rega.

111. Interview with Dmytro Bartkiw.

112. Interview with Tolek Rapf.

113. Interview with Irena Partynska-Wesolowska, Ustron, June 1997.

114. Interview with Tolek Rapf.

115. Interview with Halszka Rapf-Wierzbicka, Warsaw, June 1997.

116. Interview with Galina Skaskiv.

117. Interview with Ludmila Lubelska-Michorowska.

118. Interview with Halszka Rapf-Wierzbicka.

119. Interview with Lev Rega.

120. Gross, *Revolution from Abroad,* 226; Kaja Kazmierska, *Doswiadczenia wojenne polaków a ksztaltowanie tosamosci etnicznej: analiza narracji kresowych* (Warsaw: Wydawn. Instytutu Filozofii i Socjologii PAN, 1999), 72, 79, 93.

121. Richard C. Lukas, *The Forgotten Holocaust: The Poles under German Occupation, 1939–1944* (Lexington: University Press of Kentucky, 1986), 144.

122. Gross, *Sasiedzi: historia zaglady zydowskiego miasteczka.* See also Jan Tomasz Gross, *Upiorna dekada: trzy eseje o stereotypach na temat Zydow, Polakow, Niemcow i Komunistow, 1939–1948* (Krakow: Universitas, 1998).

123. For a discussion of Ukrainian attitudes toward Jews under German occupation, see Friedman, "Ukrainian-Jewish Relations during the Nazi Occupation," 176–

208; Wais, "Some Circles of the Ukrainian National Movement"; Taras Hunczak, "Ukrainian-Jewish Relations during the Soviet and Nazi Occupations," in *Ukraine during World War II: History and Its Aftermath*, ed. Yury Boshyk (Edmonton: Canadian Institute of Ukrainian Studies, University of Alberta, 1986), 39–57; Yaroslav Hrytsak, *Narys istoriï Ukraïny: formuvannia modernoï ukraïns'koï natsiï XIX–XX stolittia* (Kiev: Vyd-vo "Heneza," 1996), 227–347.

124. John-Paul Himka, "Ukrainian Collaboration in the Extermination of the Jews during World War II: Sorting Out the Long-Term and Conjunctural Factors," *Studies in Contemporary Jewry: An Annual* 13 (1997): 179.

125. For a discussion of personal motivations and perceptions of German executioners of Jews, see Christopher R. Browning, *Ordinary Men: Reserve Police Battalion 101 and the Final Solution in Poland* (New York: HarperCollins, 1992); and Daniel Jonah Goldhagen, *Hitler's Willing Executioners: Ordinary Germans and the Holocaust* (New York: Knopf, 1996).

6. THE AFTERMATH, 1944–1945

1. Orest Subtelny, *Ukraine: A History* (Toronto: University of Toronto Press, 1988), 487–488, 495.

2. Yaroslav Bilinsky, *The Second Soviet Republic: The Ukraine after World War II* (New Brunswick, N.J.: Rutgers University Press, 1964), 90; Subtelny, *Ukraine: A History*, 488; Bohdan Rostyslaw Bociurkiw, *The Ukrainian Greek Catholic Church and the Soviet State (1939–1950)* (Edmonton: Canadian Institute of Ukrainian Studies Press, 1996), 73, 100–115; Volodimir Sergiichuk, *Desiat' buremnykh lit: zakhidnoukraïns'ki zemli v 1944-1953 rr.: novi dokumenty i materialy* (Kiev: Vyd-vo khudozhn'oï lit-ry "Dnipro," 1998), 279.

3. Jeffrey Burds, "AGENTURA: Soviet Informants' Networks and the Ukrainian Underground in Galicia, 1944–1948," *East European Politics and Societies* 11, no. 1 (Winter 1997): 93; Subtelny, *Ukraine: A History*, 479.

4. Sergiichuk, *Desiat' buremnykh lit*, 194–195, 214–218, 239.

5. Burds, "AGENTURA: Soviet Informants' Networks and the Ukrainian Underground," 97, 110; Andrzej Chojnowski, Ukraina. (Warsaw: Wydawn. TRIO, 1997), 169.

6. Burds, "AGENTURA: Soviet Informants' Networks and the Ukrainian Underground," 106–107, 109.

7. J. Lukaszow, "Walki polsko-ukrainskie, 1943–1947," *Zeszyty Historyczne* 90 (1989): 184–185.

8. Sergii Tkachev, *Pol'sko-ukraïns'kii transfer naselenniia 1944–1946 rr.: viselenniia poliakiw z Ternopilliia* (Ternopil: Pidruchniki i posibniki, 1997), 139.

9. Lukaszow, "Walki polsko-ukrainskie," 183–184; Grzegorz Hryciuk, "Nastroje i stosunek ludnosci polskiej tzw. Ukrainy Zachodniej do przesiedlen w latach 1944–1945 w swietle sprawozdan radzieckich," in *Polska i Ukraina po II Wojnie Swiatowej*, ed. Wlodzimierz Bonusiak (Rzeszow: WSP, 1998), 217; Stanislaw Ciesielski, *Przesiedlenie ludnosci polskiej z Kresow Wschodnich do Polski, 1944–1947* (Warsaw: Wydawn. Neriton; Instytut Historii PAN, 1999), 29.

10. Lukaszow, "Walki polsko-ukrainskie," 185–186; Mikolaj Terles, *Ethnic Cleansing of Poles in Volhynia and Eastern Galicia* (Toronto: Alliance of the Polish Eastern Provinces, 1993), 22, 61–62.

11. Hryciuk, "Nastroje i stosunek ludnosci polskiej tzw," 209, 215; Sergiichuk, *Desiat' buremnykh lit,* 206–207.

12. For a discussion of the population transfers, see Jan Czerniakiewicz, *Repatriacja ludnosci polskiej z ZSRR, 1944–1948* (Warsaw: Panstwowe Wydawn. Nauk, 1987); Oleg Gaidai and Bogdan Khavarivs'kii, "Armiia Kraiova na Ternopol'shchini (Serpen' 1944–Gruden' 1945 rr.)," in Bonusiak, ed., *Polska i Ukraina po II Wojnie Swiatowej,* 103; Tkachev, *Pol'sko-ukrains'kii transfer naselenniia,* 78, 83–85, 89–91; Yosef Litvak, *Polish-Jewish Refugees in the USSR, 1939–1946* (Hebrew). (Tel-Aviv: University of Jerusalem, Institute of Contemporary Jewry, 1988), 33, 59; Ciesielski, *Przesiedlenie ludnosci polskiej z Kresow Wschodnich do Polski.*

13. For estimates of the number of Jewish survivors in eastern Galicia, see *Pinkas Hakehillot:* khaf-tet; Sergiichuk, *Desiat' buremnykh lit,* 80, 89, 99; Dieter Pohl, *Nationalsozialistische Judenverfolgung in Ostgalizien, 1941–1944* (München: Oldenbourg, 1997), 382, 385; Litvak, *Polish-Jewish Refugees in the USSR,* 332–337, 355–358; Dov Levin, *The Jews in the Soviet-Annexed Territories, 1939–1941* (Hebrew). (Tel-Aviv: ha-Kibuts ha-me'uhad, 1989), 332.

14. For a discussion of the "demographic catastrophe" of eastern Galicia, see Zhanna Kovba, *Liudianist' u bezodni pekla: povedinka mistsevoho naselennia skhidnoï Halychyny v roky "Ostatochnoho rozv'iazannia ievreis'koho pytannia"* (Kiev: Sfera, 1998), 153–154, 234.

15. Zbigniew Rusinski, *Tryptyk Brzezanski* (Wroclaw: W kolorach teczy, Oficyna Artystyczno-Wydawnicza, 1998), 87–88, 93; Tkachev, *Pol'sko-ukrains'kii transfer naselenniia,* 126–128, 131–133.

16. *Strebki* is the shortened form for a Russian term meaning "members of the 'destruction batallions.'"

17. Tkachev, *Pol'sko-ukrains'kii transfer naselenniia,* 100; Vasil' Rabik, *Trostianets': Naris istorii sela* (Berezhani: Published by the author, 1999), 65–67.

18. Collection of the Soviet Special State Commission for the Investigation of Nazi Crimes, File "On the Atrocities of the German-Fascist Aggressors and Their Collaborators in the Berezhany Region of the Ternopol Oblast, USSR," M.33/896, YVA.

19. Tkachev, *Pol'sko-ukrains'kii transfer naselenniia,* 56.

20. Eliezer Wagszal-Shaklai, "Memoirs," unpublished manuscript, n.d.

21. Interviews with Miriam Nadler and Rachel Meser-Meler, Tel-Aviv, April 1997.

22. Interview with Zbigniew Zuczkowski, Warsaw, June 1997.

23. Interview with Karol Codogni, Omer, May 1986.

24. Interview with Ivan Fanga, Berezhany, August 1997.

7. THEIR RETURN

1. *Berezhans'ka zemlia* 1, passim; Menachem Ben Shimon Katz, ed., *Brzezany Memorial Book* (Hebrew) (Haifa: Irgun yots'e Bz'ez'ani Narayuv veha-sevivah be-Yisra'el uve-Artsot ha-Berit, 1978), passim.

2. Interview with Ryszard Brzezinski, Ustron, June 1997.

3. Interview with Zbigniew Rusinski, Ustron, June 1997.

4. *Folks-sztyme,* October 27, 1989.

5. Interview with Halszka Rapf-Wierzbicka, Gdansk, July 1998.

6. Letter from Tolek Rapf to the author, December 18, 1998.

7. Interview with Israel Ne'eman-Neumann, Tel-Aviv, April 1997.

8. Interview with Natan Goldman, Haifa, March 1998.

9. Interview with Bela Feld-Danieli, Tel-Aviv, April 1998.

10. A recording of Bela Feld-Danieli's remarks at Ustron, June 1997.

11. Interview with Bela Feld-Danieli.

12. "Dokumenty istorii," *Ukrainsky visnyk* 8 (1987).

13. For biographical information on Halyna Dydyk, see "Dokumenty istorii"; *Kafedra* 10 (1989); and the permanent exhibit on Halyna Dydyk at the Berezhany Etnographic Museum.

14. E-mail letter from Michael Thaler to the author, June 16, 1998.

15. Interview with Doron Majblum, Tel-Aviv, June 1997.

16. Interview with Dmytro Bartkiw, London, October 1997.

17. Interview with Vasyl Oleskiw, London, October 1997.

18. Interview with Ivan Hrabar, London, October 1997.

BIBLIOGRAPHY

Abramsky, Chimen, Maciej Jachimczyk, and Antony Polonsky, eds. *The Jews in Poland*. Oxford: Basil Blackwell, 1986.

Amtliches Gemeinde- und Dorfverzeichnis für das Generalgouvernement. Krakau: Burgverlag Krakau g.m.b.h., 1943.

Bartal, Israel, and Antony Polonsky. "Introduction: The Jews of Galicia under the Habsburgs." In *Polin: Studies in Polish Jewry*. Vol. 12, *Focusing on Galicia: Jews, Poles and Ukrainians, 1772–1918*, edited by Israel Bartal and Antony Polonsky, 3–24. London and Portland, Ore.: Littman Library of Jewish Civilization, 1999.

———, eds. *Polin: Studies in Polish Jewry*. Vol. 12, *Focusing on Galicia: Jews, Poles and Ukrainians, 1772–1918*. London and Portland, Ore.: Littman Library of Jewish Civilization, 1999.

Berezhans'ki Visti (twice-weekly newspaper).

Berezhans'ka zemlia: Istorychno-memuarnyi zbirnyk. Vol. 1. New York: Berezhany Regional Committee, 1970.

Berezhans'ka zemlia: Istorichno-memuarnii zbirnik. Vol. 2. Toronto (Berezhany Regional Committee, 1998), 624.

Bilas, Ivan. *Represyvno-karal'na systema v Ukraini, 1917–1953*. Vol. 2. Kiev: "Lybid'," 1994.

Bilinsky, Yaroslav. *The Second Soviet Republic: The Ukraine after World War II*. New Brunswick, N.J.: Rutgers University Press, 1964.

Bociurkiw, Bohdan Rostyslaw. *The Ukrainian Greek Catholic Church and the Soviet State (1939–1950)*. Edmonton: Canadian Institute of Ukrainian Studies Press, 1996.

Bonusiak, Wlodzimierz. *Malopolska Wschodnia pod rzadami Trzeciej Rzeszy*. Rzeszow: WSP, 1990.

———, ed. *Polska i Ukraina po II Wojnie Swiatowej*. Rzeszow: WSP, 1998.

Bonusiak, Wlodzimierz, and Jozef Buszko, eds. *Galicja i jej dziedzictwo*. Vol. 1, *Historia i polityka*. Rzeszow: WSP, 1994.

Browning, Christopher R. *Ordinary Men: Reserve Police Battalion 101 and the Final Solution in Poland*. New York: HarperCollins, 1992.

Brzezany 1530–1930. Brzezany: J. Landesberg, 1930.

Brzezany: Jednodniowka Akademicka 1927. Lwow: Inauguracyjne wydawnictwo Polskiego Akademickiego Kola Brzezanczykow we Lwowie, 1927.

Burds, Jeffrey. "AGENTURA: Soviet Informants' Networks and the Ukrainian Underground in Galicia, 1944–1948." *East European Politics and Societies* 11, no. 1 (Winter 1997): 89–130.

Buszko, Jozef. "Galicyjskie dziedzictwo II Rzeczypospolitej." In *Galicja i jej dziedzictwo.* Vol. 1, *Historia i polityka,* edited by Wlodzimierz Bonusiak and Jozef Buszko, 187–199. Rzeszow: WSP, 1994.

Chervona berezhanshchina 1933–1941 (irregularly published newspaper).

Chlopecki, Jerzy. "Galicja—skrzyzowanie drog." In *Galicja i jej dziedzictwo.* Vol. 2, *Spoleczenstwo i gospodarka,* edited by Jerzy Chlopecki and Helena Madurowicz-Urbanska, 27–48. Rzeszow: WSP, 1995.

Chlopecki, Jerzy, and Helena Madurowicz-Urbanska, eds. *Galicja i jej dziedzictwo.* Vol. 2, *Spoleczenstwo i gospodarka.* Rzeszow: WSP, 1995.

Chojnowski, Andrzej. *Koncepcje polityki narodowosciowej rzadów polskich w latach 1921–1939.* Wroclaw: Zaklad Narodowy im. Ossolinskich, 1979.

———. *Ukraina.* Warsaw: Wydawn. TRIO, 1997.

Ciesielski, Stanislaw. *Przesiedlenie ludnosci polskiej z Kresow Wschodnich do Polski, 1944–1947.* Warsaw: Wydawnictwo Neriton for Instytut Historii PAN, 1999.

Czerniakiewicz, Jan. *Repatriacja ludnosci polskiej z ZSRR, 1944–1948.* Warsaw: Panstwowe Wydawn. Nauk, 1987.

Das Generalgouvernement, Reisehandbuch. Leipzig: Baedeker, 1943.

Davies, Norman. *God's Playground: A History of Poland.* Vol. 2. Oxford: Clarendon, 1981.

Drobnicka-Oleksyn, Janina. Unpublished memoirs. Olawa, 1990.

Dul, Menachem. *Z otchlani.* Haifa: Published by the author, 1967.

Folks-sztyme (Warsaw weekly newspaper).

Friedman, Philip. "Ukrainian-Jewish Relations during the Nazi Occupation." In *Roads to Extinction: Essays on the Holocaust,* edited by Ada June Friedman, 176–208. New York: Jewish Publication Society of America, 1980.

Gaidai, Oleg, and Bogdan Khavarivs'kii. "Armiia Kraiova na Ternopol'shchini (Serpen' 1944–Gruden' 1945 rr.)." In *Polska i Ukraina po II Wojnie Swiatowej,* edited by Wlodzimierz Bonusiak, 89–103. Rzeszow: WSP, 1998.

Glos Brzezanski (irregularly published newspaper).

Goldhagen, Daniel Jonah. *Hitler's Willing Executioners: Ordinary Germans and the Holocaust.* New York: Knopf, 1996.

Gross, Jan Tomasz. *Polish Society under German Occupation: The Generalgouvernement, 1939–1941.* Princeton, N.J.: Princeton University Press, 1979.

———. *Revolution from Abroad: The Soviet Conquest of Poland's Western Ukraine and Western Belorussia.* Princeton, N.J.: Princeton University Press, 1988.

———. *Upiorna dekada: trzy eseje o stereotypach na temat Zydow, Polakow, Niemcow i Komunistow, 1939–1948.* Krakow: Universitas, 1998.

———. *Sasiedzi: historia zaglady zydowskiego miasteczka.* Sejny: Pogranicze, 2000.

Grudzinska-Gross, Irena, and Jan Tomasz Gross. *War through Children's Eyes: The Soviet Occupation of Poland and the Deportations, 1939–1941.* Stanford, Calif.: Hoover Institution Press, 1981.

Grynberg, Michal, ed. *Ksiega Sprawiedliwych.* Warsaw: Wydawn. Nauk. PWN, 1993.

Gutman, Israel, Ezra Mendelsohn, Yehuda Reinharz, and Chone Shmerukl, eds. *The*

Jews of Poland between Two World Wars. Hanover, N.H.: University Press of New England, 1989.

Himka, John-Paul. "Western Ukraine in the Interwar Period." *Nationalities Papers* 22, no. 2 (Fall 1994): 347–363.

———. "Ukrainian Collaboration in the Extermination of the Jews during World War II: Sorting Out the Long-Term and Conjunctural Factors." *Studies in Contemporary Jewry: An Annual* 13 (1997): 170–187.

———. "Dimensions of a Triangle: Polish-Ukrainian-Jewish Relations in Austrian Galicia." In *Polin: Studies in Polish Jewry.* Vol. 12, *Focusing on Galicia: Jews, Poles and Ukrainians, 1772–1918,* edited by Israel Bartal and Antony Polonsky, 25–45. London and Portland, Ore.: Littman Library of Jewish Civilization, 1999.

Hoffman, Eva. *Shtetl: The Life and Death of a Small Town and the World of Polish Jews.* New York: Houghton Mifflin, 1997.

Holzer, Jerzy. "Enlightenment, Assimilation, and Modern Identity: The Jewish Elite in Galicia." In *Polin: Studies in Polish Jewry.* Vol. 12, *Focusing on Galicia: Jews, Poles and Ukrainians, 1772–1918,* edited by Israel Bartal and Antony Polonsky, 79–85. London and Portland, Ore.: Littman Library of Jewish Civilization, 1999.

Hryciuk, Grzegorz. "Nastroje i stosunek ludnosci polskiej tzw. Ukrainy Zachodniej do przesiedlen w latach 1944–1945 w swietle sprawozdan radzieckich." In *Polska i Ukraina po II Wojnie Swiatowej,* edited by Wlodzimierz Bonusiak, 209–220. Rzeszow: WSP, 1998.

Hrytsak, Yaroslav. *Narys istoriï Ukraïny: formuvannia modernoï ukraïns'koï natsiï XIX–XX stolittia.* Kiev: Vyd-vo "Heneza," 1996.

Hunczak, Taras. "Ukrainian-Jewish Relations during the Soviet and Nazi Occupations." In *Ukraine during World War II: History and Its Aftermath,* edited by Yury Boshyk, 39–57. Edmonton: Canadian Institute of Ukrainian Studies, University of Alberta, 1986.

Jablonowski, Marek, and Piotr Stawecki. *Nastepca Komendanta: Edward Smigly-Rydz. Materialy do biografii.* Pultusk: Wyzsza Szkola Humanistyczna, 1998.

Jednodniowka mlodziezy Gimnazjum Panstwowego w Brzezanach. Brzezany: Nakladem mlodziezy, 1929.

Jednodniowka mlodziezy Gimnazjum Panstwowego im. Marszalka Edwarda Smiglego-Rydza w Brzezanach. Brzezany: Nakladem Gminy Szkolnej Gimnazjum Panstwowego im. Marszalka Edwarda Smiglego-Rydza, 1937.

Jones, Eliyahu. *The Jews of Lvov during the Second World War and in the Holocaust* (Russian). Jerusalem: Rossiiskaia Biblioteka Kholokosta, 1999.

Karnilowska, Janina. "Zbrodnia na Proboszczu." *Gosc Niedzielny* (Katowice), July 23, 1989, 2.

Katz, Menachem Ben Shimon. *Path of Hope* (Hebrew). Tel-Aviv: 'Eked, 1992.

———, ed. *Brzezany Memorial Book* (Hebrew). Haifa: Irgun yots'e Bz'ez'ani Narayuv veha-sevivah be-Yisra'el uve-Artsot ha-Berit, 1978.

Kazmierska, Kaja. *Doswiadczenia wojenne polaków a ksztaltowanie tozsamosci etnicznej: analiza narracji kresowych.* Warsaw: Wydawn. Instytutu Filozofii i Socjologii PAN, 1999.

Khonigsman, Ia. S., O. Ia. Naiman, and F. Ia. Gorovskii. *Evrei Ukrainy.* Vol. 2. Kiev: Ukrainsko-finskii in-t menedzhmenta i biznesa, 1995.

Kovba, Zhanna. *Liudianist' u bezodni pekla: povedinka mistsevoho naselennia skhidnoï Halychyny v roky "Ostatochnoho rozv'iazannia ievreis'koho pytannia."* Kiev: Sfera, 1998.

Kresy Wschodnie II Rzeczypospolitej: Brzezany. Brochure. Krakow: n.p., 1993.

Kushnir, Miroslaw. "Dnevnik. Zoshit siomii." *Volia i bat'kivshchina* 2 (11/27/1998): 72–93.

Levin, Dov. *The Jews in the Soviet-Annexed Territories, 1939–1941* (Hebrew). Tel-Aviv: ha-Kibuts ha-me'uhad, 1989.

Litvak, Yosef. *Polish-Jewish Refugees in the USSR, 1939–1946* (Hebrew). Tel-Aviv: Hebrew University of Jerusalem, Institute of Contemporary Jewry, 1988.

Lukas, Richard, C. *The Forgotten Holocaust: The Poles under German Occupation, 1939–1944.* Lexington: University Press of Kentucky, 1986.

Lukaszow, J. (T. A. Olszanski). "Walki polsko-ukrainskie, 1943–1947." *Zeszyty Historyczne* 90 (1989): 159–199.

Lumans, Valdis O. *Himmler's Auxiliaries: The Volksdeutsche Mittelstelle and the German National Minorities of Europe, 1933–1945.* Chapel Hill: University of North Carolina Press, 1993.

Magocsi, Paul R. *Morality and Reality: The Life and Times of Andrei Sheptyts'kyi.* Edmonton: Canadian Institute of Ukrainian Studies, University of Alberta, 1989.

Marples, David R. "The Ukrainians in Eastern Poland under Soviet Occupation, 1939–1941: A Study in Soviet Rural Policy." In *The Soviet Takeover of the Polish Eastern Provinces,* edited by Keith Sword, 236–252. Basingstoke: Macmillan, 1991.

Maziakowski, Krzysztof. *Zycie codzienne w Brzezanach w latach 1932–1939 w swietle "Glosu Brzezanskiego."* Praca magisterska. Wroclaw: Uniwersytet Wroclawski, 1993.

Mendelsohn, Ezra. *Zionism in Poland: The Formative Years, 1915–1926.* New Haven, Conn.: Yale University Press, 1981.

———. *The Jews of East-Central Europe between the World Wars.* Bloomington: Indiana University Press, 1983.

———. "Interwar Poland: Good for the Jews or Bad for the Jews?" In *The Jews in Poland,* edited by Chimen Abramsky, Maciej Jachimczyk, and Antony Polonsky. Oxford: Basil Blackwell, 1986.

Moczarski, Kazimierz. *Rozmowy z katem.* Warsaw, 1977; Hebrew version, Tel-Aviv: ha-Kibuts ha-me'uhad, 1979.

Motyl, Alexander J. *The Turn to the Right: The Ideological Origins and Development of Ukrainian Nationalism, 1919–1929.* New York: Columbia University Press, 1980.

Musial, Bogdan. *"Konterrevolutionäre Elemente sind zu erschiessen": die Brutalisierung des deutsch-sowjetischen Krieges im Sommer 1941.* Berlin: Propyläen, 2000.

Oliner, S. P., and P. M. Oliner. *The Altruistic Personality: Rescuers of Jews in Nazi Europe.* New York: Free Press, 1988.

O'Neil, Robin. "Belzec: A Reassessment of the Number of Victims." *East European Jewish Affairs* 29, no. 1–2 (Summer–Winter 1999): 85–118.

Oren, Elyashiv. *Doctor's Come Back* (Hebrew). Tel-Aviv: Sifriyat po'alim, 1981.

Pinchuk, Ben-Cion. *Shtetl Jews under Soviet Rule: Eastern Poland on the Eve of the Holocaust.* Cambridge, Mass.: Basil Blackwell, 1990.

Pinkas Hakehillot: Encyclopedia of Jewish Communities. Poland. Vol. 2, *Eastern Galicia* (Hebrew). Jerusalem: Yad va-shem, rashut ha-zikaron la-Sho'ah vela-gevurah, 1980.

Pohl, Dieter. *Nationalsozialistische Judenverfolgung in Ostgalizien, 1941–1944*. München: Oldenbourg, 1997.

Polonsky, Antony. *Politics in Independent Poland, 1921–1939: The Crisis of Constitutional Government*. Oxford: Clarendon, 1972.

Potichnyi, P. J., and H. Aster, eds. *Ukrainian-Jewish Relations in Historical Perspective*. Edmonton: Canadian Institute of Ukrainian Studies, University of Alberta, 1988.

Prus, Edward. *Holocaust po Banderowsku: czy Zydzi byli w UPA?* Wroclaw: Wydawn. "Nortom," 1995.

Pucek, Zbigniew. "Galicyjskie doswiadczenie wielokulturowosci a problem wiezi spolecznej." In *Galicja i jej dziedzictwo*, edited by Jerzy Chlopecki and Helena Madurowicz-Urbanska. Vol. 2, *Spoleczenstwo i gospodarka*, 11–25. Rzeszow: WSP, 1995.

Rabik, Vasil'. *Trostianets' Naris istorii sela*. Berezhani: Published by the author, 1999.

Redlich, Shimon. "Sheptyts'kyi and the Jews during World War II." *Magocsi* (1989): 145–162.

————. "Jewish-Ukrainian Relations in Inter-war Poland as Reflected in Some Ukrainian Publications." In *Polin: Studies in Polish Jewry*, Vol. 11, *Focusing on Aspects and Experiences of Religion*, edited by Antony Polonsky, 232–246. Portland, Ore.: Littman Library of Jewish Civilization, 1998.

Rusinski, Zbigniew. "Hufiec Brzezany: 1911–1939." Unpublished manuscript. 1996.

————. *Tryptyk Brzezanski*. Wroclaw: W kolorach teczy, Oficyna Artystyczno-Wydawnicza, 1998.

Sandkühler, Thomas. *"Endloesung" in Galizien: Der Judenmord in Ostpolen und die Rettungsinitiativen von Bertold Beitz, 1941–1944*. Bonn: Dietz, 1996.

Sergiichuk, Volodimir. *Desiat' buremnykh lit: zakhidnoukraïns'ki zemli v 1944-1953 rr.: novi dokumenty i materialy*. Kiev: Vyd-vo khudozhn'oï lit-ry "Dnipro," 1998.

Soski, Joseph. "Memories of a Vanished World." Unpublished memoirs. 1991.

Stetkevych, Lev. *Iak z Berezhan do kadry: spogady z divizii*. Ternopil': "Dzhura," 1998.

Stulecie Gimnazyum Brzezanskiego, 1806–1906. Brzezany: Komitet Jubileuszowy, 1907.

Subtelny, Orest. *Ukraine: A History*. Toronto: University of Toronto Press, 1988.

Sword, Keith. *Deportation and Exile: Poles in the Soviet Union, 1939–1948*. London: Macmillan, 1994.

Tec, Nechama. *When Light Pierced the Darkness: Righteous Christians and the Polish Jews*. New York: Oxford University Press, 1986.

Terles, Mikolaj. *Ethnic Cleansing of Poles in Volhynia and Eastern Galicia*. Toronto: Alliance of the Polish Eastern Provinces, 1993.

Tkachev, Sergii. *Pol'sko-ukrains'kii transfer naselenniia 1944–1946 rr.: viselenniia poliakiw z Ternopilliia*. Ternopil: Pidruchniki i posibniki, 1997.

Tomaszewski, Jerzy. *Ojczyzna nie tylko Polakow: Mniejszosci narodowe w Polsce w latach 1918–1939*. Warsaw: Mlodziezowa Agencja Wydawnicza, 1985.

————. *Rzeczpospolita wielu narodow*. Warsaw: Czytelnik, 1985.

————. "Czesc II: Niepodlegla Rzeczpospolita." In *Najnowsze dzieje Zydów w Polsce w zarysie, do 1950 roku*, edited by Jerzy Tomaszewski. Warsaw: Wydawn. Nauk. PWN, 1993.

Torzecki, Ryszard. *Polacy i Ukraincy: Sprawa ukrainska w czasie II wojny swiatowej na terenie II Rzeczypospolitej*. Warsaw: Wydawn. Nauk. PWN, 1993.

Trunk, Isaiah. *Judenrat: The Jewish Councils in Eastern Europe under Nazi Occupation.* New York: Macmillan, 1972.

Ukrainians and Jews: A Symposium. New York: Ukranian Congress Committee of America, Inc., 1966.

Wagszal-Shaklai, Eliezer. "Memoirs." Unpublished manuscript. N.d.

Wais, A. "Some Circles of the Ukrainian National Movement and the Problem of Jews during the Second World War" (Russian). *Vestnik evreiskogo universiteta v Moskve* (Moscow-Jerusalem) 2, no. 9 (1995): 104–113.

Wiszniewski, Stanislaw. *Przewodnik po Brzezanach i okolicy.* N.p., n.d.

———. *Brzezany i kresy polodniowo-wschodnie Rzeczypospolitej Polskiej, 1918–1919.* Lwow: Biblioteka Kresowa, 1935.

———. *Brzezanczycy przy odbudowie Panstwa Polskiego od 1831 do 1920 r.* Lwow: Drukarnia Wydawnicza, 1938.

Wrobel, Piotr. "Czesc I: Przed odzyskaniem niepodleglosci." In *Najnowsze dzieje Zydów w Polsce w zarysie, do 1950 roku,* edited by Jerzy Tomaszewski. Warsaw: Wydawn. Nauk. PWN, 1993.

Zachuta, Leszek. *51 Pulk Piechoty Strzelcow Kresowych im. Giuseppe Garibaldiego.* Pruszkow: Oficyna Wydawnicza "Ajaks," 1992.

Zbikowski, Andrzej. "Local Anti-Jewish Pogroms in the Occupied Territories of Eastern Poland, June–July 1941." In *The Holocaust in the Soviet Union,* edited by Lucjan Dobroszycki and Jeffrey S. Gurock, 173–179. Armonk, N.J.: M. E. Sharpe, 1993.

Page numbers in italic type refer to illustrations.

SHIMON REDLICH,
born in Poland and a survivor of the Holocaust, is an internationally
distinguished specialist on the history of the Jews in Eastern Europe.
He holds degrees from Hebrew University, Harvard University, and
New York University. Redlich is Solly Yellin Chair in Lithuanian and East
European Jewry, and lectures on modern European history at Ben-Gurion
University, Israel. His publications include *War, Holocaust and Stalinism:
A Documented History of the Jewish Anti-Fascist Committee in the USSR.*